Communications in Computer and Information Science 2423

Series Editors

Gang Li ⓘ, *School of Information Technology, Deakin University, Burwood, VIC, Australia*

Joaquim Filipe ⓘ, *Polytechnic Institute of Setúbal, Setúbal, Portugal*

Zhiwei Xu, *Chinese Academy of Sciences, Beijing, China*

Rationale

The CCIS series is devoted to the publication of proceedings of computer science conferences. Its aim is to efficiently disseminate original research results in informatics in printed and electronic form. While the focus is on publication of peer-reviewed full papers presenting mature work, inclusion of reviewed short papers reporting on work in progress is welcome, too. Besides globally relevant meetings with internationally representative program committees guaranteeing a strict peer-reviewing and paper selection process, conferences run by societies or of high regional or national relevance are also considered for publication.

Topics

The topical scope of CCIS spans the entire spectrum of informatics ranging from foundational topics in the theory of computing to information and communications science and technology and a broad variety of interdisciplinary application fields.

Information for Volume Editors and Authors

Publication in CCIS is free of charge. No royalties are paid, however, we offer registered conference participants temporary free access to the online version of the conference proceedings on SpringerLink (http://link.springer.com) by means of an http referrer from the conference website and/or a number of complimentary printed copies, as specified in the official acceptance email of the event.

CCIS proceedings can be published in time for distribution at conferences or as post-proceedings, and delivered in the form of printed books and/or electronically as USBs and/or e-content licenses for accessing proceedings at SpringerLink. Furthermore, CCIS proceedings are included in the CCIS electronic book series hosted in the SpringerLink digital library at http://link.springer.com/bookseries/7899. Conferences publishing in CCIS are allowed to use Online Conference Service (OCS) for managing the whole proceedings lifecycle (from submission and reviewing to preparing for publication) free of charge.

Publication process

The language of publication is exclusively English. Authors publishing in CCIS have to sign the Springer CCIS copyright transfer form, however, they are free to use their material published in CCIS for substantially changed, more elaborate subsequent publications elsewhere. For the preparation of the camera-ready papers/files, authors have to strictly adhere to the Springer CCIS Authors' Instructions and are strongly encouraged to use the CCIS LaTeX style files or templates.

Abstracting/Indexing

CCIS is abstracted/indexed in DBLP, Google Scholar, EI-Compendex, Mathematical Reviews, SCImago, Scopus. CCIS volumes are also submitted for the inclusion in ISI Proceedings.

How to start

To start the evaluation of your proposal for inclusion in the CCIS series, please send an e-mail to ccis@springer.com.

Shina Sheen · Latha R. · Sridevi U. K. ·
Thanalakshmi P. · Thilaga M.
Editors

Computational Intelligence, Cyber Security and Computational Models

Emerging Trends in Computational Models, Intelligence and Security Systems

6th International Conference, ICC3 2023
Coimbatore, India, December 14–16, 2023
Revised Selected Papers

Editors
Shina Sheen
PSG College of Technology
Coimbatore, Tamil Nadu, India

Latha R.
PSG College of Technology
Coimbatore, Tamil Nadu, India

Sridevi U. K.
PSG College of Technology
Coimbatore, Tamil Nadu, India

Thanalakshmi P.
PSG College of Technology
Coimbatore, Tamil Nadu, India

Thilaga M.
PSG College of Technology
Coimbatore, Tamil Nadu, India

ISSN 1865-0929　　　　　　　ISSN 1865-0937　(electronic)
Communications in Computer and Information Science
ISBN 978-3-031-88296-8　　　ISBN 978-3-031-88297-5　(eBook)
https://doi.org/10.1007/978-3-031-88297-5

© The Editor(s) (if applicable) and The Author(s), under exclusive license to Springer Nature Switzerland AG 2025

This work is subject to copyright. All rights are solely and exclusively licensed by the Publisher, whether the whole or part of the material is concerned, specifically the rights of translation, reprinting, reuse of illustrations, recitation, broadcasting, reproduction on microfilms or in any other physical way, and transmission or information storage and retrieval, electronic adaptation, computer software, or by similar or dissimilar methodology now known or hereafter developed.
The use of general descriptive names, registered names, trademarks, service marks, etc. in this publication does not imply, even in the absence of a specific statement, that such names are exempt from the relevant protective laws and regulations and therefore free for general use.
The publisher, the authors and the editors are safe to assume that the advice and information in this book are believed to be true and accurate at the date of publication. Neither the publisher nor the authors or the editors give a warranty, expressed or implied, with respect to the material contained herein or for any errors or omissions that may have been made. The publisher remains neutral with regard to jurisdictional claims in published maps and institutional affiliations.

This Springer imprint is published by the registered company Springer Nature Switzerland AG
The registered company address is: Gewerbestrasse 11, 6330 Cham, Switzerland

If disposing of this product, please recycle the paper.

Preface

In the modern era, various models of computation and advanced technologies are becoming essential to facilitate the interpretation and summarisation of complex data. Mathematical models are simulated using computation to gain scientific insights and seek technological innovations. Rigorous mathematical algorithms are in high demand for computational paradigms.

The Department of Applied Mathematics and Computational Sciences of PSG College of Technology, Coimbatore, India has been conducting the biennial International Conference on Computational Intelligence, Cyber Security and Computational Models (ICC^3) since 2013. The intent of the conference is to provide a forum for researchers and practitioners across the globe to discuss the most recent innovations, trends, concerns, practical challenges encountered and solutions adopted in the fields of Computational Models, Intelligence and Cyber Security. The sixth edition of the ICC^3 conference was organised with the theme "Emerging Trends in Computational Models, Intelligence and Security Systems" during 14–16th December, 2023. The conference was funded by Science and Engineering Research Board (SERB) and Visteon Corporation.

The increased use of social media imposes challenges to the security of systems connected through the Internet. The surge of digital attacks in the Internet era creates an increasing demand for sophisticated cyber security solutions to mitigate cyber risk. Cyber threats such as data theft, phishing scams and other cyber vulnerabilities mandate that users should remain vigilant about protecting data.

Computational modelling formulates real-world problems and develops solutions using computing. The goal of computational modelling is to use mathematical models to simulate and analyse any complex system for better understanding and efficient decision making. Computational models help various stakeholders of the system to visualize, predict, optimize, regulate and control any complex system using high-end computing technologies.

Computational Intelligence is a branch of AI which deals with the systematic study of adaptive mechanisms to facilitate intelligent behaviour in complex and changing environments. The adaptive mechanisms are paradigms that exhibit an ability to learn and adapt to new situations. Being an evolving field, computational intelligence involves different computing paradigms such as artificial neural networks, ambient intelligence, evolutionary computing, social reasoning, fuzzy systems, cultural learning, artificial immune systems etc.

ICC^3 2023 included 14 keynote talks by experts from world-class academic institutions and top-notch industries from across the globe. ICC^3 2023 received 86 technical submissions, of which 10 papers were selected for publication. Each submitted paper underwent a rigorous (double-blind) review process, with three reviews per submission.

We, the organisers of ICC^3, express our gratefulness to all the keynote speakers, Advisory Committee Members, Technical Program Committee members and authors of the papers for their invaluable contribution to the success of the conference. We appreciate the reviewers for their comments and suggestions, which helped us to ensure the quality of the proceedings. We extend our warmest gratitude to Springer for their continuous support in publishing the ICC^3 proceedings. The plenary talks, discussions and paper presentations were fruitful for the participants, with critical suggestions for improvement of their research ideas.

July 2024

Shina Sheen
Latha R.
Sridevi U. K.
Thanalakshmi P.
Thilaga M.

Organisation

Chief Patron

L. Gopalakrishnan   PSG & Sons Charities Trust, India

Patron

K. Prakasan   PSG College of Technology, India

Organizing Chair

Shina Sheen   PSG College of Technology, India

Program Chair

R. Latha   PSG College of Technology, India

Program Co-chair

Ivan Garibay   University of Central Florida, USA

Computational Intelligence Track Chair

U.K. Sridevi   PSG College of Technology, India

Computational Intelligence Track Co-chair

Manuel Grana   University of the Basque Country, Spain

Cyber Security Track Chair

P. Thanalakshmi PSG College of Technology, India

Computational Models Track Chair

M. Thilaga PSG College of Technology, India

Advisory Committee

Mohammad S. Obaidat	University of Jordan, Jordan
Bella Bose	Oregon State University, USA
Bojan Mohar	Simon Fraser University, Canada
Theodoros Tsiftsis	University of Thessaly, Greece
Balaraman Ravindran	Indian Institute of Technology Madras, India
Soumya Banerjee	Trasna-Solutions Ltd., Ireland
R. Nadarajan	PSG College of Technology, India
R. Anitha	PSG College of Technology, India
G. Sai Sundara Krishnan	PSG College of Technology, India
R. S. Lekshmi	PSG College of Technology, India
M. Senthilkumar	PSG College of Technology, India

Technical Programme Committee

Dariusz Jakobczak	Koszalin University of Technology, Poland
Kevin Curran	Ulster University, Derry-Londonderry Campus, UK
Manuel Grana	University of the Basque Country, Spain
Igor Kotenko	St. Petersburg Federal Research Center of the Russian Academy of Sciences, Russia
Tan Saw Chin	Multimedia University, Malaysia
Gerald Penn	University of Toronto, Canada
Vijayalakshmi Ramasamy	University of Wisconsin-Parkside, USA
Gyanendra Prasad Joshi	Sejong University, South Korea
Gokul Kumari Govindasamy	Saudi Electronic University, Saudi Arabia
Ismail Naci Cangul	Bursa Uludağ University, Turkey
Parameswaran Raman	Amazon, USA
Sridhar Venkatesan	Peraton Labs, USA
Akshaya Mani	Optable, Canada

Arfat Ahmad Khan	Khon Kaen University, Thailand
Anitha Anandhan	University of Malaya, Malaysia
R. Sumithra	Centre for Development of Advanced Computing, India
Natarajan Venkatachalam	Society for Electronic Transactions and Security, India
Phalguni Gupta	Indian Institute of Technology, Kanpur, India
Sudeesh Kumar Kattumannil	Indian Statistical Institute, Chennai, India
Ashok Kumar M.	Indian Institute of Technology, Palakkad, India
Ram Bilas Pachori	Indian Institute of Technology, Indore, India
Shivashankar B. Nair	Indian Institute of Technology, Guwahati, India
R. B. V. Subramaanyam	National Institute of Technology, Warangal, India
Debashisha Jena	National Institute of Technology, Surathkal, India
V. Masilamani	Indian Institute of Information Technology, Design and Manufacturing, Kancheepuram, India
Ashok Kumar Das	International Institute of Information Technology, Hyderabad, India
Ruhul Amin	International Institute of Information Technology, Naya Raipur, India
S. K. Hafizul Islam	Indian Institute of Information Technology, Kalyani, India
Elizabeth Sherly	Indian Institute of Information Technology and Management, Trivandrum, India
G. Sethuraman	Anna University, Chennai, India
J. Baskar Babujee	Anna University, Chennai, India
E. Chandra	Bharathiar University, India
P. V. S. S. R. Chandra Mouli	Central University of Tamil Nadu, India
H. S. Ramane	Karnatak University, India
B. H. Shekar	Mangalore University, India
Vishal Jain	Sharda University, India
V. Viswanathan	Vellore Institute of Technology, Chennai, India
G. Sudha Sadasivam	PSG College of Technology, India
Nidhi Saxena	Madhav Institute of Technology and Science, India
N. Anbazhagan	Alagappa University, India
A. P. Nirmala	New Horizon College of Engineering, India
Nidhi Arora	University of Delhi, India
P. Venketesh	Vellore Institute of Technology, Chennai, India
Kaja Mohideen	Vellore Institute of Technology, Chennai, India
Manimegalai Rajkumar	PSG Institute of Technology and Applied Research, India

B. Surendiran	National Institute of Technology, Puducherry, India
M. Sethumadhavan	Amrita Vishwa Vidyapeetham, Coimbatore, India
N. Radhika	Amrita Vishwa Vidyapeetham, Coimbatore, India
B. R. Shankar	National Institute of Technology, Surathkal, India
Santhi Thilagam	National Institute of Technology, Surathkal, India
A. V. Chithra	National Institute of Technology, Calicut, India
M. Prem Laxman Das	Society for Electronic Transactions and Security, India
S. Parthasarathy	Thiagarajar College of Engineering, India
S. Mary Saira Bhanu	National Institute of Technology, Trichy, India
G. R. Karpagam	PSG College of Technology, India
K. Umamaheswari	PSG College of Technology, India
B. K. Tripathy	Vellore Institute of Technology, Vellore, India
C. Oswald	National Institute of Technology, Trichy, India
Rajamanickam Natarajan	Infosys, India
S. Rooban	KL University, India
Rubell Marion Lincy	Indian Institute of Information Technology, Kottayam, India
Ramesh Thanappan	Bharathiar University, India
Priti Sehgal	University of Delhi, India
Anand Mahendran	Vellore Institute of Technology, Vellore, India

Sponsors

Science and Engineering Research Board, India

Visteon Corporation

Keynote Abstracts

Approximation Algorithms for the Genus of Graphs

Bojan Mohar[1,2]

[1] Simon Fraser University, Canada
[2] University of Ljubljana, Slovenia
bojan.mohar@fmf.uni-lj.si

Abstract. The speaker gives an overview of computational issues related to representations of a given graph G by a drawing on a surface whose genus is as small as possible for given G. The task of finding if the graph can be drawn in the plane (the surface of genus 0) is well understood and solvable by fast linear-time algorithms. The talk will discuss known FPT extension to surfaces of larger genus and will discuss approximation algorithms for this problem.

Do Language Models Know Language?

Gerald Penn
Department of Computer Science, University of Toronto, Canada
gpenn@cs.toronto.edu

Abstract. Triumphalist portraits of large language models (LLMs) boast that language models have mastered a level of language understanding that natural language processing (NLP) researchers have laboured for years to attain using complex architectures consisting of diverse component models that each require large amounts of training data.

Do they? How do we know? And, if so, how do they manage this? In this talk, we will examine two recent experiments with LLMs that cast doubt upon these claims, while affirming the utility of LLMs in present-day NLP.

Knowledge Graphs: Question Answering Systems

Ramasuri Narayanam
Senior Research Scientist, Adobe Research – Bangalore, India
`nrsuri@gmail.com`

Abstract. The first part of the talk focuses on highlighting certain important problems that are tackled inside Adobe Research. Then the later part of the talk focuses on covering detailed technical aspects of one research problem of interest: Knowledge graphs and Question Answering Systems. In particular, the talk highlights the associated research challenges and their approach to tackle the same.

Equitable and Inclusive AI- Assistants

Tanuja Ganu
Principal Research SDE Manager, Microsoft Research Lab, India
Tanuja.Ganu@microsoft.com

Abstract. The technology landscape is being rapidly transformed by Large Language Models (LLMs), allowing users to address real-world applications in various domains. However, a digital divide exists that may exclude large populations from benefiting and contributing to this technological revolution due to factors such as language, income, digital awareness, and access to information. This talk covers the current gaps in applying of SOTA GenAI models in real-world use-cases in Education, Agriculture etc. and the ongoing efforts to make the GenAI model equitable, inclusive and accessible for the entire world population.

Steps Towards Networked Autonomy: Spatial Perception, Certifiable–and–Adaptive Learning Models, and Time-Sensitive Information Exchange

Rajat Talak
Research Scientist, Massachusetts Institute of Technology, USA
rajatalak@gmail.com

Abstract. Networked Autonomy aspires to build a team of robots that can seamlessly communicate, perceive, and interact with humans and the environment. The ultimate tool for humankind is such a networked autonomous system, which humans can direct, for example, to (i) organize inventory in a hospital and manage patients; (ii) help cook, clean floors, wash dishes and laundry at home; (iii) assemble pre-fabricated parts, ferry construction material, plaster, and paint walls, install wirings and lighting, at a construction site; (iv) carry out system checks and repairs, setup experiments, and perform routine cleaning operations, on the international space station; (v) and even enable space exploration and asteroid mining. This is not possible today!

His work has focused on building the next generation of robot perception and communication algorithms that can enable networked autonomy. For perception, robots need to build an actionable scene representation in real-time that is scalable for long-horizon autonomy. With deep-learning models (and their failure-prone behavior) finding their place in the robot perception system, it becomes necessary to develop mechanisms that can certify the correct workings of a model, and adapt the model, using real and unannotated data, to again, make it work to its desired specifications. Finally, networked autonomous systems operating in a constantly changing environment need to exchange time-sensitive information.

Knowledge-Augmented Reinforcement Learning for Safe Systems

Mayukh Das

Senior Researcher, Microsoft Research, India
mayukhdas@microsoft.com

Abstract. Operational efficiency and reliability are the key aspects of successful and sustainable enterprise level services and systems, be it cloud platforms, edge or hybrid, and to ensure optimal efficiency and reliability we have to solve a plethora of critical challenges including resource and capacity optimization, platform tuning, incident detection and mitigation etc. To develop dynamic and adaptive solutions for such problems we leverage online optimization or Reinforcement Learning based techniques and methods. While extremely powerful, these methods come with high risk, especially for real systems, where environments are noisy or uncertain, non-stationary, feedback is sparse and often ambiguous or sometimes unobservable. This leads to learning unsafe policies that can cause catastrophic issues in real production level deployments. We explore and investigate knowledge augmented RL techniques to quantify, characterize and alleviate such risks and create safe and robust adaptive solutions. This talk aims to highlight the general conceptual details of such methods as well as their impacts on real scenarios through real case studies on Microsoft Cloud systems.

A Single-Server Delay/Retrial Model with Two Phases of Service and Non-preemptive Priority for the Queued Customers

Rein Nobel[1] and Hylke Muntinghe[1]

[1] Department of Operations Analytics, Vrije Universiteit Amsterdam
r.d.nobel@vu.nl

Abstract. In mobile cellular communication systems handover calls must be given priority over originating calls to avoid undesired interruptions of handover calls when entering the region of a new base station. One protocol is to queue the handover calls and block the originating calls in case upon arrival at the base station no channels are free. In this paper a one-server (channel) mixed delay/retrial queueing model is considered to study the performance of this protocol. Calls arrive at the base station according to a Poisson process, and if the single server (channel) is busy the handover calls are put in a queue and the originating calls are sent to an unlimited virtual waiting place, called the orbit. Any call which finds the server idle upon arrival starts its service immediately. From the orbit calls try to approach the server anew after a random time and because non-preemptive priority is given to the queued (handover) calls, calls in the orbit can approach the server successfully only when the queue is empty and the server is idle. Every call requires two service phases. The First Essential Service phase (FES) can fail, and upon failure the call is (re)sent into the orbit (in that case a handover call looses his handover status). The Second Essential Service phase (SES) is always successful. Both phases are exponentially distributed with different parameters. The probability generating function (PGF) of the joint steady-state distribution of the queue length and the orbit size is derived, and from this PGF several performance measures are calculated, such as the queue-length distribution, the mean queue length, the waiting-time distribution of a handover call in the queue, and the mean orbit size, amongst others. Extensive numerical results illustrate the sensitivity of these performance measures for the parameters, such as the fraction of handover calls and the success probability of the FES.

Enhancing Healthcare with AI-in-the-Loop

Sriraam Natarajan

Department of Computer Science, The University of Texas at Dallas, Texas, USA
Sriraam.Natarajan@utdallas.edu

Abstract. Historically, Artificial Intelligence has taken a symbolic route for representing and reasoning about objects at a higher-level or a statistical route for learning complex models from large data. To achieve true AI in complex domains such as healthcare, it is necessary to make these different paths meet and enable seamless human interaction. The talk introduces learning from rich, structured, complex and noisy data. One of the key attractive properties of the learned models is that they use a rich representation for modeling the domain that potentially allows for seam-less human interaction. It includes the recent progress that allows for more reasonable human interaction where the human input is taken as "advice" and the learning algorithm combines this advice with data. The talk highlights the algorithms in the context of several healthcare problems – learning from electronic health records, clinical studies, and surveys – and demonstrate the value of involving experts during learning.

Leveraging Mathematics for Biomedical Informatics Data – Solving Micro to Macro Image Processing Challenges

Surya Prasath

Departments of Biomedical Informatics, University of Cincinnati, USA

prasatsa@ucmail.uc.edu

Abstract. The big data era is well and truly underway and the deluge of data in biomedical imaging provides promising solutions for personalized medicine and computer-aided diagnosis. The talk covers a gamut of imaging modalities from microscopy to endoscopy, and corresponding challenging image analysis problems. It includes case studies across micro to macro scale biomedical imaging along with challenges that are successfully tackled with computational image processing, computer vision, machine and deep learning techniques.

Controlling Diffusion Model Generation to User Constraints

Balaji Vasan Srinivasan
Principal Scientist, Adobe Research, India
balsrini@adobe.com

Abstract. Recent advancements in text-guided image synthesis have revolutionized creative workflows, opening up a lot of possibilities in the realms of image generation. However, in many scenarios, the user would like to control specific aspects of the generation. The talk covers a few practical scenarios that gives raise to such constraints/controls and present some of the explorations that tailor diffusion models to provide such control and flexibility. The talk begins with EMILIE, that allows iterative image generation where a user can retain parts of a generated image while customizing other parts to their needs. To allow for exemplar based image control, MATTE, a textual inversion based framework and TINTIN, a T2I adaptor based framework that provides user to control generation on aspects like color, style from an example image(s) are introduced. To address the computational costs associated with such custom generation, the talk finally introduces the recent exploration on zero-shot customization of the generation by leveraging the latents.

Ensemble Methods in Spatiotemporal Applications

Jaya Sreevalsan Nair
International Institute of Information Technology, Bangalore (IIIT-B), India
jnair@iiitb.ac.in

Abstract. In several spatiotemporal data applications across several domains, we encounter the need to use validation from the data itself given the absence of ground truth. Uncertainty in the data that manifests in several analytical operations must also be derived from the data itself, in several cases. Thus, ensemble methods have been a useful tool in understanding spatial data with more confidence. In a second line of applications, it is useful to stop reinventing the wheel and improve the reusability of deep learning models used for spatial analysis. Thus, existing methods can be integrated together using an ensemble approach. The talk covers such methods for specific case studies of probabilistic flood extent estimation from SAR images and object detection of automotive LiDAR point clouds.

Contents

Computational Intelligence

Deep Learning in Stock Market Forecasting: A Comparative Study 3
   Manas Rahman and V. Kumar

Enhancing Resolution: Harnessing Generative Adversarial Networks
for Domain-Specific Super-Resolution 15
   Divya Mohan, Jeswin Roy Dcouth, and Puthin Kumar

Audio Tagging – Deep Learning Approach 37
   *E. Sophiya, S. Sudharsan, S. K. Mukhil Varnan, T. P. Nithishvaran,
   and M. S. Mohan Vamsi*

A Design Pattern Based Forecasting Model for Predicting Time Series
Data in Kaggle Ecosystem 55
   Naman Bhargava, B. Malar, and G. Priyalakshmi

Cyber Security

An Anonymous and Unlinkable Security Protocol for the Communication
in Cloud-Enabled Smart Agriculture Environment 69
   Sundararaju Mugunthan and Venkatasamy Sureshkumar

Mitigating Malware Threats in Wireless Sensor Networks: A Fractional
Approach with Infected Mutant and Traced Nodes 88
   Abilasha Balakumar, Sumathi Muthukumar, and Veeramani Chinnadurai

Exploring Post-quantum Hash-Based Signature Schemes for IoT Motes 100
   P. Thanalakshmi and N. K. J. Ashwinkumaar

Computational Models

Describing Regular Closure of Linear Languages by Semi Conditional
Insertion Deletion Systems 117
   Indhumathi Raman

Predicting the Toxicity of Biomolecules Using Graph Kernel 127
   R. Manimegalai, A. Susmeta, V. R. Umayal, and M. Venkateshwaran

A New Modified Juchez Distribution: Induced Juchez Distribution with Its
Properties and Application in Intelligent Irrigation System Data 140
  M. Subhashree and C. Subramanian

Author Index 153

Computational Intelligence

Deep Learning in Stock Market Forecasting: A Comparative Study

Manas Rahman(✉) and V. Kumar

Department of Computer Science, Central University of Kerala, Periye, Kasaragod, India
manasrahmanpadiyoor@gmail.com, vkumar@cukerala.ac.in

Abstract. Due to the potential for profits and the opportunity to invest instantaneously in specific businesses, stocks remain people's most common investment option. Forecasting the stock market flow is crucial for market individuals because even a tiny increase in estimation preciseness could result in making better trading choices than their competitors. Various studies focused on forecasting stock market movement using different learning methods and parameters. These market data are commonly forecasted using statistical methods, machine learning, deep-learning models, and combinations. This research seeks to take advantage of the Long Short-Term Memory(LSTM) layers' efficiency in detecting both short-term and long-term relationships and the convolutional layers' capacity for grasping the internal structure of stock market data. The study used the Agricultural Development Bank Limited (ADBL) stock price data from the Nepal stock market for demonstration. In experimentation, we compared the suggested model to state-of-the-art deep learning techniques. The results illustrate that the Convolutional Neural Network-LSTM (CNN-LSTM) model performs significantly better than typical deep-learning models.

Keywords: Nepal stock market · Forecasting · Deep-learning · CNN · CNN-LSTM

1 Introduction

The stock market, also known as an equity or share market, is the collection of individuals purchasing and selling stocks(also known as shares), indicating ownership stakes in corporations [1]. These assets are either displayed on an open exchange or just exchanged privately, like shares of private corporations that are offered to purchasers via stock crowdfunding channels. The stock market offers numerous benefits to investors[2]. Despite the possibility that one will occasionally lose money, compared to other asset types like bonds or savings accounts, the stock marketplace offers higher rates of return over the long run. One can diversify the portfolio and lower the risk of losing by owning various securities in different companies and sectors in the stock market [3]. Unlike other assets, like land and savings accounts, stocks are incredibly flexible, making them simple and fast to purchase and trade. When purchasing the stocks, one becomes a shareholder in the business, gaining the opportunity to gain from any profits the company makes via dividends or financial gains.

Since the stock market has numerous advantages over other assets, the usage of the stock market has achieved exponential growth in the modern world [4]. Even though the pandemic has affected the stock market negatively in many organizations, the overall performance has a positive trend. The investors are regaining their assets and profits through their investment plans. An investment plan is typically present while buying or selling stocks [5]. Each person involved in stock trading will have their own strategies. Usually, they will develop these strategies based on the experiences they gained in the market. The complicated interactions among investors, companies, and the political and financial environment are all reflected in the share market [6], constituting a rapidly changing structure. A thorough grasp of finance and economics and the complex links between market factors and human behavior are necessary to comprehend the nature of stock markets.

The increasing usage of the stock market has pointed to a question; How can a beginner in the stock market earn profit by investing? If the investor is not aware of the factors influencing stock prices, the more possibility is that he will make a loss [7]. Here comes the importance of data mining technologies. Analyzing historical data through mining techniques makes forecasting the stock price flow possible [8]. Historical aspects are a single element to predict the flow. However, it significantly impacts stock flow more than other elements because the stock provider(a company) gains consumers' trust through its history. Hence, analyzing historical aspects will assist investors in making decisions and profits.

The objective of this study is to effectively forecast future trends by analyzing the historical data obtained from a particular stock. The study uses deep learning models in the historical data to learn the relationship among the stock market features. The core idea is to help traders to analyze the market effectively and gain more profit than their competitors. Even in the case of a beginner who does not have any experience in the stock market can benefit from this research. In short, the study seeks to undertake a standardized evaluation of the stock market prediction abilities of different deep-learning models under identical circumstances. And give an insight into trading policies the traders can take in the future.

The rest of the paper structure is as follows: the review of related works is in Sect. 2; Sect. 3 describes the methodologies used in the study along with the dataset; Sect. 4 will describe the experimental setup and compare the results obtained to state-of-art methods; Sect. 5 concludes the study with future directions.

2 Literature Review

Numerous deep-learning approaches have recently been used in various stock markets all over the globe to forecast the market's movements. Different studies used different parameters and feature space to increase the performance of their model over specific data. Even though, without question, the unpredictability of the market makes it challenging to accurately forecast future stock returns using the currently used methods [9]. The phenomena, such as those marked by recessions, expansions, and high or low-volatility times, must be considered for accurate modeling. The authors [10] understood that, in market values, there are two primary causes of uncertainty. The first risk factor relates to broader economic factors like interest rates, currency exchange costs, inflation rates, and business cycles. Firm-specific inconsistency is the next cause of uncertainty. According to their analysis, it has to do with the firm's projections, the administration, the outcomes of the company's research and development division, and many more.

The authors [11] implemented the Recurrent Neural Network(RNN) with LSTM for stock market analysis. They compared the model to well-known machine-learning algorithms, including Backpropagation, Support Vector Machine, Random Forest, and Feed Forward Neural Networks. According to the findings, the RNN-LSTM model is more likely to produce precise results than conventional machine learning methods. To effectively forecast future FOREX currency closing values, the study [12] introduces a novel model that integrates GRU and LSTM, two effective neural networks frequently utilized for time series forecasting. After preprocessing, the system will circulate the time series data to a GRU layer following an LSTM layer. The experiment's findings indicate that the system works better than all comparable models.

Deep Neural Networks (DNN), which are bigger and more intense, are more likely to increase accuracy if there is enough data. In contrast, massive networks are ineffective because of overfitting if insufficient data exists. It is crucial to conquering the lack of accessible data in finance time-series analyses using DNNs to prevent overfitting. Data augmentation is one of the commonly suggested options. However, since time series created by changing the original data are artificial, it is not advisable to use them for prediction. Hence, the study [13] suggest a novel augmentation method for economic time-series forecasting that avoids creating an inflated time series to supplement the training data and instead strengthens the model against overfitting. The outcomes support the suggested model's outstanding forecasting precision.

The study [14] investigates the performance of RNN with LSTM in the data collected from the National Stock Exchange(NSE), India, to predict future stock returns. The suggested algorithm forecasts the stock yields for the following 24 h in the future using trading information from recent times as input. Through assessment, they discovered that the RNN with an LSTM framework works better than a feed-forward artificial neural network. The research [15] introduced a novel share market forecasting structure NuNet that can effectively gain high-level characteristics from high dimensional time series. A high-dimensional marketplace feature extractor and a desired(target) feature extractor are the two feature extractor modules that comprise the end-to-end interconnected neural network architecture known as NuNet. The high-dimensional feature extractor for the market consists of several ConvLSTM layers, and the target extractor contains LSTMs. The outcomes show that the suggested model works better than all benchmark models.

Even though many studies on stock market forecasting are available, a single-digit precision improvement in prediction will make a huge difference. Since every study in this area uses different data, considering a single study as the best model is unreliable. Deep learning models can help market forecasting much better by extracting inner patterns. This study demonstrates the effectiveness of incorporating two deep-learning models(CNN and LSTM) to create the CNN-LSTM architecture. Hence, the study compares the results with [16] because they have recently used other popular deep-learning models, LSTM and GRU, for stock market forecasting on Nepal stock data. Incorporating news events and other factors may help to predict the market. However, there is a chance of getting negative results also. Historical data has a massive impact on any market. Because, as a customer, we always look for firms we can trust. Any business will gain the trust of its users from past dealings(history). Hence, using historical data in efficient deep-learning models will effectively forecast the market. The finding of an effective model is still an open area.

3 Methodology

For forecasting the stock market, this study used two deep-learning models; CNN and CNN-LSTM. The training in these models takes place in a supervised model setting. Figure 1 illustrates the complete architecture and workflow used in the study. At first, the raw stock data will be preprocessed and scaled. The two models under consideration use the data obtained after the preparation. After inverse transform(inverse scaling), the evaluation will take place. The matrices used for assessment include; Root Mean Square Error(RMSE), Mean Absolute Error(MAE), and Coefficient of determination(R^2).

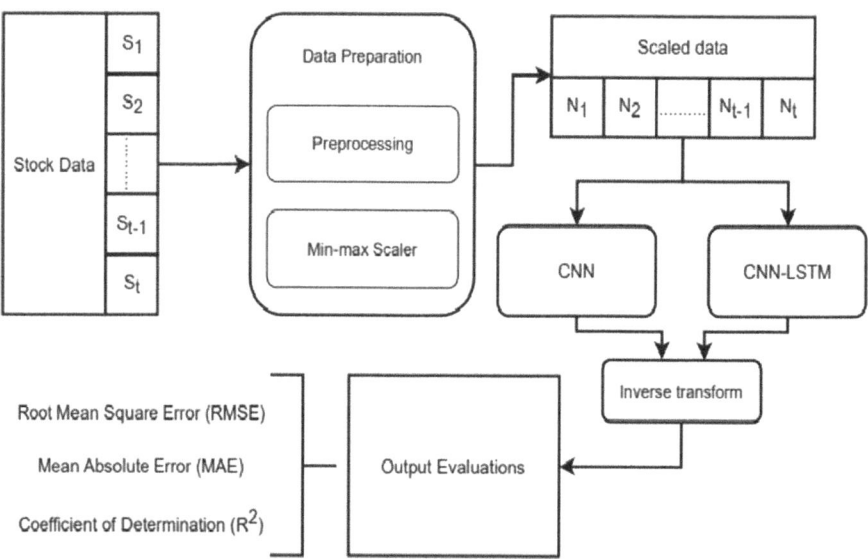

Fig. 1. Deep learning architecture in the study

3.1 Dataset

The study used Nepal stock data collected from ShareSansar (https://www.sharesansar.com/) website, just like in [16] to ensure the effectiveness of the proposed methodology. The data contains the stock parameters of Agricultural Development Bank Limited(ADBL) from 20th March 2011 to 14th November 2019. The data parameters include Date, Open, High, Low, LTP, Qty, and Turnover. Table 1 describes the feature descriptions of the dataset.

Table 1. ADBL stock data description

Feature	Description
Date	The Day at which all the stock indices are considered
Open	The price of a particular security or stock once the market opens. This is the amount at which a day's first trade is executed
High	During a trading session, the high price of a specific stock or asset refers to its maximum price. This is typically the day's highest price for the stock
Low	The cheapest cost at which a given asset or security was traded on a given trading day is referred to as its low price
LTP	Last Traded Price(LTP) is the stock's last transacted price for that particular day
Qty	The precise number(quantity) of shares delivered by vendors and received by purchasers in a given trade
Turnover	The aggregate worth of all transactions that take place on a specific stock exchange during a specified time period. It represents the quantity of money exchanged on the market during the specified time period

3.2 Preprocessing

Data preprocessing is an essential face in any learning method. This phase involves feature selection, normalization, splitting data(training, validation, testing splits), target variable identification, and many more. The target variable under consideration is LTP. Figure 2 presents the correlation heatmap of features in the dataset. The brighter color represents a higher correlation, and the darker color represents a lesser correlation [17]. From the heatmap, it is clear that the feature 'Qty' is less correlated to LTP and avoided in the study, considering the remaining five features for experimentation.

The values were then scaled using a min-max scaler [18] in the range from 0 to 1. When a single parameter extensively surpasses others in scale, it may alter distance estimation. It will affect the behavior of the method. The scaling is essential during machine learning as numerous algorithms depend on Euclidean distance, depending on how the parameter scales. The scaling guarantees an equilibrium effect from every parameter in distance estimations, thereby improving algorithm efficiency, particularly for approaches such as neural networks that often demand normalized input data. Then we convert the data to a supervised learning problem by setting different lag values(look-back values). The original dataset under consideration contains 1996 days of traded information(1996 records). If the lag value is 10, the data size will decrease by 10(1996 to 1986). We will do the experimentation for different lag values. The data size will change to (*1996-lag, lag*n_features*) depending on the lag value chosen. After this, since the data is time series, data splitting should be done sequentially. Hence, from the updated data, we will consider the first 1200 samples for training, the following 300 samples for validation, and the remaining samples for testing. The testing sample size will vary according to the lag value we chose each time.

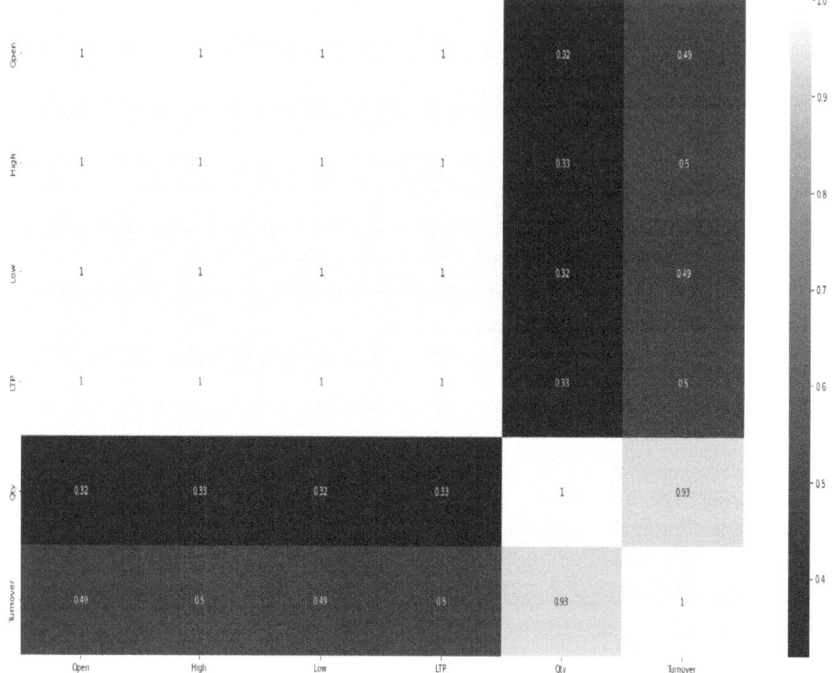

Fig. 2. Feature correlation heat map

3.3 Deep-Learning Models

The study used two deep learning models; Convolutional Neural Network(CNN) and CNN-Long Short Term Memory(CNN-LSTM). The same preprocessed data is given as input to each model and evaluated their performance under different lag values.

CNN. CNN is an advanced artificial neural network that substitutes the mathematical process known as convolution for basic matrix multiplication at least in one of its levels [19]. The CNN framework on time series assessment extends the conventional CNN architecture for handling sequential data over a single dimension. The traditional CNN uses 2D convolutional layers for image analysis. In contrast, the time series utilizes 1D convolutional layers to identify local trends. These convolutional layers moved over the input stream using filters to identify characteristics at various points. Convolution layers are specifically data exploration layers tasked with filtering the incoming data and extracting usable information that will typically serve as input on a wholly connected network layer. The convolutional layers perform a convolution strategy using kernels on the raw incoming data to create new feature values.

CNN-LSTM. The state-of-art methods show the popularity of LSTM networks for forecasting stock data [20]. The LSTM networks are good at detecting both short-term and long-term dependencies, convolution layers expertise at extracting usable information, and learning the internal architecture of time-series data. Our suggested model's core idea is effectively integrating these deep learning methods for stock market forecasting. To achieve this, we present the CNN-LSTM model with two parts: a CNN layer and an LSTM layer. Figure 3 represents the architecture of the CNN-LSTM model used in this study. The input data(preprocessed data) flows from a convolution layer that will extract valuable pieces of information to an LSTM layer. The LSTM layer will forecast the output sequence.

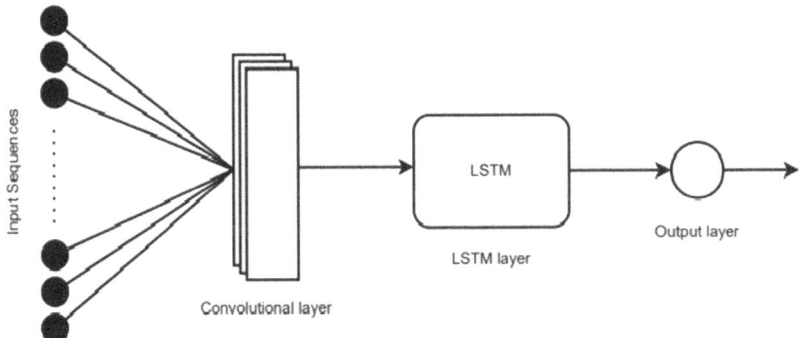

Fig. 3. Proposed CNN-LSTM architecture

3.4 Assessment Metrices

The evaluation of each day's stock price and trends in forecasting takes place using different metrics. The R^2 value determines how well the actual and predicted data match [21]. At the same time, the RMSE and MAE help to assess the forecasting error [22]. The equations to find all these measures are;

$$RMSE = \sqrt{\frac{1}{n}\sum_{i=1}^{n}(a_i - p_i)^2} \quad (1)$$

$$MAE = \frac{1}{n}\sum_{i=1}^{n}|a_i - p_i| \quad (2)$$

$$R^2 = 1 - \frac{\sum_{i=1}^{n}(a_i - p_i)^2}{\sum_{i=1}^{n}(a_i - \overline{a})^2} \quad (3)$$

where, $\overline{a} = \frac{1}{n}\sum_{i=1}^{n} a_i$; p_i, a_i are the predicted and actual price at day i.

4 Experimentation and Results

To compare our work, we used the state-of-art method [14] that experimented with the GRU and LSTM models for stock price forecasting in the same dataset. They have incorporated the news sentiment scores with the models to improve performance. Their results show that LSTM performed better than GRU and observed that the performance varies depending on the lag value chosen.

This study evaluates the performance of both CNN and CNN-LSTM by considering different lag values and comparing the results with the existing work mentioned above. We have chosen the lag values 10, 12, 14, 16, 18, and 20, which are the same as the method mentioned for better comparison. The CNN model in the study has a single one-dimensional convolutional hidden layer with 120 filters of size 5. The CNN-LSTM model contains a one-dimensional convolutional hidden layer and an LSTM layer with 120 units. Table 2 describes the other parameters used in the models. We evaluated the results using the performance measures such as RMSE, MAE, and R^2. We have considered the RMSE as the primary measure for evaluation, intending to reduce the loss. Figure 4 and Fig. 5 reveals the RMSE and MAE values obtained in the CNN and CNN-LSTM models, respectively. CNN is giving better performance, having minimum loss at lag value 16. The CNN-LSTM model gives fewer errors(per form better) while the lag value is 14. Figure 6 exposes the R^2 values in CNN and CNN-LSTM. Figure 7 demonstrates the fitting of the predicted and actual value of LTP in CNN and CNN-LSTM by choosing a lag of 14. In the case of the R^2 value, CNN is giving better performance while the lag is 16, and CNN-LSTM is giving better performance while the lag is 14. The model's error metrics and R^2 value clearly show that the RMSE and MAE have a positive correlation and R^2 is negatively correlated to them.

Table 2. ADBL stock data description

Parameters	Values
Nodes in input layer	Number of input features × look back value
Number of epochs	100
Batch size	30
Lag in number of days	10, 12, 14, 16, 18, 20
Output layer	1

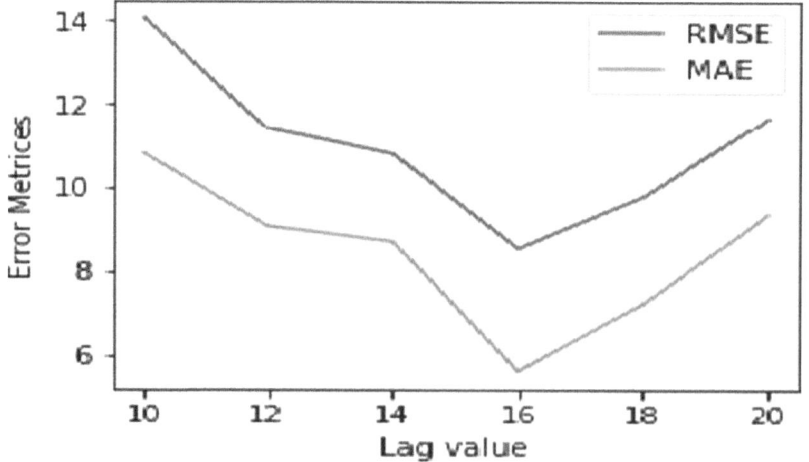

Fig. 4. RMSE and MAE of CNN

The summary of performance evaluation of the methods in our study(CNN and CNN-LSTM) with the state-of-art methods(LSTM and GRU) are in Table 3. The results show that the CNN-LSTM model performs better than CNN, LSTM, and GRU. The CNN model performs better than LSTM and GRU while considering the loss.

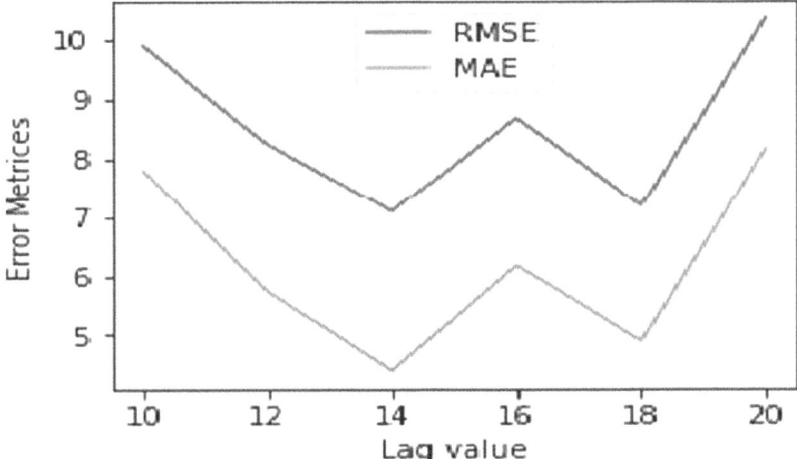

Fig. 5. RMSE and MAE of CNN-LSTM

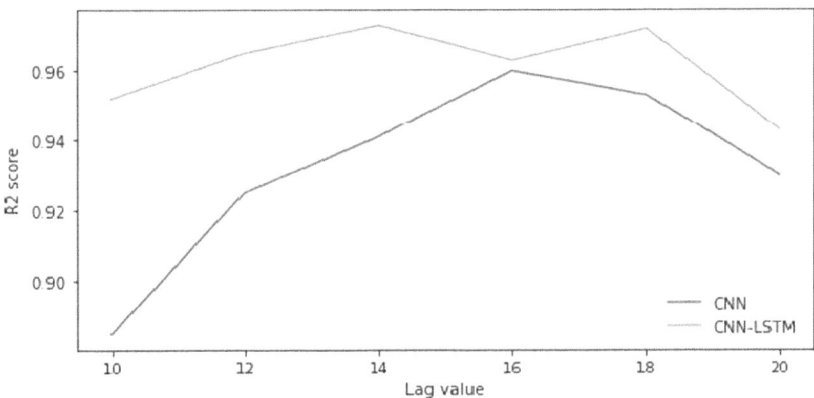

Fig. 6. R^2 Score of CNN and CNN-LSTM

Table 3. Comparison with state-of-art methods

Assessment Metrics	GRU News [16]	LSTM News [16]	CNN (proposed)	CNN-LSTM (proposed)
RMSE	29.153	23.070	10.792	7.081
MAE	24.472	17.689	8.705	4.398
R^2	0.967	0.979	0.941	0.973

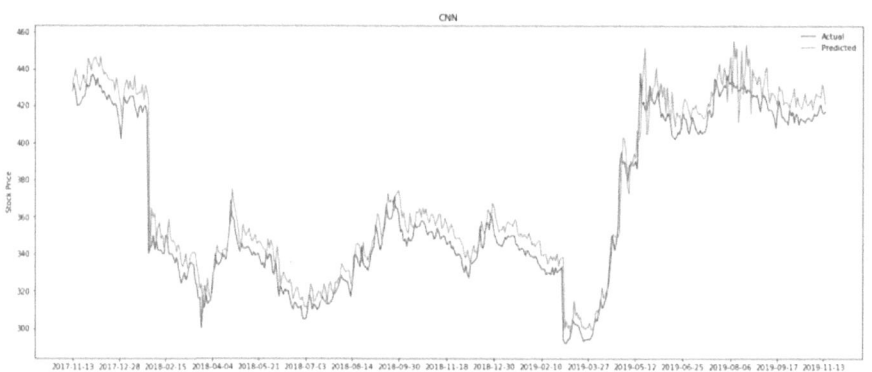

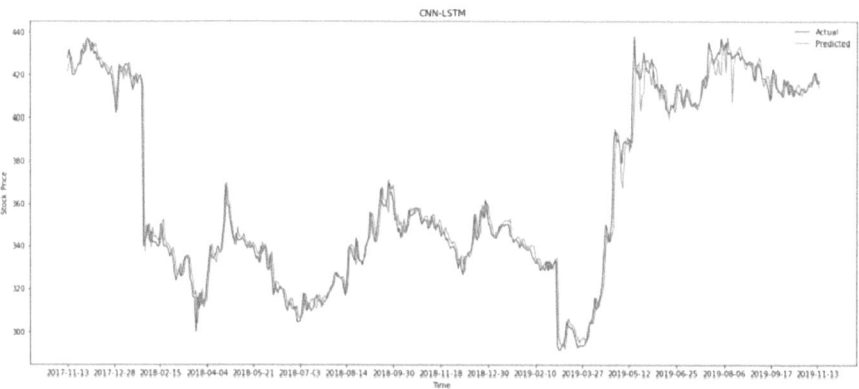

Fig. 7. Performance of CNN and CNN-LSTM at lag = 14.

5 Conclusion

The stock market is a crucial part of the business and the financial market. It makes systematic, safe dealing in stocks easier. Investors can purchase and trade securities on the stock market under well-established rules and regulations. Businesses can acquire funds as well as trade openly on the stock exchange. Additionally, it enables buyers to benefit from trading in securities. To benefit from the stock market, an individual must apply a trading strategy he developed from his experiences. The more you know about a specific stock, the more you make a benefit. It is challenging to enter the stock market without thoroughly understanding the market flow or without a trading strategy. Understanding and developing these strategies is a herculean task for humanity. Here comes the involvement of AI and deep-learning techniques. Deep-learning architectures are more suitable for learning within the stock data.

This study seeks the use of a convolutional neural network for understanding the inner patterns in the stock data, along with the capability of the LSTM model to forecast future values effectively. This study used a CNN-LSTM architecture that will use the properties of a convolutional network and long short-term memory. The study compared the performance of CNN and CNN-LSTM models with state-of-art methods: LSTM and GRU, on stock market data with different lag values. The result shows that the CNN and CNN-LSTM architecture perform better than the compared methods(LSTM and GRU). And CNN-LSTM gives a much better performance than CNN. The reason is that LSTM is excellent for modeling temporal patterns, and CNN specializes in spatial patterns. These spatial and temporal patterns have equal value in a time series analysis, and the CNN-LSTM model is sufficient to handle that. In short, rather than using CNN and LSTM models separately to forecast stock market data, incorporating both methods(CNN-LSTM) can significantly improve the results.

This study examined the effect of the proposed models only on a single stock data from the Nepal stock exchange. A possible expansion of this study is to verify the impact of the CNN-LSTM model on different stock data from various stock exchanges. Another possibility is incorporating market-influencing parameters such as news with historical data for better results. The development of new hybrid deep-learning models that can improve forecasting efficiency is another considerable expansion of this study.

References

1. Teweles, R.J., Bradley, E.S.: The stock market. John Wiley & Sons, vol. 64 (1998)
2. Li, Q., Wang, S., Song, V.: Product competition, political connections, and the costs of high leverage. J. Empirical Finance, 101430 (2023)
3. Guidi, F., Ugur, M.: An analysis of south-eastern European stock markets: evidence on cointegration and portfolio diversification benefits. J. Inter. Financial Markets, Institutions Money **30**, 119–136 (2014)
4. Shanken, J., Weinstein, M.I.: Economic forces and the stock market revisited. J. Empir. Financ. **13**(2), 129–144 (2006)
5. Siman, B.P., Orencia, A.J.B.: Understanding financial resiliency: a qualitative inquiry into the experiences and strategies of the employees in an engineering and consultancy firm. Inter. J. Multi.: Appl. Bus. Edu. Res. **4**(7), 2391–2400 (2023)
6. Alanyali, M., Moat, H.S., Preis, T.: Quantifying the relationship between financial news and the stock market. Sci. Rep. **3**(1), 1–6 (2013)
7. Ritter, J.R.: Behavioral finance. Pac. Basin Financ. J. **11**(4), 429–437 (2003)
8. Bustos, O., Pomares-Quimbaya, A.: Stock market movement forecast: a systematic re-view. Expert Syst. Appl. **156**, 113464 (2020)
9. Atsalakis, G.S., Valavanis, K.P.: Surveying stock market forecasting techniques–part ii: soft computing methods. Expert Syst. Appl. **36**(3), 5932–5941 (2009)
10. Liagkouras, K., Metaxiotis, K.: Stock market forecasting by using support vector ma-chines. Mach. Learn. Paradigms: Adv. Deep Learn. Technol. Appl. 259–271 (2020)

11. Pawar, K., Jalem, R.S., Tiwari, V.: Stock market price prediction using LSTM RNN. In: Emerging Trends in Expert Applications and Security: Proceedings of ICETEAS 2018. Springer, pp. 493–503 (2019)
12. Islam, M.S., Hossain, E.: Foreign exchange currency rate prediction using a GRU LSTM hybrid network. Soft Comput. Lett. **3**, 100009 (2021)
13. Baek, Y., Kim, H.Y.: Modaugnet: a new forecasting framework for stock market index value with an overfitting prevention LSTM module and a prediction LSTM module. Expert Syst. Appl. **113**, 457–480 (2018)
14. Naik, N., Mohan, B.R.: Study of stock return predictions using recurrent neural net-works with lstm. In: Engineering Applications of Neural Networks: 20th International Con-ference, EANN 2019, Xersonisos, Crete, Greece, May 24-26, 2019, Proceedings 20. Springer, pp. 453–459 (2019).
15. Lee, S.W., Kim, H.Y.: Stock market forecasting with super-high dimensional time-series data using convlstm, trend sampling, and specialized data augmentation. Expert syst. Appl. **161**, 113704 (2020)
16. Shahi, T.B., Shrestha, A., Neupane, A., Guo, W.: Stock price forecasting with deep learning: a comparative study. Mathematics **8**(9), 1441 (2020)
17. DeBoer, M.: Understanding the heat map. Cartographic Perspect. **80**, 39–43 (2015)
18. Martin, R.D., Yohai, V.J., Zamar, R.H.: Min-max bias robust regression. Ann. Stat. **17**(4), 1608–1630 (1989)
19. I. Goodfellow, Y. Bengio, and A. Courville, Deep Learning. MIT Press (2016). http://www.deeplearningbook.org
20. Kim, H.Y., Won, C.H.: Forecasting the volatility of stock price index: a hybrid model integrating LSTM with multiple garch-type models. Expert Syst. Appl. **103**, 25–37 (2018)
21. Barrett, J.P.: The coefficient of determination—some limitations. Am. Stat. **28**(1), 19–20 (1974)
22. Chai, T., Draxler, R.R.: Root mean square error (rmse) or mean absolute error (mae). Geoscientific Model Dev. Discuss. **7**(1), 1525–1534 (2014)

Enhancing Resolution: Harnessing Generative Adversarial Networks for Domain-Specific Super-Resolution

Divya Mohan, Jeswin Roy Dcouth[✉], and Puthin Kumar

Albertian Institute of Science and Technology, Kochi, Kerala, India
jespro89@gmail.com

Abstract. In the current era, super-resolution has emerged as a prominent field of research aimed at enhancing the resolution and visual quality of low-resolution images. Generative Adversarial Networks (GANs) have demonstrated remarkable success in numerous computer vision domains, such as synthesis of images and restoration. In this work, we introduce an innovative approach for domain-specific super-resolution utilizing GANs. Our method focuses on leveraging the domain knowledge inherent in specific types of images to achieve superior results. In this work, we improve upon Enhanced Super-Resolution Generative Adversarial Network (ESRGAN) and introduce domain-specific super-resolution networks that are trained using datasets of homogenous images. By adopting this approach, we effectively reduce the overall complexity associated with the super-resolution problem. Our findings demonstrate that the output of general-purpose networks lacks consistency. While these networks exhibit decent generalization capabilities for super-resolution tasks, their results often exhibit artifacts and subpar textures. Consequently, these models prove unsuitable for practical applications. Conversely, domain-specific models demonstrate high consistency within their trained problem domain. When comparing the outcomes of domain-specific models to the general-purpose ESRGAN model, we observe that the former achieves superior perceptual quality and texture, while exhibiting minimal to no artifacts. By emphasizing domain-specific features during training, our approach achieves super-resolution results which are enhanced and are tailored to the characteristics of the target domain. Experimental evaluations on various domain-specific datasets showcase the efficacy of our proposed approach. Our approach outperforms state-of-the-art super-resolution techniques in terms of both quantitative metrics, such as Peak Signal-to-Noise Ratio (PSNR) and Structural Similarity Index (SSIM), as well as subjective visual quality. The results showcase the ability of our method to effectively enhance resolution and preserve domain-specific details in images.

Keywords: Artificial Neural Network · Computer Vision · Convolutional Neural Network · Deep Learning · Image Processing · Machine Learning · Super Resolution · Generative Adversarial Network

1 Introduction

The process of reconstructing a high-resolution (HR) image from a corresponding low-resolution (LR) image is called Super-Resolution (SR). It is widely recognized as an underdetermined inverse problem, lacking a unique solution. The challenge of the discussed problem becomes increasingly evident with higher upscaling factors, as the reconstructed SR images often fail to capture fine texture details. This limitation is largely attributed to the optimization objectives used in traditional supervised SR algorithms. Over the years, significant advancements have been made in the field of super-resolution, particularly with the introduction of Super-Resolution Generative Adversarial Network (SRGAN) [1] and Enhanced Super-Resolution Generative Adversarial Network (ESR-GAN) [2]. These models have not only established a new state-of-the-art in single image super-resolution but have also shifted the emphasis from simple interpolation techniques to the utilization of DCNNs, which comprise a generator and a discriminator. In the current age of high-definition displays and demanding computational needs in computer graphics, the utilization of super-resolution methods can greatly empower computing systems to excel. The most common solution to super-resolution remains interpolation. This is done by increasing the spatial size of an LR image and using an interpolation approach such as nearest neighbour, bilinear, or bicubic to approximate missing pixel values. These methods produce overly smooth results which lack texture details. Recently, Generative Adversarial Networks were used for the task of super-resolution. Experimental evidence has demonstrated that conventional metrics used to compare super-resolution (SR) algorithms, such as Peak Signal-to-Noise Ratio, fail to effectively capture perceptually significant distinctions, particularly in terms of high texture detail. This inadequacy arises from the reliance on pixel-level discrepancies as the basis for evaluation.

As depicted in Fig. 1, it becomes evident that relying solely on PSNR/SSIM metrics does not accurately reflect the pictorial fidelity of the generated image. Notably, both Bicubic interpolation and SRGAN exhibit comparable PSNR/SSIM values, but SRGAN significantly outperforms Bicubic interpolation in terms of visual appeal. Conversely, SRResNet, trained with a Mean Squared Error based loss function, achieves higher PSNR/SSIM values; however, the resulting images lack the same level of visual satisfaction as those generated by SRGAN, which employs a perceptual loss function.

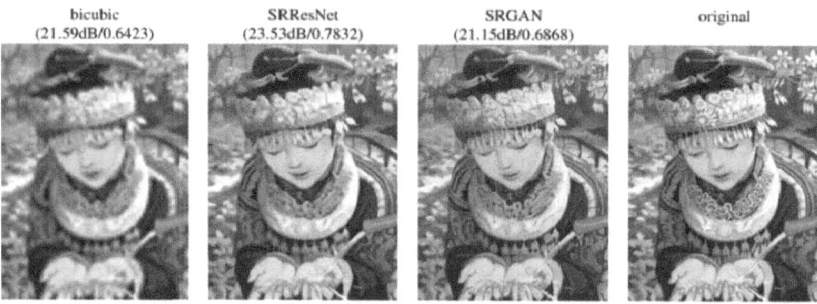

Fig. 1. The PSNR and SSIM values are indicated in brackets for HR image, deep residual generative adversarial network and bicubic interpolation

SRGAN [1] pioneered the introduction of a perceptual loss function by incorporating high-level feature maps from the VGG network [3]. This innovative approach aimed to capture more meaningful and perceptually relevant differences between the generated and ground truth high-resolution images. By utilizing the VGG network's feature maps, which capture semantic information rather than relying solely on pixel-wise comparisons, SRGAN successfully enhanced the overall image fidelity and realism of the upscaled images. This breakthrough opened up new possibilities for improving the perceptual fidelity of super-resolution algorithms and paved the way for subsequent advancements in the field.

ESRGAN [2] advanced these developments by integrating a relativistic discriminator and Residual-in-Residual Dense Blocks (RRDB) into its architecture, aiming to enhance the quality and realism of super-resolved images. Despite these improvements, however, the resulting models still exhibited artifacts, primarily attributable to the inherent complexity of the super-resolution task. The challenge arises from the fact that training a single GAN model to upscale all conceivable image categories would be impractical and inefficient. Different image categories possess unique characteristics and textures, making it essential to consider domain-specific knowledge during the training process. Failure to account for these specific attributes often results in the generation of artifacts and inconsistencies within the super-resolved images.

To overcome these limitations, researchers have recognized the need for domain-specific models that focus on particular image categories. By training models specifically tailored to these domains, it becomes possible to achieve higher quality super-resolution results with reduced artifacts. This approach highlights the importance of considering the domain-specific nature of images in order to address the complexities and challenges associated with the super-resolution task. In Fig. 2, the super-resolved image on the left exhibits a remarkable resemblance to the original image on the right, demonstrating nearly indistinguishable quality. This impressive result was achieved using a $4\times$ upscaling factor.

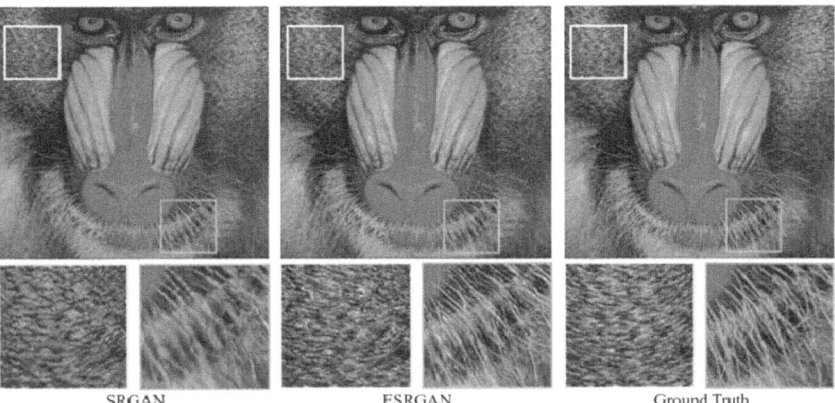

Fig. 2. Super-resolved image (left) original (right) [$4 \times$ upscaling]

Consequently, we propose the utilization of domain-specific super-resolution techniques, which focus on upscaling images belonging to a specific heterogeneous category. This approach significantly simplifies the complexity associated with super-resolution, allowing for faster training using shallower network architectures. By tailoring the model specifically to the characteristics and intricacies of a particular domain, it outperforms general-purpose models in terms of super-resolution performance within that specific domain. The advantages of domain-specific super-resolution models are twofold. Firstly, their specialization enables a more targeted and efficient learning process, resulting in improved accuracy and higher-quality outputs. Secondly, the reduced complexity allows for faster training times, making the approach more practical and feasible for real-world applications. By leveraging domain-specific knowledge, these models can better capture and preserve the unique features and textures specific to the targeted image category. As a result, the super-resolved images exhibit enhanced visual fidelity, with minimized artifacts and increased perceptual quality. Domain-specific super-resolution proves to be a promising direction in addressing the challenges of the super-resolution task and catering to the diverse needs of different image categories.

2 Related Works

The initial scenarios of super-resolution domain heavily relied on interpolation techniques rooted in sampling theory. These approaches sought to estimate missing high-resolution information by interpolating and extrapolating from the available low-resolution data. By leveraging principles from sampling theory, these methods aimed to reconstruct the high-resolution image with increased detail and clarity. However, as the field progressed, more advanced and sophisticated techniques, such as deep learning and GANs, emerged, surpassing limitations from traditional interpolation-based approaches [4–6].

A popular explored area to augment the quality and in particular resolution of images is Single Image Super-Resolution. To achieve this, prediction-based methods are commonly employed. These methods leverage techniques such as linear filtering, bicubic filtering, or Lanczos filtering to predict higher-resolution details based on the available low-resolution information. These prediction-based methods serve as the foundation for many Single Image SR algorithms. Through prediction and estimation of missing high resolution details from inputs of lower resolution, these techniques contribute to the improvement of quality and pictorial fidelity in diverse applications, including digital image processing, computer vision and content upscaling.

Example-based methods [17, 18] employ sophisticated techniques to establish a complex linkage between low-res and high-res images. These methods leverage a dataset of paired low-res and high-res image examples for learning underlying relationship and generate super-resolved outputs. By effectively capturing the intricate details and structures from the provided examples, these methods achieve impressive results in enhancing image resolution.

In addition to example-based methods, another approach frequently employed in the domain of image super-resolution is compressed sensing [12], [62, 69]. Compressed sensing techniques exploit the sparsity of images in certain domains to reconstruct high-resolution images from limited and undersampled measurements. By exploiting the prior knowledge of the sparsity or compressibility of images, compressed sensing enables the recovery of fine details and enhances the resolution effectively.

Example-based methods and compressed sensing ways have a vital role in advancing image super-resolution, offering robust tools to generate high-definition, detailed, and aesthetically compelling high-res images from low-res inputs.

Sparse-Coding [25] significantly enhances the consistency of image processing by taking into account the entirety of the image rather than relying on overlapping patches. This approach ensures a more comprehensive understanding of the visual information and promotes a more coherent representation of the image. By considering the complete context, Sparse-Coding can capture global patterns and relationships, resulting in improved image interpretation and analysis. Tai et al. [52] employ a novel approach to achieve realistic texture reconstruction while mitigating the occurrence of edge artifacts. Their approach combines a super-resolution edge-directed (SR) algorithm [50], with the advantages of learning-enabled texture synthesis. This hybrid strategy effectively balances traditional edge-preserving techniques with modern learning-driven methods. As a result, it enhances the reconstruction of fine textures while maintaining structural integrity in super-resolved images. By integrating these two techniques, they are able to generate high-quality textures that maintain visual fidelity and avoid undesirable artifacts at edges. This innovative fusion of edge-guided super resolution and learning-driven synthesis offers a promising solution for enhancing texture detail in an accurate and visually pleasing manner.

Neighborhood embedding approaches [54, 55] aim to upsample a less resolution image by leveraging concept of locating comparable LR patches for training within a reduced feature space. By identifying these similar LR patches, these methods can extract corresponding high-resolution (HR) patches and utilize them for the reconstruction process. This technique allows for the integration of local context from the HR patches, resulting in a more accurate and visually appealing upsampled image. The use of neighborhood embedding approaches in image reconstruction showcases their ability to exploit the intrinsic structure of the LR image and efficiently capture relevant information from its surroundings. This combination of patch-based similarity searching and HR patch synthesis facilitates the production of superior quality high-res outputs from low-quality inputs. In addition to Kernel Ridge Regression [35], alternative methods such as Gaussian Process Regression [27], decision trees [46], and Random Forests [47] can also be employed to address the regression problem. These approaches offer different modeling techniques and algorithms that can effectively handle various types of regression tasks. By exploring these alternative methods, investigators and specialists have broader array of choices to choose from based on the particular needs of their regression problem, allowing them to select the most suitable approach for achieving accurate and reliable regression results.

The Super-Resolution CNN (SRCNN) is a two-layer CNN that incorporates sparse coding techniques. Dong et al. in their contribution [9, 10] adopted a method of interpolation i.e. bicubic to magnify the initial image. To attain cutting edge performance super-resolution (SR) performance, they trained a three-layer deep fully convoluted model end-to-end. This approach allowed them to learn and extract intricate details from the low-quality (LR) input and generate high-quality, super-resolved images. By combining sparse coding and deep learning techniques, the SRCNN demonstrated its ability to surpass previous SR methods and achieve remarkable results in enhancing image resolution and visual fidelity. The Deeply-Recursive CNN (DRCN) [34] is an architecture designed for achieving high performance in image processing tasks. This innovative network excels in capturing long-range pixel dependencies, enabling it to effectively capture and utilize contextual information from distant pixels. Remarkably, the DRCN accomplishes this while maintaining a small number of predictive factors, which is advantageous in terms of computational efficiency and memory requirements. The DRCN's ability to leverage long-range dependencies while remaining parameter-efficient makes it a compelling choice for tasks requiring comprehensive understanding of image structures and intricate relationships between pixels.

Training deeper CNN network architectures [49, 51] can pose challenges due to issues like vanishing gradients and overfitting. However, these architectures hold immense ability for significantly boosting the accuracy of the model. By increasing the depth of the network, we enable the modeling of mappings with a much higher level of complexity. This enables the network to learn and represent intricate patterns and relationships within the data, leading to enhanced performance in tasks such as image classification or object detection. Although the training process may be more intricate, the rewards of leveraging deeper CNN architectures are substantial, as they allow for more expressive and sophisticated feature representations, ultimately leading to enhanced accuracy and performance. Batch normalization [32] aids in the training of these deeper network architectures. Residual blocks [29] and skip-connections [30, 34] are utilized for training deeper networks. Skip-connections provide a solution to the challenge of training the identity mapping, which is a simple task but can be difficult to represent accurately using convolutional kernels alone. By incorporating skip-connections, the network architecture is relieved of the burden of explicitly learning the identity mapping, allowing it to focus on capturing more complex and non-trivial patterns in the data. This approach facilitates the training of deeper networks by enabling smoother gradient flow and mitigating the vanishing gradient problem. The combination of residual blocks and skip-connections enhances the network's ability to learn deep representations, leading to enhanced results and increased accuracy in various tasks such as image recognition or semantic segmentation. Learning upscaling filters [11, 48, 57] offers advantages in both accuracy and speed. By training specific filters for the upscaling process, the network can tailor the transformation to the characteristics of the input data, resulting in improved accuracy. These learned filters can capture the intricate details and patterns necessary for high-quality upscaling. Moreover, by employing learned filters, the network can efficiently perform the upscaling operation, leading to faster processing times compared to traditional fixed filters. The combination of improved accuracy and enhanced computational efficiency makes learning upscaling filters a valuable approach in various tasks such as image super-resolution, where both quality and speed are crucial factors.

MSE (Mean Squared Error) encounters difficulties when dealing with the inherent uncertainty involved in recovering lost high-frequency details, such as texture. The nature of MSE minimization tends to encourage the finding of pixel-wise averages among plausible solutions, resulting in excessively smooth outputs that lack satisfactory perceptual quality. As a result, MSE optimization alone may fail to capture and preserve the fine-grained details and textures that are vital for visually appealing and realistic image reconstruction. Therefore, alternative evaluation metrics or optimization objectives that prioritize perceptual quality and preserve high-frequency information should be considered to address this limitation. By incorporating perceptual loss functions or other suitable measures, it becomes possible to mitigate the drawbacks of MSE and achieve more visually pleasing and faithful reconstructions [5, 13, 33, 42]. Li and Wand [38] explain process about Generative Adversarial Networks (GANs) learning to sync from one manifold to another for style transfer. In a recent study, Li and Wand [38] conducted an investigation into the impact of contrasting and merging patches in either space or Visual Geometry Group feature space.

In [54] the model has been expanded upon to enhance the overall visual quality of generated images. To achieve this, a new network architecture has been developed, featuring a unique basic block that replaces the one originally employed in ESRGAN. Additionally, a new element has been introduced into the generator network, namely, noise inputs. This addition enables the model to take advantage of stochastic or random variations, resulting in images that exhibit more realistic textures.

3 Proposed Method

The progress of screen resolution has been remarkable over the years. However, the availability of native high-resolution images is still limited due to constraints in storage space and computational resources. As a result, interpolated images are commonly used as a solution, but they often result in excessively smooth outputs that lack fine details. While significant progress has been made in improving the accuracy and speed of single-image super-resolution using faster and deeper convolutional neural networks, a critical challenge remains unresolved. This challenge lies in effectively reconstructing fine texture details, particularly at high upscaling factors. Traditional methods often struggle to balance detail restoration and overall image consistency. Addressing this issue is vital for advancing the practical application of super-resolution techniques across diverse domains. Many online image upscaling applications offer limited features and often require preprocessing of the input image before applying their algorithms. The use of Mean Squared Error (MSE) as the loss function fails to accurately enhance texture details during the upscaling process. Similarly, the Peak Signal-to-Noise Ratio (PSNR) metric falls short in capturing perceptual quality, as it primarily focuses on objective quality evaluation rather than subjective visual perception.

Our approach focuses on fine-tuning the generator network specifically for related categories of images, resulting in an enhanced perceptual quality of the generated high-resolution (HR) images. The generator network generates estimations of the HR image by utilizing low-resolution (LR) counterparts as input. To prioritize perceptual quality over objective quality (PSNR), we train the generator network using an adversarial network and a perceptual loss function. Superior perceptual quality was attained by making the generator to produce solutions that align with the natural image manifold.

To further enhance the visual quality of the generated images, we employ model chaining and network interpolation techniques. Model chaining enables us to combine the outputs from two distinct models. Additionally, network interpolation helps reduce artifacts in the generated images by blending a PSNR-oriented network with a GAN-based network.

For our GAN-based models, we divide them into two categories. The first category consists of a general-purpose model trained on diverse image datasets with no inherent relationship between the images. The second category comprises domain-specific models trained on image datasets belonging to a particular category. These domain-specific models are specialized in super-resolving images within their respective category but may perform sub optimally for images from other categories. In summary, for a super resolution task, the generator is responsible for upscaling low-resolution images using a specialized architecture with enhanced basic blocks and noise inputs, while the discriminator is part of a GAN and focuses on distinguishing real from generated high-resolution images. The interplay between these two networks results in the generation of high-quality super-resolved images with improved perceptual quality, including more realistic textures.

3.1 Generator

The generator network in our model is responsible for estimating the high-resolution (HR) image, also known as the Super-Resolved (SR) image, from its corresponding low-resolution (LR) counterpart. Our generator is built upon the architecture of the generator network presented in ESRGAN [2]. The generator in our model incorporates a variable number of Residual-in-Residual Dense (RRDB) blocks, which is determined based on the specific image domain. Increasing the depth of the network can enhance the generator's ability to generate accurate estimations. However, it is important to note that deeper networks also result in longer training times. Therefore, our ESRGAN model offers flexibility and can be adjusted to meet the requirements of different image domains. Some image categories may be less complex and diverse than others, allowing the generator network to be trained with a smaller number of RRDB blocks (such as 16) instead of the recommended number proposed in [2].

The output of the generator is compared to the ground-truth high-resolution (HR) image. The generator tries to minimize the following loss function:

$$L(G(LR), HR)$$

where L is the loss function, G is the generator function, LR is the input low-resolution image and HR is the original ground-truth image.

3.2 Discriminator

We augment the discriminator by employing the Relativistic GAN [20] framework. This approach enhances the discriminator's ability to distinguish between real and generated images by introducing a relativistic formulation. By considering the relative quality of the generated and real images, the Relativistic GAN provides a more accurate assessment of the discriminator's performance. This technique helps improve the overall training stability and encourages the generator to produce higher-quality images that better align with the distribution of real images. The Relativistic GAN framework has proven to be an effective enhancement in the adversarial training process for super-resolution tasks. While the conventional discriminator in SRGAN estimates the likelihood of an input image being the true HR image, a relativistic discriminator takes on the task of predicting the probability that a real image is comparatively more realistic than a generated one. By adopting a relativistic perspective, this discriminator aims to assess the relative quality of real and fake images rather than making an absolute determination. This approach provides a more nuanced understanding of the realism of generated images and contributes to the overall training process of SRGAN.

The adversarial loss is defined as:

$$L_G = -E_{Xr}\left[\log(1 - D_{Ra}(Xr, Xf))\right] - E_{Xf}[log(DRa(Xf, Xr))] \tag{1}$$

where Xr is the real image and Xf is the fake image and D_{Ra} is the relativistic discriminator.

In Eq. (1) definition of the adversarial loss (LG) in the context of a Generative Adversarial Network (GAN) for a super resolution task is depicted. The components of this loss function are:

LG: This represents the adversarial loss, which is a key component of training the generator in a GAN. The goal of the generator is to minimize this loss, as it indicates how well the generator is performing in generating realistic images.

EXr: This term represents the expectation (average) over real high-resolution images (Xr). In GAN training, this is typically calculated as an average over a batch of real high-resolution images drawn from the dataset.

EXf: This term represents the expectation over fake high-resolution images (Xf), which are generated by the generator.

DRa(Xr, Xf): This is the output of the discriminator (D) when given both a real high-resolution image (Xr) and a fake high-resolution image (Xf) as inputs. The discriminator produces a probability score indicating the likelihood that the input is a real image (in the case of Xr) or a fake image (in the case of Xf).

log(1−DRa(Xr, Xf)): This part of the loss measures how well the discriminator is at correctly identifying that Xr is a real image. The generator aims to minimize this term by making Xf (the fake image) more convincing as a real image.

log(DRa(Xf, Xr)): This part of the loss measures how well the discriminator is at correctly identifying that Xf is a fake image. The generator aims to minimize this term by making Xf more difficult to distinguish from real images.

The overall objective of the generator is to minimize the adversarial loss LG, which encourages it to generate high-resolution images (Xf) that are so convincing that the discriminator cannot easily differentiate them from real high-resolution images (Xr). In other words, the generator's goal is to "fool" the discriminator into assigning high probabilities to the fake images.

Through a process of adversarial training, the generator gets better at generating high-quality super-resolved images that are visually similar to real high-resolution images. This competition between the generator and discriminator results in improved image quality during training.

During the generator training phase, we utilize both high-resolution (HR) images and their corresponding low-resolution (LR) counterparts. However, only the HR images are provided during the training process. The low-resolution (LR) images are generated by downscaling the high-resolution (HR) images using a bicubic kernel function. By presenting the generator with LR images and expecting it to produce HR images that closely resemble the ground-truth images, we encourage the generator to deceive the discriminator network. The goal is to generate super-resolved images that are challenging for the discriminator to differentiate from the actual HR images. This approach promotes the generation of visually superior results. Additionally, to ensure stability and facilitate the training process, we implement residual scaling and smaller initialization techniques as proposed in [2].

3.3 Network Interpolation

To mitigate the noise and artifacts commonly observed in the results of GAN-based super-resolution networks, we employ network interpolation. Our approach involves training a PSNR-oriented network, which typically produces results with minimal artifacts due to its use of MSE as the loss function. Additionally, we train a GAN-based network using a new perceptual loss function. By combining these two networks through interpolation, we create an improved interpolated model that effectively removes noise and unwanted artifacts from the upscaled image. It is important to note that there is a trade-off between noise reduction and the potential for slight blurring in the resultant network. This trade-off can be adjusted according to the specific requirements of the model.

3.4 Model Chaining

In addition to network interpolation, which blends a PSNR-oriented model and a GAN-based model, we employ model chaining as another approach. Model chaining involves combining the output of two GAN-based approaches to achieve a final result. For example, we can merge the output of a general-purpose model, which excels at generating images with high perceptual quality but may have minor artifacts, with that of a domain-specific model, which specializes in preserving textures and reducing artifacts. This combined result maintains the desired perceptual quality while mitigating some of the artifacts present. Model chaining can also be applied to restore images affected by camera noise, artifacts, and other imperfections, resulting in improved image quality and fidelity.

3.5 General Purpose Model

Training a general-purpose model involves using image datasets that encompass diverse categories of images without any inherent relationship between them. This approach necessitates a large collection of images and lengthy training times. However, even when these prerequisites are met, the resulting model often falls short in delivering satisfactory outcomes for various image categories or complex images, such as textures. There are several reasons contributing to the underperformance of general-purpose models. Firstly, the super-resolution problem itself is highly challenging, making it difficult for a single model to accurately capture the necessary information required for high-quality super-resolution across all image categories. Additionally, there is no single dataset that encompasses all possible image categories, which further hinders the training of a comprehensive general-purpose model. As a result, general-purpose models typically yield suboptimal results and fail to fully exploit the capabilities of generative adversarial networks (GANs).

3.6 Domain-Specific Model

Specialized models tailored to specific domains are trained using image datasets that focus on a particular category, such as anime datasets. These models are specifically designed to enhance the resolution of images belonging to that specific category and exhibit significantly lower performance when applied to images from other categories. However, when applied to images within their intended category, these domain-specific models often outperform general-purpose models by a substantial margin. This highlights the effectiveness of training models that are specialized for specific image categories, enabling them to better capture the unique characteristics and nuances associated with those categories.

4 Experiments

4.1 Training Details

In the case of SRGAN, the training process involved utilizing a random sample of 350 thousand images sourced from the ImageNet database [45]. It is important to note that these training images were distinct from the images used for testing. To generate the low-resolution (LR) images, we downscaled the high-resolution (HR) images using a bicubic kernel with a downsampling factor of r = 4. During the training process, each mini-batch consisted of 16 randomly cropped 96×96 HR sub-images, ensuring a diverse representation of training images. We scaled to the range of 0 to 1 the low resolution input images, while the range of -1 to 1 was selected for the high resolution images. For optimization purposes, we employed the Adam optimizer [36] with a β1 value of 0.9. Our generator network was designed with 16 identical residual blocks (B = 16). During the testing phase, we disabled the batch-normalization update to ensure that the output of the network is solely dependent on the input in a deterministic manner [32].

In the case of ESRGAN, the training procedure is carried out in two separate phases. Initially, a Peak Signal Noise Ratio-oriented model is trained using the L1 loss. The learning rate is initialized to $2 \times 10^{(-4)}$ and is reduced by half after every 2×10^5 mini-batch updates. Subsequently, the trained PSNR-oriented model is utilized as an initialization for the generator. The generator is then trained using a loss function with parameters λ set to $5 \times 10^{(-3)}$ and η set to $1 \times 10^{(-2)}$. The learning rate for this stage is established as $1 \times 10^{(-4)}$ and is halved at iterations [50k, 100k, 200k, 300k]. Pre-training the model with a pixel-wise loss aids GAN-based methods in achieving visually appealing results. For the optimization process, the Adam optimizer is employed with β1 set to 0.9 and β2 set to 0.999. The generator and discriminator networks are alternatively updated until the model converges. This iterative process helps refine the model's performance. We utilize two different configurations for our generator network. The first configuration consists of 16 residual blocks, which provides a similar capacity to that of SRGAN. The second configuration is a deeper model that incorporates 23 RRDB (Residual-in-Residual Dense Blocks) blocks.

4.2 Data

The SRGAN experiments were conducted on three commonly used benchmark datasets, namely Set5 [3], Set14 [69], and BSD100, utilizing the testing set of BSD300 [41]. In all experiments, a scale factor of 4× was employed to compare low-resolution and high-resolution images. This scale factor corresponds to a reduction of 16× in terms of image pixels. To prepare the low-resolution (LR) images for ESRGAN, we utilize the MATLAB bicubic kernel function to down-sample the high-resolution (HR) images. In our experiments, the mini-batch size of 16 is utilized and the spatial size of the cropped HR patch is fixed at 128 × 128 pixels. We have observed that training a deeper network tends to benefit from using larger patch sizes, as it allows for a wider receptive field to capture additional semantic information. However, it is important to note that this increase in patch size also leads to longer training times and higher consumption of computing resources. This phenomenon holds true not only for ESRGAN but also for PSNR-oriented methods. To train the general-purpose GAN model, we employ the DIV2K, Flickr2K, and Outdoor Scene Training datasets. These datasets offer a wide range of diverse textures that are suitable for training the model. The evaluation of the general images was conducted using the Set5, Set14, and BSD100 datasets. For the domain-specific model dedicated to upscaling anime images, we curated a custom dataset comprising high-resolution anime footage, which we refer to as Anime4x. The evaluation of the super-resolved anime images was performed using images sourced from Danbooru. Similarly, the model focused on upscaling digital art was trained using a custom dataset created from images obtained from DeviantArt. The evaluation of the super-resolved digital art images was conducted using the same custom dataset, which we refer to as DigArt4x. Throughout the experiments, a scale factor of 4× is consistently used to compare low-resolution and high-resolution images. This scale factor corresponds to a significant reduction of 16× in terms of image pixels. In order to ensure a fair and standardized comparison, all reported PSNR [dB] and SSIM measures are calculated specifically on the y-channel of center-cropped images. Additionally, a 4-pixel wide strip is removed from each border of the images before applying the measurements, following the guidelines provided by the daala package (Fig. 3).

4.3 Mean Opinion Score (MOS) Testing

To evaluate and compare the performance of various SR algorithms, we employ the Mean Opinion Score (MOS) test. This test serves as a superior comparison metric compared to traditional metrics such as PSNR (Peak Signal-to-Noise Ratio) and SSIM (Structural Similarity Index). MOS allows for subjective assessment by human observers, taking into account perceptual quality and overall user preference, providing more reliable and comprehensive results. In the MOS test, a group of 26 raters is tasked with assigning integral scores ranging from 1 (representing bad quality) to 5 (representing excellent quality)

Fig. 3. BSD100 Dataset

to the super-resolved images. Each rater evaluates 12 different versions of each image from the Set5, Set14, and BSD100 datasets. The versions of the images include different upscaling methods such as nearest neighbor (NN), bicubic, SRCNN [9], SelfExSR [31], DRCN [34], ESPCN [48], SRResNet-MSE, SRResNet-VGG22, SRGAN-MSE, SRGAN-VGG22, SRGANVGG54, and the original high-resolution (HR) image. The raters assessed a total of 1128 instances, which included 12 versions of 19 images and 9 versions of 100 images, all presented in a randomized order. Before conducting the evaluations, the raters underwent calibration by rating the NN (score 1) and HR (score 5) versions of 20 images from the BSD300 training set. This calibration step ensured consistency and provided a reference point for the subsequent ratings. In an initial study, we conducted an assessment of the calibration procedure and test-retest reliability involving a group of 26 raters. This evaluation was performed on a subset of 10 images extracted from BSD100. As part of this assessment, we included duplicate images of a particular method in a larger test set. The results of this pilot study demonstrated good reliability and indicated no significant differences between the ratings of the identical images. The raters consistently assigned a rating of 1 to the test images interpolated with nearest neighbor (NN) method, while the original high-resolution (HR) images consistently received a rating of 5. These findings suggest a high level of consistency among the raters in their assessment of image quality.

5 Results

We evaluate the performance of SRResNet and SRGAN against NN, bicubic interpolation, and four other state-of-the-art methods. The quantitative results are presented in Table 1, demonstrating that SRResNet achieves a new state-of-the-art performance in terms of PSNR/SSIM on the three benchmark datasets. Moreover, the results in

Table 1 show that SRGAN surpasses all the reference methods by a significant margin, establishing a new state-of-the-art for photorealistic image super-resolution (Fig. 4).

Table 1. Comparison of NN, bicubic, SRCNN [9], SelfExSR [31], DRCN [34], ESPCN [48], SRResNet, SRGAN-VGG54 and the original HR on benchmark data. Highest measures (PSNR [dB], SSIM, MOS). [4 × upscaling].

		PSNR	SSIM	MOS
Set 5 Dataset	nearest	26.26	0.7552	1.28
	Bicubic	28.43	0.8211	1.97
	SRCNN	30.07	0.8627	2.57
	SelfExSR	30.33	0.872	2.65
	DRCN	31.52	0.8938	3.26
	ESPCN	30.76	0.8784	2.89
	SRResNet	32.05	0.9019	3.37
	SRGAN	29.40	0.8472	3.58
	HR	∞	1	4.32
Set 14 Dataset		**PSNR**	**SSIM**	**MOS**
	nearest	24.64	0.7100	1.20
	Bicubic	25.99	0.7486	1.80
	SRCNN	27.18	0.7861	2.26
	SelfExSR	27.45	0.7972	2.34
	DRCN	28.02	0.8074	2.84
	ESPCN	27.66	0.8004	2.52
	SRResNet	28.49	0.8184	2.98
	SRGAN	26.02	0.7397	3.72
	HR	∞	1	4.32
BSD100 Dataset		**PSNR**	**SSIM**	**MOS**
	nearest	25.02	0.6606	1.11
	Bicubic	25.94	0.6935	1.47
	SRCNN	26.68	0.7291	1.87
	SelfExSR	26.83	0.7387	1.89
	DRCN	27.21	0.7493	2.12
	ESPCN	27.02	0.7442	2.01
	SRResNet	27.58	0.7620	2.29
	SRGAN	25.16	0.6688	3.56
	HR	∞	1	4.46

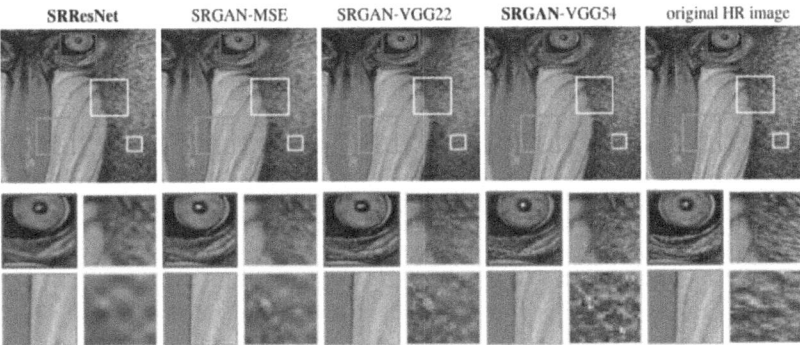

Fig. 4. Output from the different GAN networks

We conduct a comprehensive comparison of our models on various benchmark datasets, comparing them with basic bicubic and nearest neighbor interpolation methods, as well as the general-purpose upscaling model ESRGAN based on GAN. To provide a more comprehensive assessment of perceptual quality, we present multiple relevant visual examples, as existing measurements may not accurately capture human perceptual preferences at a fine-grained level. Additionally, we include quantitative results below for reference.

Our Anime4x model and DigArt4x model demonstrate superior performance compared to the general-purpose model and other approaches in upscaling anime images and digital art, respectively. These domain-specific models exhibit improved texture details and fewer artifacts compared to the general-purpose model. Conversely, it is worth noting that the general-purpose model outperforms the domain-specific models when applied to images that do not fall into the anime or digital art categories. Despite providing a reasonable generalization for super-resolution tasks, the general-purpose model's results fall short of being satisfactory. Hence, domain-specific models remain the optimal choice for achieving high perceptual quality, preserving texture details, and minimizing artifacts (Table 2).

Even when combined with the adversarial loss, the Mean Squared Error (MSE) loss produces solutions with high Peak Signal-to-Noise Ratio (PSNR) values. However, these solutions tend to be visually smooth and less convincing compared to results achieved with a loss component that is more sensitive to visual perception. On Set14, the SRGAN-VGG54 variant significantly outperforms other SRGAN and SRResNet variants in terms of Mean Opinion Score (MOS). This improvement can be attributed to the use of higher-level VGG feature maps, which capture better texture detail. The competition between the MSE-based content loss and the adversarial loss in SRGAN can lead to perceptually smooth but less visually convincing results, and in some cases, minor reconstruction artifacts may be observed. For SRResNet or SRGAN, no significantly superior loss function could be determined based on the MOS score on Set5. However, SRGAN-VGG54 outperforms other variants on Set14 in terms of MOS (Table 3 and Figs. 5, 6 and 7).

Table 2. Comparison of bicubic, NN, ESRGAN(General)[X], Anime4x and Digart4x on benchmark data. [4 × upscaling]

	Metric	Bicubic	Nearest Neighbor	ESRGAN (General)	Anime 4x	Digart4x
Anime images	PSNR	34.25	33.38	33.40	34.05	32.66
	SSIM	0.8407	0.7514	0.8042	0.8517	0.8125
Digital Art	Metric	Bicubic	Nearest Neighbor	ESRGAN (General)	Anime 4x	Digart4x
	PSNR	28.66	26.37	28.35	26.02	28.51
	SSIM	0.8292	0.7727	0.8271	0.7949	0.8368
General	Metric	Bicubic	Nearest Neighbor	ESRGAN (General)	Anime 4x	Digart4x
	PSNR	26.87	25.59	25.84	24.94	25.18
	SSIM	0.7969	0.6598	0.7608	0.6766	0.6284

Table 3. Investigation of content loss

			PSNR	SSIM	MOS
SRResNet	Set5 Dataset	MSE	32.05	0.9019	3.37
		VGG22	30.51	0.8803	3.46
	Set14 Dataset	MSE	28.49	0.8184	2.98
		VGG22	27.19	0.7807	3.15
SRGAN	Set5 Dataset	MSE	30.64	0.8701	3.77
		VGG22	29.84	0.8486	3.78
		VGG54	29.40	0.8472	3.58
	Set14 Dataset	MSE	26.92	0.7611	3.43
		VGG22	26.44	0.7518	3.57
		VGG54	26.02	0.7397	3.72

Esper is a Windows application that leverages Python for both its front and back end. It incorporates advanced GAN networks such as SRGAN, ESRGAN, and ESPER-GAN, utilizing the PyTorch library. Additionally, it offers basic interpolation algorithms for users who wish to interpolate results from the GAN networks. The models have been trained for various upscaling factors and support up to 4x upscaling. Users are

Fig. 5. Qualitative Results on Amine Images Domain

Fig. 6. Qualitative Results on Digital Art Images Domain

Fig. 7. Qualitative Results on General Images Domain

provided with the flexibility to compare different super-resolution algorithms within the application (Fig. 8).

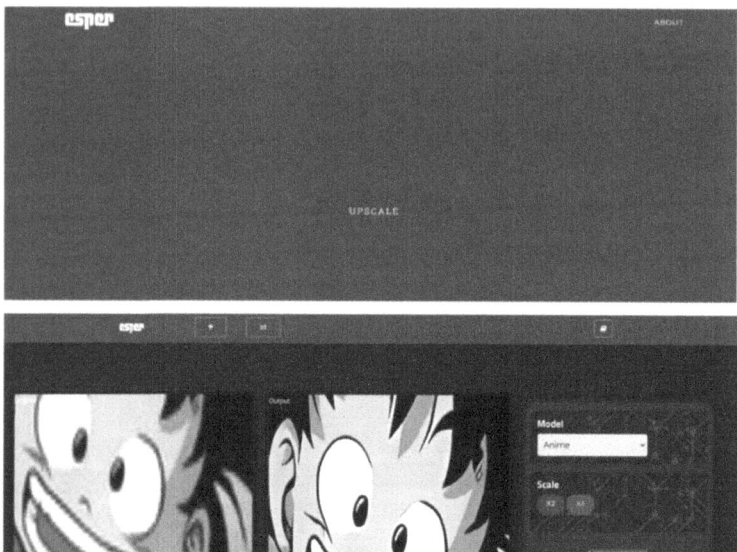

Fig. 8. User Interface

6 Conclusion

By leveraging GANs, we have addressed the limitations of general-purpose models in producing high-quality super-resolved images across diverse image categories. We introduced domain-specific models tailored to specific image domains such as anime and digital art, which outperformed the general-purpose model in terms of texture details and artifact reduction. Our research highlights the importance of considering the unique characteristics and requirements of different image domains when designing super-resolution models. The use of domain-specific models allows for better preservation of perceptual quality and texture details, resulting in superior visual results. Furthermore, we introduced techniques such as network interpolation and model chaining to further enhance the visual quality of the super-resolved images. These techniques enable us to combine the strengths of different models and mitigate their individual limitations, resulting in improved image quality and reduced artifacts. The experimental results presented in the paper, along with the quantitative evaluations, demonstrate the superiority of our domain-specific models over existing approaches, including general-purpose models and traditional interpolation methods. We have also provided an intuitive user interface in the Esper application, enabling users to compare and visualize the results of various super-resolution algorithms.

In summary, our work underscores the significance of leveraging GANs and domain-specific models to achieve remarkable enhancements in super-resolution. The proposed techniques contribute to advancing the field of image resolution enhancement and offer promising avenues for further research and application in various domains.

References

1. Allebach, J., Wong, P.W.: Edge-directed interpolation. In: Proceedings of International Conference on Image Processing, vol. 3, pp. 707–710 (1996)
2. Aly, H.A., Dubois, E.: Image up-sampling using total-variation regularization with a new observation model. IEEE Trans. Image Process. **14**(10), 1647–1659 (2005)
3. Bevilacqua, M., Roumy, A., Guillemot, C., Alberi-Morel, M.L.: Low-complexity single-image super-resolution based on nonnegative neighbor embedding. In: BMVC (2012)
4. Borman, S., Stevenson, R.L.: Super-resolution from image sequences - a review. In: Midwest Symposium on Circuits and Systems, pp. 374–378 (1998)
5. Bruna, J., Sprechmann, P., LeCun, Y.: Super-resolution with deep convolutional sufficient statistics. In: International Conference on Learning Representations (ICLR) (2016)
6. Dai, D., Timofte, R., Van Gool, L.: Jointly optimized regressors for image super-resolution. Comput. Graph. Forum **34**, 95–104 (2015)
7. Denton, E., Chintala, S., Szlam, A., Fergus, R.: Deep generative image models using a Laplacian pyramid of adversarial networks. In: Advances in Neural Information Processing Systems (NIPS), pp. 1486–1494 (2015)
8. Dieleman, S., et al.: Lasagne: First release (2015)
9. Dong, C., Loy, C.C., He, K., Tang, X.: Learning a deep convolutional network for image super-resolution. In: European Conference on Computer Vision (ECCV), pp. 184–199. Springer (2014)
10. Dong, C., Loy, C.C., He, K., Tang, X.: Image super-resolution using deep convolutional networks. IEEE Trans. Pattern Anal. Mach. Intell. **38**(2), 295–307 (2016)

11. Dong, C., Loy, C.C., Tang, X.: Accelerating the super-resolution convolutional neural network. In: European Conference on Computer Vision (ECCV), pp. 391–407. Springer (2016)
12. Dong, W., Zhang, L., Shi, G., Wu, X.: Image deblurring and superresolution by adaptive sparse domain selection and adaptive regularization. IEEE Trans. Image Process. **20**(7), 1838–1857 (2011)
13. Dosovitskiy, A., Brox, T.: Generating images with perceptual similarity metrics based on deep networks. In: Advances in Neural Information Processing Systems (NIPS), pp. 658–666 (2016)
14. Duchon, C.E.: Lanczos filtering in one and two dimensions. J. Appl. Meteorol. **18**, 1016–1022 (1979)
15. Farsiu, S., Robinson, M.D., Elad, M., Milanfar, P.: Fast and robust multiframe super resolution. IEEE Trans. Image Process. **13**(10), 1327–1344 (2004)
16. Ferwerda, J.A.: Three varieties of realism in computer graphics. In: Electronic Imaging, pp. 290–297. International Society for Optics and Photonics (2003)
17. Freeman, W.T., Jones, T.R., Pasztor, E.C.: Example-based superresolution. IEEE Comput. Graphics Appl. **22**(2), 56–65 (2002)
18. Freeman, W.T., Pasztor, E.C., Carmichael, O.T.: Learning low level vision. Int. J. Comput. Vision **40**(1), 25–47 (2000)
19. Gatys, L.A., Ecker, A.S., Bethge, M.: Texture synthesis using convolutional neural networks. In: Advances in Neural Information Processing Systems (NIPS), pp. 262–270 (2015)
20. Gatys, L.A., Ecker, A.S., Bethge, M.: Image style transfer using convolutional neural networks. In: IEEE Conference on Computer Vision and Pattern Recognition (CVPR), pp. 2414–2423 (2016)
21. Glasner, D., Bagon, S., Irani, M.: Super-resolution from a single image. In: IEEE International Conference on Computer Vision (ICCV), pp. 349–356 (2009)
22. Goodfellow, I., et al.: Generative adversarial nets. In: Advances in Neural Information Processing Systems (NIPS), pp. 2672–2680 (2014)
23. Gregor, K., LeCun, Y.: Learning fast approximations of sparse coding. In: Proceedings of the 27th International Conference on Machine Learning (ICML-10), pp. 399–406 (2010)
24. Gross, S., Wilber, M.: Training and investigating residual nets (2016). http://torch.ch/blog/2016/02/04/resnets.html
25. Gu, S., Zuo, W., Xie, Q., Meng, D., Feng, X., Zhang, L.: Convolutional sparse coding for image super-resolution. In: IEEE International Conference on Computer Vision (ICCV), pp. 1823–1831 (2015)
26. Gupta, P., Srivastava, P., Bhardwaj, S., Bhateja, V.: A modified PSNR metric based on HVS for quality assessment of color images. In: IEEE International Conference on Communication and Industrial Application (ICCIA), pp. 1–4 (2011)
27. He, H., Siu, W.-C.: Single image super-resolution using Gaussian process regression. In: IEEE Conference on Computer Vision and Pattern Recognition (CVPR), pp. 449–456 (2011)
28. He, K., Zhang, X., Ren, S., Sun, J.: Delving deep into rectifiers: surpassing human-level performance on imagenet classification. In: IEEE International Conference on Computer Vision (ICCV), pp. 1026–1034 (2015)
29. He, K., Zhang, X., Ren, S., Sun, J.: Deep residual learning for image recognition. In: IEEE Conference on Computer Vision and Pattern Recognition (CVPR), pp. 770–778 (2016)
30. He, K., Zhang, X., Ren, S., Sun, J.: Identity mappings in deep residual networks. In: European Conference on Computer Vision (ECCV), pp. 630–645. Springer (2016)
31. Huang, J.B., Singh, A., Ahuja, N.: Single image super-resolution from transformed self-exemplars. In: IEEE Conference on Computer Vision and Pattern Recognition (CVPR), pp. 5197–5206 (2015)

32. Ioffe, S., Szegedy, C.: Batch normalization: accelerating deep network training by reducing internal covariate shift. In: Proceedings of the 32nd International Conference on Machine Learning (ICML), pp. 448–456 (2015)
33. Johnson, J., Alahi, A., Li, F.: Perceptual losses for real-time style transfer and super-resolution. In: European Conference on Computer Vision (ECCV), pp. 694–711. Springer (2016)
34. J. Kim, J. K. Lee, and K. M. Lee. Deeply-recursive convolutional network for image super-resolution. In IEEE Conference on Computer Vision and Pattern Recognition (CVPR), 2016. 3, 6, 8 [35] K. I. Kim and Y. Kwon. Single-image super-resolution using sparse regression and natural image prior. IEEE Transactions on Pattern Analysis and Machine Intelligence, 32(6):1127–1133, 2010
35. Kingma, D., Ba, J.: Adam: a method for stochastic optimization. In: International Conference on Learning Representations (ICLR) (2015)
36. Krizhevsky, A., Sutskever, I., Hinton, G.E.: ImageNet classification with deep convolutional neural networks. In: Advances in Neural Information Processing Systems (NIPS), pp. 1097–1105 (2012)
37. Li, C., Wand, M.: Combining Markov random fields and convolutional neural networks for image synthesis. In: IEEE Conference on Computer Vision and Pattern Recognition (CVPR), pp. 2479–2486 (2016)
38. Li, X., Orchard, M.T.: New edge-directed interpolation. IEEE Trans. Image Process. **10**(10), 1521–1527 (2001)
39. Mahendran, A., Vedaldi, A.: Visualizing deep convolutional neural networks using natural pre-images. Int. J. Comput. Vis. **120**, 1–23 (2016)
40. Martin, D., Fowlkes, C., Tal, D., Malik, J.: A database of human segmented natural images and its application to evaluating segmentation algorithms and measuring ecological statistics. In: IEEE International Conference on Computer Vision (ICCV), vol. 2, pp. 416–423 (2001)
41. Mathieu, M., Couprie, C., LeCun, Y.: Deep multi-scale video prediction beyond mean square error. In: International Conference on Learning Representations (ICLR) (2016)
42. Nasrollahi, K., Moeslund, T.B.: Super-resolution: a comprehensive survey. Mach. Vis. Appl. **25**, 1423–1468 (2014)
43. Radford, A., Metz, L., Chintala, S.: Unsupervised representation learning with deep convolutional generative adversarial networks. In: International Conference on Learning Representations (ICLR) (2016)
44. Russakovsky, O., et al.: ImageNet large scale visual recognition challenge. Int. J. Comput. Vis. Pp. 1–42 (2014)
45. Salvador, J., Perez-Pellitero, E.: Naive bayes super-resolution forest. In: IEEE International Conference on Computer Vision (ICCV), pp. 325–333 (2015)
46. Schulter, S., Leistner, C., Bischof, H.: Fast and accurate image upscaling with super-resolution forests. In: IEEE Conference on Computer Vision and Pattern Recognition (CVPR), pp. 3791–3799 (2015)
47. Shi, W., et al.: Real-time single image and video super-resolution using an efficient sub-pixel convolutional neural network. In: IEEE Conference on Computer Vision and Pattern Recognition (CVPR), pp. 1874–1883 (2016)
48. Simonyan, K., Zisserman, A.: Very deep convolutional networks for large-scale image recognition. In: International Conference on Learning Representations (ICLR) (2015)
49. Sun, J., Sun, J., Xu, Z., Shum, H.-Y.: Image super-resolution using gradient profile prior. In: IEEE Conference on Computer Vision and Pattern Recognition (CVPR), pp. 1–8 (2008)
50. Szegedy, C., et al.: Going deeper with convolutions. In: IEEE Conference on Computer Vision and Pattern Recognition (CVPR), pp. 1–9 (2015)
51. Tai, Y.-W., Liu, S., Brown, M.S., Lin, S.: Super resolution using edge prior and single image detail synthesis. In: IEEE Conference on Computer Vision and Pattern Recognition (CVPR), pp. 2400–2407 (2010)

52. Theano Development Team. Theano: a python framework for fast computation of mathematical expressions. arXiv preprint arXiv:1605.02688 (2016)
53. Timofte, R., De, V., Van Gool, L.: Anchored neighborhood regression for fast example-based super-resolution. In: IEEE International Conference on Computer Vision (ICCV), pp. 1920–1927 (2013)
54. Rakotonirina, N.C., Rasoanaivo, A.: ESRGAN+ : Further Improving Enhanced Super-Resolution Generative Adversarial Network. Laboratoire d'Informatique et Mathematiques, Université d'Antananarivo, Madagascar (2020)

Audio Tagging – Deep Learning Approach

E. Sophiya[1(✉)], S. Sudharsan[2], S. K. Mukhil Varnan[2], T. P. Nithishvaran[2], and M. S. Mohan Vamsi[2]

[1] Department of Computer Science and Engineering, Vel Tech Rangarajan Dr. Sagunthala R&D Institute of Science and Technology, Chennai, India
venus.sophiya@gmail.com
[2] Amrita School of Computing, Amrita Vishwa Vidyapeetham, Chennai, India

Abstract. Having multiple applications in areas such as music curation, voice identification, and identifying environmental sounds, audio tagging proves to be a pivotal task within the realm of audio analysis and categorization. Due to their ability to capture complex characteristics from raw audio data, convolutional neural networks (CNNs) have found extensive utility in the context of audio tagging tasks. The selection of the feature extraction technique is an important component of CNN-based audio tagging. In this study, we investigate how three well-liked features such as MFCC, GFCC, and Spectrograms affect the precision of a CNN-based audio tagging model. Using a sizable dataset of labelled audio clips, we train a base CNN model with three convolutional layers and two fully connected layers, and we compare the model's performance using each feature extraction technique. According to the outcomes of our experiments, Spectrograms perform better than MFCCs and GFCCs in terms of accuracy and F1 score. Finally, the performance of the model is evaluated on several performance matrices and this approach enables us to effectively classify audio files into various categories.

Keywords: Audio analysis · Audio tagging system · Audio Signals · MFCC · GFCC · Spectrogram · LSTM · CNN

1 Introduction

The ability to listen to everyday sounds and recognize them is so natural for humans. However, creating efficient machine learning algorithms that can automatically recognize sounds is a difficult task for computers. The problem of accurately identifying sound events in multimedia content remains unsolved, with a vast amount of such content being uploaded to social media and personal collections. At present, the majority of indexing systems depend on textual explanations offered by users or originators, a process that can be both time-consuming and inaccuracy.

Nonetheless, the advancement of algorithms capable of autonomously creating depictions for multimedia material might pave the way for more accurate search algorithms grounded in the content's intrinsic attributes. Computational sound analysis can also be utilized to capture and analyse the unique characteristics of audio signals for classification and detection purposes.

The technique of providing descriptive tags or labels to an audio clip to pinpoint the origin of music or sound it includes is known as audio tagging. The objective of the suggested research is to assign a singular label to each audio file. Due to the growth of multimedia content on the internet in recent years, audio tagging has grown in significance. The demand for efficient audio tagging systems has increased dramatically with the introduction of massive multimedia-sharing sites like YouTube and Sound Cloud. Applications like music information retrieval, content-based multimedia search, and recommendation algorithms all depend on audio tagging.

Since audio data is complicated, audio tagging is a difficult task. As a result of being often represented as a collection of discrete samples, audio signals are high-dimensional and noisy. Moreover, audio data is very varied, with various sound kinds having various temporal and spectral properties. In order to create efficient audio tagging systems, numerous aspects like feature extraction, classification models, and optimization strategies must be carefully taken into account (Fig. 1).

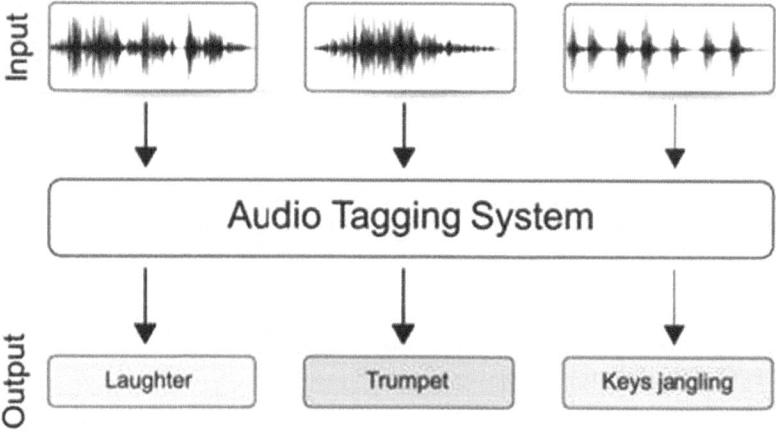

Fig. 1. Audio Tagging System Architecture

Deep learning-based methods have become a potent audio tagging tool in recent years. CNNs have proven highly valuable in this domain due to their capacity to extract advanced insights from unprocessed audio inputs. Speech recognition, music genre identification, and environmental sound categorization are just a few of the many audio classification tasks for which CNNs have been used. The underlying factor contributing to the effectiveness of CNNs in audio classification is their capability to learn features directly from the unprocessed audio signals, eliminating the need for manually engineered features.

The subsequent sections of this paper are organized as follows: Sect. 2 presents an overview of pertinent research concerning CNN-based audio tagging. In Sect. 3, we provide a succinct explanation of the feature extraction methods. Section 4 offers an intricate delineation of the proposed system architecture. Finally, Sect. 5 concludes the study and deliberates on potential avenues for future research.

2 Related Work

Content-based automatic music labelling systems are now being developed more quickly because to recent developments in deep learning. Numerous architectural designs have been conceived by researchers in the realm of music information retrieval (MIR) have proposed use convolutional neural networks (CNNs) as a common foundation. When it comes to this multi-label binary classification challenge, CNNs produce cutting-edge results. Directly comparing the proposed architectures becomes a challenge due to variations in experimental configurations utilized by researchers, including distinct dataset divisions and software editions for assessment.

In [4], short-chunk-based techniques outperformed models trained with bigger input segments in terms of performance (FCN, CRNN). The CNN model could perform well on a short dataset because of its design decisions, but it was unable to gain more knowledge from larger datasets. Given that numerous tags within the datasets don't demand extensive sequences for identification, sequential models (like CRNN and self-attention) exhibited commendable outcomes but fell short of surpassing alternative models. By testing with altered inputs, the models' generalization capabilities were further evaluated. It is noted that the models perform differently on each deformation in terms of ranking. This implies that relying solely on ROC-AUC and PR-AUC metrics is inadequate for evaluating music tagging techniques. Harmonic CNN and Short-Chunk CNN consistently yield superior scores compared to other models in their experimentation. Harmonic CNN demonstrates the most effective generalization across all deformation types, except for instances involving considerable amounts of white noise.

The author in [8] divides the stages of the approach into two categories: categorization and sound representation. During the sound representation phase, the audio waveform undergoes transformation into a sequence of feature vectors in the spectral domain, obtained from short time intervals. A deep convolutional neural network (CNN) is trained to determine source presence probabilities for each frame during the classification step. By averaging the probabilities over the brief recording periods, the source presence probability for each recording are determined.

In [5, 6], Comprehensive investigation into the automation of audio captioning has been somewhat limited. In this research, a CNN-Transformer model undergoes a pretraining phase.

According to experimental findings, automated audio captioning can be directly accomplished using the features gleaned from the multi-label categorization challenge. The pre-training method improves the feature extraction and language modelling capabilities of the model and considerably improve the performance. It illustrates that Transformer has stronger language modelling capabilities than LSTM in this challenge by utilizing a different decoder. The experiments also supported the efficiency of the proposed model's Spec Augment and Label smoothing.

In [9], The author provides a distinctive regularising method for the encoder that processes the audio sequence using data preprocessing and a multi-task learning setup.

Sequence-to-sequence classifier built using deep learning and feature and target extraction are the two stages of the proposed methodology. Log mel band energies are employed as acoustic features to preprocess the captions for feature and target extraction. Two types of target outputs are provided by the sequence-to-sequence deep learning classifier: captions and content words. The classifier is trained and evaluated using the SPIDEr metric.

A CNN-Transformer model for audio captioning is proposed in [10]. The model is a typical sequence to sequence system with the addition of Transformer layers in the decoder component and more conventional CNN layers in the encoder. The encoder employs a 10-layer CNN that utilises ReLU activation function and is utilised for feature extraction from the spectrogram. The decoder employs a two layer transformer with 4 heads and a concealed size of 192. To enhance performance and prevent overfitting, SpecAugment and Label smoothing are applied to CNN encoder and Transformer decoder.

In [11], the author presents an AAC method which continuously adapts to new information. A pre-optimized technique for Automated Audio Captioning (AAC) known as WaveTransformer (WT) is integrated with the Learning without Forgetting (LwF) strategy, enabling it to dynamically adjust to fresh data within the same task. To assimilate new knowledge, the author employs a neutral model characterized by an iterative procedure, a regularization-driven loss, a duplicate of the AAC model, a pre-optimized AAC model, and an influx of novel audio data paired with captions. Employing the Mbase and WT pre-optimized AAC model, the model undergoes training and evaluation.

A novel encoder-decoder framework using contrastive learning is proposed in [12]. The Contrastive Loss for Audio Captioning (CL4AC) model uses a Transformer decoder and Convolutional Neural Network (CNN) encoder in a sequence-to-sequence architecture. Utilising CNN-10 of Pre-trained audio neural networks (PANNs), CL4AC is implemented, with ReLU activation function being applied after each layer. In the inference phase, the encoder and decoder are provided with distinct inputs: the mel-spectrogram of an audio clip and the special token "sos>" to initiate the first token. Subsequently, tokens are predicted based on preceding tokens until the "eos" token is encountered. The model's performance is assessed using SPIDEr.

In [13], Reconstruction Latent Space Similarity Regularisation (RLSSR), a novel self-supervised module presented by the author, employs Transfer Learning with Pre-trained Audio Neural Networks (PANNs) to improve the similarity among the latent spaces of the encoder and the decoder. The encoder is made up of CNN10, and a two-layer transformer encoder receives the output. A transformer decoder with two layers is used by RLSSR. The module is tested using METEOR, SPICE, and SPIDEr metrics after being trained using the clotho dataset. The RLSSR module exhibited notable superiority over the baseline model and even performed competitively against advanced models employing transfer learning, underscoring the value of integrating the transformer encoder into the encoder.

An AAC module with Contrastive Learning using an innovative image-text pre-trained model, named CLIP is proposed by [14]. For the AAC challenge, the CLIP-AAC module teaches cross-modality embedding utilising both audio and text input. The encoder consists of a text-head and an audio-head. The ESResNeXt model is used for audio-head because it has proven to be effective at learning reliable Time-Frequency transformation of audios. The 12-layer Transformer is additionally utilised to extract the text-head input embedding's deep characteristics. The encoder output is harnessed to mitigate domain disparities by integrating and implementing contrastive learning to grasp the correlation among the audio signal and its corresponding captions. Empirical outcomes, evaluated through diverse metrics, substantiate that the introduced CLIP-AAC method outperforms the top-performing baseline method by a notable margin.

In [15], The author amalgamates Automatic Speech Recognition (ASR) techniques with audio captioning, incorporating a Transformer encoder enriched with convolutions and a Transformer decoder, thereby furnishing natural Verbal depictions. The CNN14 PANNs model is utilised to increase the model's generalizability. Shallow fusion is used to combine the word-token RNN language model (RNNLM), which is constructed through the utilization of captions from the training dataset, with the involvement of the decoder. The model greatly outperformed the baseline model, according to an evaluation using SPIDEr.

3 Proposed Methodology

3.1 Feature Extraction

The audio processing segment comprises numerous processing phases and yields acoustic attributes, given that realworld audio analysis seldom depends on the audio signal alone, but rather on a streamlined signal representation accompanied by distinctive features. In order to make the subsequent modelling stage computationally affordable and simpler to accomplish with a limited amount of development material, the objective of feature extraction is to gather sufficient information for the identification or classification of the intended sounds. Frame blocking, windowing, spectrum computing, and subsequent analysis make up the feature extraction processing pipeline, which is the same for many different kinds of auditory characteristics used in the study. Because of the swift temporal variations in signal statistics (such as frequency component magnitudes), audio signals often exhibit nonstationarity. Thus, to capture the signal within a nearly stationary state, the feature extraction employs the short-time processing technique. This approach involves conducting analysis at regular intervals using short segments called analysis frames. Frame blocking separates an audio stream into analysis frames of a given length that move with a set timestep. The frame sizes range from 20 to 60 ms, and the frameshift is often chosen so that the following frames at least partially overlap. Windowing serves the purpose of refining the analysis frames to avoid abrupt shifts at frame boundaries, which might otherwise result in spectral irregularities. Subsequently, the framed window is transformed into a spectrum to facilitate the extraction of additional features. Three separate inputs are supplied into the deep learning network in this study. Feature extraction methods that have been used for audio categorization tasks include Mel Frequency Cepstral Coefficients (MFCCs), Gammatone Frequency Cepstral Coefficients (GFCCs), and Spectrograms.

3.2 Mel Frequency Cepstral Coefficients

For audio tagging, MFCC a popular feature extraction method, are used. The goal of MFCC is to extract pertinent information from the audio input by simulating the human auditory system through a sequence of mathematical processes. The procedure entails applying a filter bank to the audio input before performing the Discrete Cosine Transform (DCT) of the filter bank energies that have been logarithmically scaled. The generated coefficients—also referred to as MFCCs—represent the spectral properties of the audio signal and are frequently utilized as input features for machine learning models for tasks like audio classification and tagging. So, using it we have tried extracting 13 features and 40 features and fed to our model to compare results (Fig. 2).

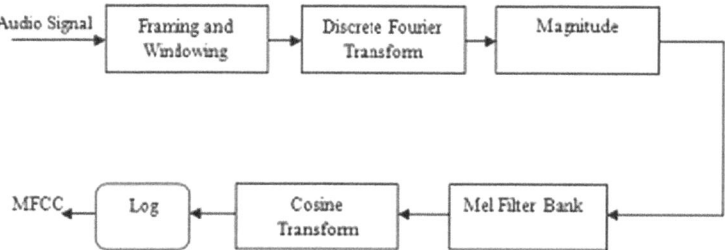

Fig. 2. MFCC feature extraction

The linear association [1] between the mel scale (f) and the Hertz scale f has been determined by

$$mel(f) = (1000/log2)log(1 + f/1000) \quad (1)$$

3.3 Gammatone Frequency Cepstral Coefficients

The feature GFCC is modeled after the human auditory system and intended to record key acoustic features of sounds (Fig. 3).

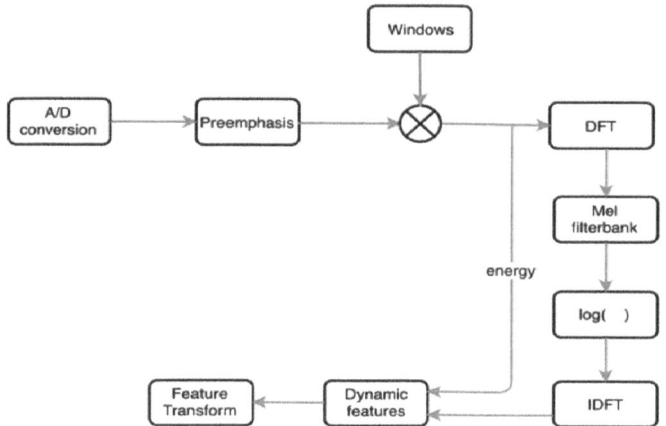

Fig. 3. GFCC feature extraction

Gammatone filters, which resemble the actions of the cochlea in the ear, are used to filter the audio signal before calculating GFCCs. A cepstral analysis is then used to analyze the filtered signals to extract pertinent features. Gamma distribution function [1] can be defined by

$$gamma[n] = an^{\gamma-1}e^{-2\pi bn}cos(2\pi f_c n) + \phi \qquad (2)$$

Here, "a" denotes the amplitude, γ stands for the filter order, "b" represents a temporal attenuation coefficient (linked to the filter's bandwidth), f_c signifies the carrier frequency (associated with the filter's central frequency), and ϕ indicates the carrier phase (related to the envelope's position on the carrier).

GFCCs have been proven to work well for tasks including speech recognition, classifying music by genre, and identifying environmental sounds. In here we have tried extraction the first 40 features and the results weren't as close to the results obtained from the extracted features from MFCC so we didn't prefer trying it out with 13 features this will be explained in detail in the experimental result section.

3.4 Spectrogram

A popular feature extraction technique for audio tagging is the spectrum. It is a visual representation of a signal's changing frequency spectrum over time. The application of Fourier transform to a short audio signal results in the creation of a spectrogram, which is then produced by graphing the magnitudes as a function of frequency and time. Due to their thorough depiction of the frequency content and temporal structure of the signal, spectrograms can be used to recognize and categorize various forms of sounds. Several audio tagging applications, such as voice recognition, music transcription, and environmental sound classification, have successfully utilized them. With the spectrogram, we were able to obtain the highest accuracy with our model again which will be explained in detail in the experimental result part (Fig. 4).

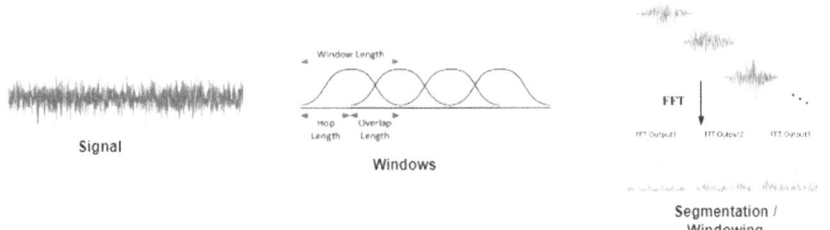

Fig. 4. Spectrogram feature extraction

3.5 Dataset Description

The UrbanSound8k audio dataset is a collection of ultrasound recordings of human vocal folds during phonation. There are 8,730 audio recordings in the collection.

The dataset contains sound clips with varying durations, ranging from 0.3 to 30 s, with a total duration of approximately 10 h. All sound clips have a sampling rate of 44.1 kHz and are saved in uncompressed WAV format. The categories include 'Air Cooling Apparatus', 'Car Horn Signal', 'Sounds of Children Playing', 'Dog Barking sound', 'Drilling Activities', 'Stationary Engine Noise', 'Gunshot Sound', 'Operation of a Heavy-Duty Hammer', 'Warning Siren', 'Urban Street Music'.

The organization of the dataset includes 6.4 k audio samples as train set and the 1.4 k audio samples as test set. The train set is equally distributed with a maximum of 873 samples per category.

3.6 Proposed 1D CNN Architecture

A 1D convolutional neural network(CNN) architecture with 4 convolution layers has been proposed because it demonstrated great performance on many existing research works. It consist of Input, convolutional, pooling, and fully linked layers. Convolutional layer: At the core of a CNN lies the convolutional layer, comprised of diverse filters that necessitate training. Generally, these filters are smaller in size compared to the original image. Following the convolution of each filter with the image, an activation map is generated (Fig. 5).

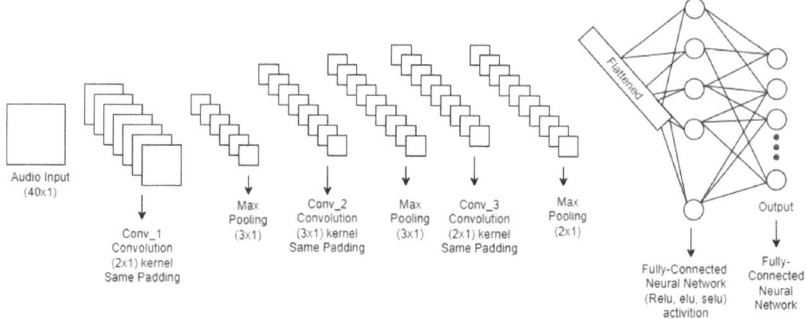

Fig. 5. CNN model Architecture Diagram

Pooling layer: Pooling layers are incorporated to diminish the dimensions of the hidden layer. This is achieved by consolidating outputs from neuron clusters in the preceding layer into a single neuron in the subsequent layer.

Input layer: Input layer takes the features as raw input. Number of neurons at input layer is based on size of input features.

Output layer: Final predictions are done at this layer. Number of neurons at this layer is based on the number of target classes.

Fully linked layer: Each neuron in a neural network with fully connected layers linearly transform the input vector by utilizing a matrix of weights. All layer-to-layer linkages are therefore present since every input of the input vector influences every output of the output vector.

4 Experimental Results

4.1 CNN Model with MFCC

The baseline 1D CNN model was trained with 13 MFCC feature vectors. The model consists of three 1D convolution layers with the relu activation function at each hidden layer. It activates the neuron using

$$f(x) = argmax(0, x) \tag{3}$$

The rectified linear unit (ReLU) function optimises model computation by activating only a few neurons. It deactivates the neurons whose linear transformation is less than 0. It is represented as

$$f(x) = \begin{cases} 0, & \textit{if } x < 0 \\ 1, & \textit{if } x \geq 0 \end{cases} \tag{4}$$

It further improves gradient descent convergence significantly compared to sigmoid or tanh activation functions. 1D max pool operation at each hidden layer down samples the input representation and softmax classifier is used at output layer that output the probability of each audio tags. The training of the model is conducted using a batch size of 64. Dropout layers are used in CNN training because they avoid overfitting on the training data. If they are not there, then the initial batch of training data has a disproportionately large influence on learning. As a result, learning of MFCC features that occur only in later samples or batches would be prevented. A summary of the trained model is shown in Fig. 6.

```
Model: "sequential"
_____
Layer (type)                 Output Shape              Param #
=================================================================
max_pooling1d (MaxPooling1D) (None, 7, 1)              0
)
batch_normalization (BatchN  (None, 7, 1)              4
ormalization)
conv1d_1 (Conv1D)            (None, 5, 64)             256
max_pooling1d_1 (MaxPooling  (None, 3, 64)             0
1D)
batch_normalization_1 (Batc  (None, 3, 64)             256
hNormalization)
conv1d_2 (Conv1D)            (None, 2, 128)            16512
max_pooling1d_2 (MaxPooling  (None, 1, 128)            0
1D)
batch_normalization_2 (Batc  (None, 1, 128)            512
hNormalization)
flatten (Flatten)            (None, 128)               0
dense (Dense)                (None, 40)                5160
dropout (Dropout)            (None, 40)                0
dense_1 (Dense)              (None, 10)                410
_____
Total params: 23,110
Trainable params: 22,724
Non-trainable params: 386
_____
```

Fig. 6. 1D CNN summary for 13 features

The same baseline model is trained with 40 MFCC feature vector with a batch size of 64. A summary of the trained model is shown in the Fig. 7.

```
Model: "sequential"
_____
Layer (type)                 Output Shape              Param #
=================================================================
max_pooling1d (MaxPooling1D  (None, 20, 1)             0
)

batch_normalization (BatchN  (None, 20, 1)             4
ormalization)

conv1d_1 (Conv1D)            (None, 18, 64)            256

max_pooling1d_1 (MaxPooling  (None, 9, 64)             0
1D)

batch_normalization_1 (Batc  (None, 9, 64)             256
hNormalization)

conv1d_2 (Conv1D)            (None, 8, 128)            16512

max_pooling1d_2 (MaxPooling  (None, 4, 128)            0
1D)

batch_normalization_2 (Batc  (None, 4, 128)            512
hNormalization)

flatten (Flatten)            (None, 512)               0

dense (Dense)                (None, 40)                20520

dropout (Dropout)            (None, 40)                0

dense_1 (Dense)              (None, 10)                410

=================================================================
Total params: 38,470
Trainable params: 38,084
Non-trainable params: 386
_____
```

Fig. 7. 1D CNN summary for 40 features

The proposed CNN model has been trained with same parameters by varying activation function as selu and elu. Exponential linear unit (ELU) is similar to ReLU to handle non negative inputs. The function helps to improve the model accuracy by reducing the training time and it is defined by.

$$f(x) = \begin{cases} \alpha(e^{-2} - 1), & if x < 0 \\ x, & if x \geq 0 \end{cases} \quad (5)$$

ELU gradually smoothes until its output equals $-\alpha$, whereas RELU sharply smoothes. In the above equation, α is a positive constant which is always 1.0 in order to maintain the saturation level for negative inputs. Scaled Exponential linear unit (SELU) is an activation function that self-normalizes and it is a subset of the ELU. Because of its self-normalizing behaviour, it is certain that the output will always be standardised. This eliminates the requirement for Batch-Normalization layers. The working of SELU function is represented by

$$f(x) = \begin{cases} \lambda x, & if x > 0 \\ \lambda \alpha(e^x - 1), & if x \leq 0 \end{cases} \quad (6)$$

Among different activation functions, SeLU function outperformed others with an accuracy of 80%. The Accuracy of SeLU activation function is shown in Fig. 8. In contrast to ReLU, it is capable of dropping below zero, allowing the system to have a zero average output. As a result, the model may converge more quickly.

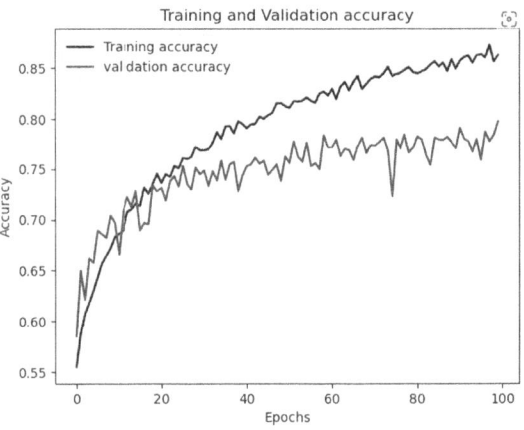

Fig. 8. Selu accuracy

The identical training and test data were utilised to compare the performance of the baseline CNN, and the feature parameter extraction method was mfcc (13 and 40 coefficients respectively). As shown in Table 1, the accuracy has been increased by 20% for 40 coefficients using ReLU function and 27% using SELU function.

Table 1. Comparison of optimized accuracy for mfcc with different activation functions.

No of features	ReLU	SeLU	eLU
13	54.6%	53.5%	59.2%
40	77.9%	79.6%	75.5%

The overall prediction report of the proposed baseline model is shown in Table 2.

4.2 CNN Model with GFCC

The baseline 1D CNN model was trained with 13 GFCC feature vectors. The model consists of three 1D convolution layers with the relu activation function, 1D max pool at each hidden layers and softmax classifier at output layer. The model is trained with a batch size of 64. A summary of the trained model is shown in Fig. 9.

The same baseline model is trained with 40 GFCC feature vector with a batch size of 64. A summary of the trained model is shown in the Fig. 10.

Table 2. Prediction Report for Baseline Model with MFCC

Label	Precision	Recall	F1-score
Air Cooling Apparatus	0.82%	0.98%	0.89%
Car Horn Signal	0.92%	0.98%	0.94%
Sounds of Children Playing	0.79%	0.73%	0.76%
Dog Barking sound	0.91%	0.73%	0.81%
Drilling Activities	0.96%	0.88%	0.92%
Stationary Engine Noise	0.90%	0.90%	0.94%
Gunshot Sound	0.86%	0.87%	0.86%
Operation of a Heavy-Duty Hammer	0.95%	0.95%	0.095%
Warning Siren	0.86%	0.98%	0.91%
Urban Street Music	0.78%	0.84%	0.81%

```
Model: "sequential"
_____
Layer (type)                 Output Shape              Param #
=================================================================
max_pooling1d (MaxPooling1D) (None, 7, 1)              0
)
batch_normalization (BatchN  (None, 7, 1)              4
ormalization)
conv1d_1 (Conv1D)            (None, 5, 64)             256
max_pooling1d_1 (MaxPooling  (None, 3, 64)             0
1D)
batch_normalization_1 (Batc  (None, 3, 64)             256
hNormalization)
conv1d_2 (Conv1D)            (None, 2, 128)            16512
max_pooling1d_2 (MaxPooling  (None, 1, 128)            0
1D)
batch_normalization_2 (Batc  (None, 1, 128)            512
hNormalization)
flatten (Flatten)            (None, 128)               0
dense (Dense)                (None, 32)                4128
dropout (Dropout)            (None, 32)                0
dense_1 (Dense)              (None, 10)                330
=================================================================
Total params: 21,998
Trainable params: 21,612
Non-trainable params: 386
_____
```

Fig. 9. 1D CNN summary for 13 features.

To compare the performance of the baseline CNN, and the feature parameter extraction method was GFCC (13 and 40 coefficients respectively). As shown in Table 3, the accuracy has been increased by 5% for 40 coefficients using ReLU function and 8% using SELU function. The Accuracy of reLU activation function is shown in Fig. 11.

It is observed that the baseline model trained with GFCC feature vector could not recognize most of the audio classes with various activation functions.

The overall prediction report of the proposed baseline model is shown in Table 4.

```
Model: "sequential_1"
_____
Layer (type)                 Output Shape              Param #
=================================================================
max_pooling1d_3 (MaxPooling  (None, 20, 1)             0
1D)

batch_normalization_3 (Batc  (None, 20, 1)             4
hNormalization)

conv1d_4 (Conv1D)            (None, 18, 64)            256

max_pooling1d_4 (MaxPooling  (None, 9, 64)             0
1D)

batch_normalization_4 (Batc  (None, 9, 64)             256
hNormalization)

conv1d_5 (Conv1D)            (None, 8, 128)            16512

max_pooling1d_5 (MaxPooling  (None, 4, 128)            0
1D)

batch_normalization_5 (Batc  (None, 4, 128)            512
hNormalization)

flatten_1 (Flatten)          (None, 512)               0

dense_2 (Dense)              (None, 32)                16416

dropout_1 (Dropout)          (None, 32)                0

dense_3 (Dense)              (None, 10)                330
=================================================================
Total params: 34,286
Trainable params: 33,900
Non-trainable params: 386
_____
```

Fig. 10. 1D CNN summary for 40 features

Table 3. Comparison of optimized accuracy for GFCC with various activation functions.

No of features	ReLU	SeLU	eLU
13	59.2%	48.2%	52.4%
40	64.5%	56.9%	48.6%

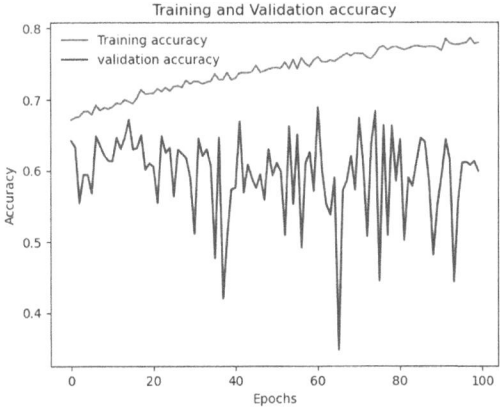

Fig. 11. Relu accuracy.

Table 4. Prediction Report for Baseline Model with GFCC

Label	Precision	Recall	F1-score
Air Cooling Apparatus	0.00%	0.00%	0.00%
Car Horn Signal	0.80%	0.04%	0.88%
Sounds of Children Playing	0.15%	0.00%	0.80%
Dog Barking sound	0.43%	0.19%	0.26%
Drilling Activities	0.00%	0.00%	0.00%
Stationary Engine Noise	0.30%	0.06%	0.11%
Gunshot Sound	0.44%	0.05%	0.09%
Operation of a Heavy-Duty Hammer	0.80%	0.08%	0.14%
Warning Siren	0.19%	0.33%	0.24%
Urban Street Music	0.13%	0.85%	0.23%

Feature vector could not recognize most of the audio classes with various activation functions.

4.3 CNN Model with Spectrogram

The baseline CNN model was trained with spectral values of the audio signal. The model consists of three 2D convolution layers with the relu activation function, 2D max pool layers, and softmax layer. The model is trained with a batch size of 64. A summary of the trained model is shown in Fig. 12.

The same CNN model has been trained with same parameters by varying activation function as selu and elu. Among different activation functions, reLU function outperformed others with an accuracy of 87%. The Accuracy of reLU activation function is shown in Fig. 13 and the comparison is shown in Table 5.

The generated system output is matched against the reference annotations given for the test data, which remains consistent throughout the evaluation procedure. Some of the metrics considered for Audio tagging include accuracy, precision, recall, and F-score. The metrics are computed based on the number of right predictions and the sorts of errors made by the algorithm.

Accuracy is defined as the ratio of accurate system outputs to the total number of outputs, and it measures how frequently the classifier makes the correct evaluation. It is given by

$$Accuracy = \frac{TP + TN}{TP + TN + FP + FN} \quad (7)$$

True positive (TP): An accurate prediction signifies the concurrence of both the system's output and the reference in indicating the existence or activity of the sound class.

True negative (TN): Both the system output and the referenced show whether the sound class exists or not.

```
Model: "sequential"
_____
Layer (type)                 Output Shape              Param #
=================================================================
conv2d (Conv2D)              (None, 126, 126, 16)      160
max_pooling2d (MaxPooling2D  (None, 63, 63, 16)        0
)
dropout (Dropout)            (None, 63, 63, 16)        0
conv2d_1 (Conv2D)            (None, 61, 61, 32)        4640
max_pooling2d_1 (MaxPooling  (None, 30, 30, 32)        0
2D)
dropout_1 (Dropout)          (None, 30, 30, 32)        0
conv2d_2 (Conv2D)            (None, 28, 28, 64)        18496
max_pooling2d_2 (MaxPooling  (None, 14, 14, 64)        0
2D)
dropout_2 (Dropout)          (None, 14, 14, 64)        0
conv2d_3 (Conv2D)            (None, 12, 12, 128)       73856
max_pooling2d_3 (MaxPooling  (None, 6, 6, 128)         0
2D)
dropout_3 (Dropout)          (None, 6, 6, 128)         0
flatten (Flatten)            (None, 4608)              0
dense (Dense)                (None, 128)               589952
dropout_4 (Dropout)          (None, 128)               0
dense_1 (Dense)              (None, 10)                1290
=================================================================
Total params: 688,394
Trainable params: 688,394
Non-trainable params: 0
_____
```

Fig. 12. CNN summary with spectral values

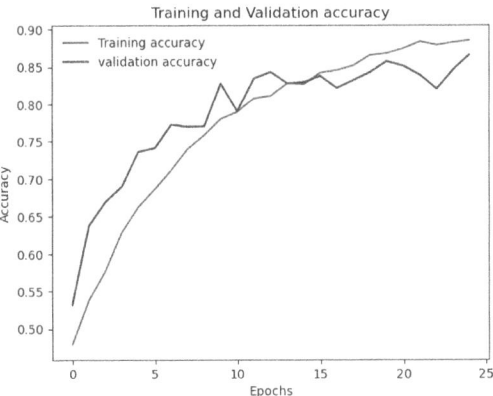

Fig. 13. Relu accuracy.

Table 5. Comparison of optimized accuracy for Spectrogram with different activation functions.

ReLU	SeLU	eLU
87.3%	77.4%	79.7%

False positive (FP): The system's output implies the presence or activation of a sound class even when the reference signifies the absence or inactivity of that sound class.

Table 6. Prediction Report for Baseline Model with Spectrogram

Label	Precision	Recall	F1-score
Air Cooling Apparatus	0.82%	0.82%	0.82%
Car Horn Signal	0.97%	0.77%	0.80%
Sounds of Children Playing	0.55%	0.42%	0.47%
Dog Barking sound	0.81%	0.59%	0.68%
Drilling Activities	0.93%	0.69%	0.88%
Stationary Engine Noise	0.65%	0.95%	0.78%
Gunshot Sound	0.90%	0.55%	0.69%
Hammer	0.87%	0.98%	0.89%
Warning Siren	0.92%	0.67%	0.77%
Urban Street Music	0.48%	0.83%	0.81%

False negative (FN): The system result shows that the sound class is not existent or has been removed. The reference indicates that the sound class is not existing or is active.

Precision (P), Recall(R), and F-Score(F) is given as follows.

$$P = \frac{TP}{TP + FP} \quad (8)$$

$$R = \frac{TP}{TP + FN} \quad (9)$$

$$F = \frac{2PR}{P + R} \quad (10)$$

According to our experiments, among the various feature extraction methods used for audio tagging, it was observed that Spectrogram features performed better than others with an accuracy of 87.3%. The optimized accuracy of the proposed audio tagging system is compared with existing ones and presented the results in Table 7.

Table 7. Comparison of optimized accuracy for the proposed audio tagging system with the existing system

Features	Existing work: DCASE 2016	Proposed work accuracy
MFCC	CNN, 77.20%	1D-CNN, 77%
GFCC	DenseNet, 77.57%	1D-CNN, 64.5%
Spectrogram	CNN, 78.6%	1D-CNN, 87.3%

The test data along with predicted labels are presented and visualized using Ipython and it is shown below.

Audio File	Actual Label	Predicted Label
100032-3-0-0.wav	Dog Barking sound	Dog Barking sound

5 Conclusion

This study proposed a deep-learning method for tagging different acoustic sound categories. In this work, different acoustic modeling and feature learning methods have been contributed. The Proposed 1D CNN Architecture incorporated supervised learning for single-label tagging. The performance of CNN with Spectrogram features is superior to the baseline system compared to other feature vectors. In the Future, Audio tagging will be enhanced as the contextual description for every audio file using free language which will be trained on large-scale of data.

References

1. Berg, J., Drossos, K.: Continual learning for automated audio captioning using the learning without forgetting approach (Barcelona, 2021). In: Proceedings of the 6th Detection and Classifcation of Acoustic Scenes and Events Workshop, pp. 140–144 (2021)
2. Emre, C., Heittola, T., Virtanen, T.: Domestic audio tagging with convolutional neural networks. In: Proceedings of the Detection and Classification of Acoustic Scenes and Events (2016)
3. Cakir, E., Drossos, K., Virtanen, T.: Multi-task regularization based on infrequent classes for audio captioning. In: Proceedings of the Detection and Classifcation of Acoustic Scenes and Events, pp. 6–10 (2020)
4. Chen, C., Hou, N., Hu, Y., Zou, H., Qi, X., Chng, E.S.: Interactive audiotext representation for automated audio captioning with contrastive learning. arXiv preprint arXiv:2203.15526 (2022)
5. Chen, K., et al.: Audio captioning based on transformer and pre-trained CNN (Tokyo, 2020). In: Proceedings of the Detection and Classifcation of Acoustic Scenes and Events Workshop, pp. 21–25 (2020)
6. Humberto Ochoa-Dominguez, K.R.R.: Discrete Cosine Transform, 2nd edn. CRC Press (2019)
7. Smith III, J.O.: Spectral Audio Signal Processing. W3K Publishing (2011)
8. Koh, X.F., Siong, C.E.: Automated audio captioning using transfer learning and reconstruction latent space similarity regularization. In: IEEE International Conference on Acoustics, Speech and Signal Processing, pp. 7722–7726 (2022)
9. Drossos, K., Lipping, S., Virtanen, T.: Clotho: an audio captioning dataset. arXiv preprint arXiv:1910.09387 (2021)
10. Drossos, K., Adavanne, S., Virtanen, T.: Automated audio captioning with recurrent neural networks. In: IEEE Workshop on Applications of Signal Processing to Audio and Acoustics (2017)
11. Liu, X., et al.: CL4AC: a contrastive loss for audio captioning. In: Proceedings of the 6th Detection and Classifcation of Acoustic Scenes and Events Workshop, pp. 196–200 (2021)
12. Won, M., Ferraro, A., Bogdanov, D., Serra, X.: Evaluation of CNN-based automatic music tagging models. arXiv:2006.00751v1 (2020)

13. Narisetty, C.P., Hayashi, T., Ishizaki, R., Watanabe, S., Takeda, K.: Leveraging state-of-the-art ASR techniques to audio captioning. In: Proceedings of the 6th Detection and Classifcation of Acoustic Scenes and Events Workshop, pp. 160–164 (2021)
14. Lipping, S., Drossos, K., Virtanen, T.: Crowdsourcing a dataset of audio captions. In: International Workshop on Detection and Classification of Acoustic Scenes and Events (2019)
15. Virtanen, T., Plumbley, M.D., Ellis, D.: Computational analysis of sound scenes and events (2017), https://doi.org/10.1007/978-3-319-63450-0

A Design Pattern Based Forecasting Model for Predicting Time Series Data in Kaggle Ecosystem

Naman Bhargava[1(✉)], B. Malar[2], and G. Priyalakshmi[3]

[1] Department of Statistics, University of Michigan, Ann Arbor 48109, USA
nambhprac@gmail.com
[2] Department of Applied Mathematics and Computational Sciences, PSG College of Technology, Coimbatore 641004, India
bmr.amcs@psgtech.ac.in
[3] Sri Ethiraja Technologies, Coimbatore 641004, India

Abstract. With the development of online communities, exploring and publishing of datasets and collaborative development with data scientists and machine learning engineers is exponentially increasing. The participation in competitions to solve data science challenges and the formation of machine learning communities has matured. Kaggle is one of the well-known machine learning hub to explore competitions, datasets, notebooks, and forums. Knowing the evolution and the mere future of datasets, competitions, and courses would benefit not only for users of Kaggle but also Kaggle administrators. This paper aims to develop a novel design pattern-based decision support system using a sequence model, Auto Regressive Integrated Moving Average (ARIMA) model to predict the total number of competitions, the number of competitions in the top 5 tags and the number of datasets using sequence models.

Experiments are conducted using the Meta Kaggle dataset to evaluate the performance of the design pattern-based ARIMA model and the results show that the proposed forecasting model provides significant results in terms of MAPE (Mean Absolute Percentage Error) and other design pattern-based evaluation measures. Experimental results of the proposed system are compared with Long-Short Term Memory (LSTM) based models and the results reveal that the proposed system is superior to LSTM based system in terms of minimizing the error.

Keywords: Time series data · ARIMA · Kaggle Ecosystem · Design Patterns · Reusability · Maintainability

1 Introduction

Kaggle is an open-source online community that allows people to find and publish datasets and participate in competitions. It offers machine learning competitions, a public data platform, and a cloud-based workbench for data science. This research analyzes the Meta Kaggle dataset [8], consisting of complete information regarding competitions, datasets, forums, kernels, and users in Kaggle. This can be considered as a major concern. This motivates us to develop a reusable system for predicting competitions in different domains using metadata available in Kaggle about competitions, tags, and datasets.

The proposed system studies the tag-wise frequency of contributions, notebooks, and datasets on a monthly basis. The system helps to popularize Kaggle competitions. The proposed system helps better visualize and predict different parameters such as competitions, tags, datasets, and notebooks and proposes a reusable system using design patterns.

The contributions of the paper are three-fold:

1. To propose an ARIMA model for predicting the usage of Kaggle competitions, tags, and
2. Experiments are conducted on the forecasting model, ARIMA using Meta Kaggle and results are compared with the Deep Learning sequential model, Long Short Term Memory (LSTM).
3. Experiments are also conducted on the Design Pattern-based framework and the results are compared with the same model without design patterns.

This paper is organized in the following manner. Section 2 discusses the background study of forecasting models in software development. Section 3 defines the problem statement. Section 4 details the steps of the proposed design pattern-based forecasting model. Section 5 reports the experimental results of the proposed method with the dataset. Section 6 concludes the work with the scope for future work.

2 Related Works

In recent years, a plethora of research has been conducted on open-source software repositories and ecosystems. However, there is little consensus on the definition of open-source software ecosystems and the dominant features of open-source software projects. Liao et al. [9] proposed a model to predict the health of GitHub, a software ecosystem. They proposed that ecosystem health refers to the behavior of its participants (developers, users, etc.), the project's survival and development, continuous service in the event of disruption and meeting people's needs for the project's capabilities. Capiluppi et al. [4] analyzed different attributes on which a project depends. Mohamed et al. [2] use quality attributes at system level, information level and service level, for the selection of the appropriate open-source software.

Recently there has been an interest among researchers towards developing design pattern-based systems and implementing them as reusable and easily maintainable solutions. There are two kinds of patterns: Architecture and Design patterns. Architectural patterns are primary concepts in the field of software architecture: These patterns are firmly established solutions to architectural problems and illustrate the quality attributes of a software system as forces [1]. Out of the patterns from the preliminary and elementary catalogs and categorizations that deal with components and connectors, the Pipes and Filters architectural pattern caters to a composition of systems operating on a data stream [3]. This work applies design patterns so that people can use the design effectively. Design patterns make it easier to reuse successful designs and architectures [6].

The adoption of architectural and design patterns leads to better software reusability, extensibility, and maintainability. This motivates us to develop a reusable architecture for the proposed forecasting model which promotes design and code reusability using architecture and design patterns.

Time series analysis describes data that fluctuates over time. ARIMA model is a class of models that describe time series based on its past values, i.e., lagged values and lagged forecast errors. Recently, the ARIMA model has been applied in different realms where forecasting is required. Gencer et al. explored Android vulnerabilities using time series, Multilayer Perceptron (MLP), Convolutional Neural Network (CNN), Long Short-Term Memory (LSTM), Convolutional LSTM (ConvLSTM) and CNN-LSTM-based models, and it was found that the ARIMA model provided the lowest error rates for the prediction of future security vulnerabilities [7]. The forecasting of the time series data Kaggle can help get an understanding of the health of competitions, tags and datasets by predicting future events, based on the assumption that future trends will hold similar to historical trends. In addition, the prediction of competitions, datasets and tags supports Kaggle administrators in decision making on releasing new data sets in prominent domains to organize competitions.

3 Problem Statement

Given a collection of time series data (Y1, Y2, ..., Yn) arranged over the time steps (t1, t2, ..., tn), the key objective of the proposed work is to develop a reusable design pattern-based forecasting model to predict the value at future time steps tn + 1, tn + 2, ..., based on the previous values with minimum error. The time series data considered in this research work are:

1. Total number of Competitions (year-wise)
2. Number of Competitions Tag-wise (year-wise)
3. Number of Datasets (year-wise)

Kaggle collects data about other factors like submission scores, and kernels as well, the significant factors for the prediction of the Kaggle community are competitions, tags, and datasets due to them being the most important and active features of the website.

4 Design Pattern Based Forecasting Model

The proposed method first collects the time series data from Kaggle, checks stationarity and seasonality in the data, applies the ARIMA model, and conducts experiments. The proposed forecasting model works in four phases:

1. Data Collection
2. Stationarity checking
3. Seasonality checking
4. Building a design pattern based ARIMA model

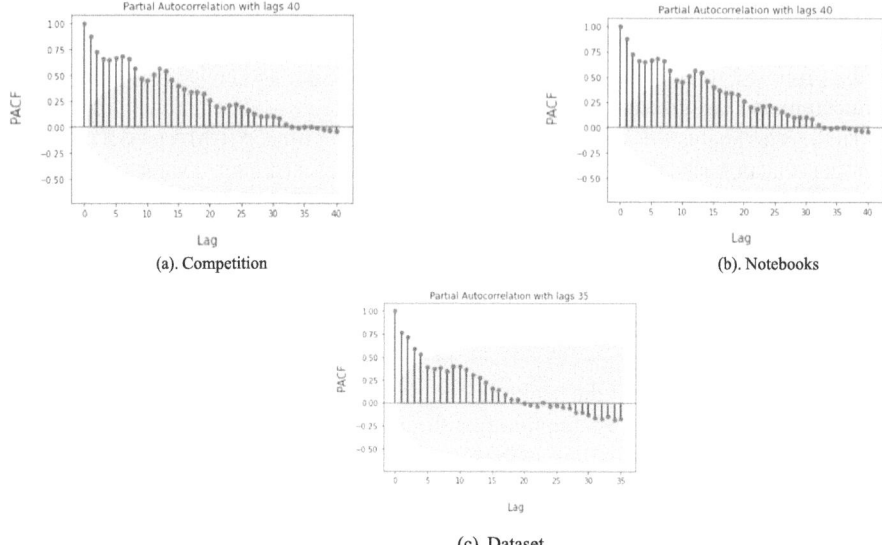

Fig. 1. No. of Contributions for Different categories in Kaggle (for the contributions of different tags, competitions, datasets and notebooks related to tag are considered)

4.1 Data Collection

The dataset used in this paper is Meta Kaggle which is updated frequently (usually weekly) by the Kaggle team. With 8 GB of data, it contains detailed information about competitions, datasets, forums, kernel, organizations, submissions, etc. The data regarding creation and update namely time, author, etc. are logged and available in this dataset. For this research, the number of competitions held per month, the number of tags added per month, and the number of datasets added per month between years 2010–20 are extracted from Meta Kaggle and stored in a separate dataset.

4.2 Building a Design Pattern-Based ARIMA Model

The time series modeling of the analysis of Meta Kaggle data can be designed with an architectural pattern - Pipes and Filter pattern and three design patterns – Factory Method pattern, Adapter pattern and Iterator pattern. This subsection explains the ARIMA model for Kaggle data and the implementation of the proposed method using architecture and design patterns.

4.3 Architectural Pattern

Architectural patterns are a fundamental theory in the domain of software architecture and they provide authentic solutions to architectural problems. Pipes and Filters architectural pattern caters to a composition of systems that operates on a stream of data [10]. Every execution stage is wrapped in a filter component. Data is pushed forward through

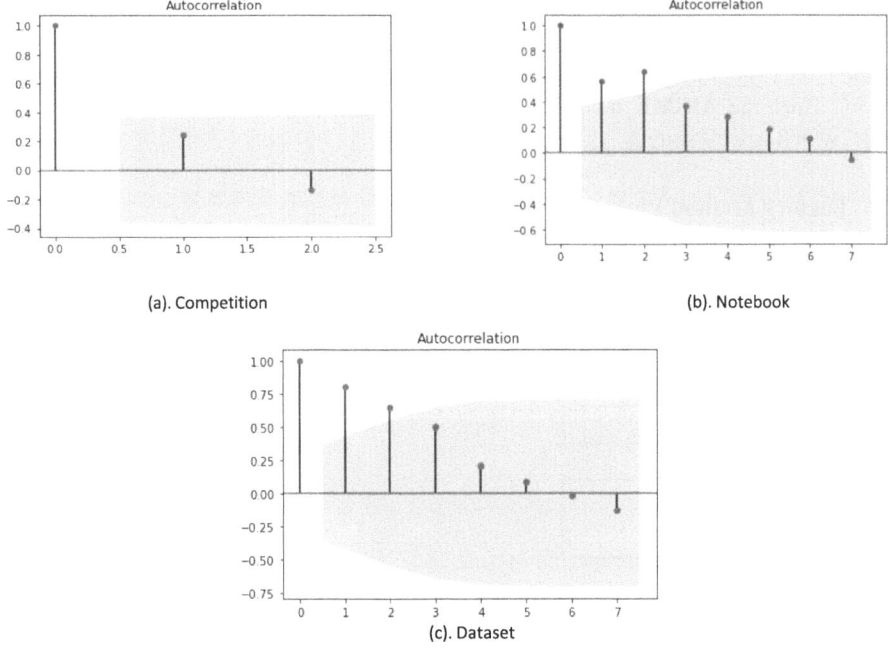

Fig. 2. Sample Autocorrelation Graph

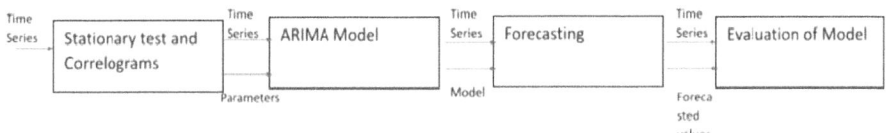

Fig. 3. Pipes and Filters Architectural Pattern applied to ARIMA model

pipes between neighboring filters. Therefore, we decided to apply the Pipes and Filters architectural pattern to our problem.

The Pipes and Filters architectural pattern was applied to the forecasting model at a higher level as shown in Fig. 3. The time series data is input to the first filter, which checks stationarity and seasonality and obtains the order of AR and MA. If the data is not stationary, then differencing is done to make it stationary. The outcome of this phase of data analysis is given as input to the second filter, which trains the data and builds the model using ARIMA. ARIMA model requires two parameters, p, and q, where p is the parameter of the AutoRegressive model and q is the order of the Moving Average model. The parameter q is obtained from the sample Autocorrelation Function plot and is the number of lags after which a sharp drop is noticed in autocorrelation. Based on this conjecture, the q value for competitions, tags and datasets are 2, 7 and 6 respectively, as shown in Fig. 2. Partial Autocorrelation Function is used to obtain the parameters p, 10,7 and 6 are taken as p for competition, tags, and dataset respectively, as displayed in Fig. 1. The model parameters are fed into the third filter, where the forecasting of Kaggle metadata is done. The output pipe holds the forecasted values which are pushed into the fourth filter, which evaluates the model. This stage is the final stage in the architecture of the forecasting model, which assesses the performance of the model through forecast errors. Thus, the ARIMA model is designed using the Pipes and Filters architectural style, which is well suited.

4.4 Factory Method Pattern

Factory Method Pattern enables us to create objects without affecting the behavior of other classes. This helps in increasing the Reusability and Maintainability of classes. Therefore, we use it in our work to keep three forecasting components- Competitions, Tags and Datasets.

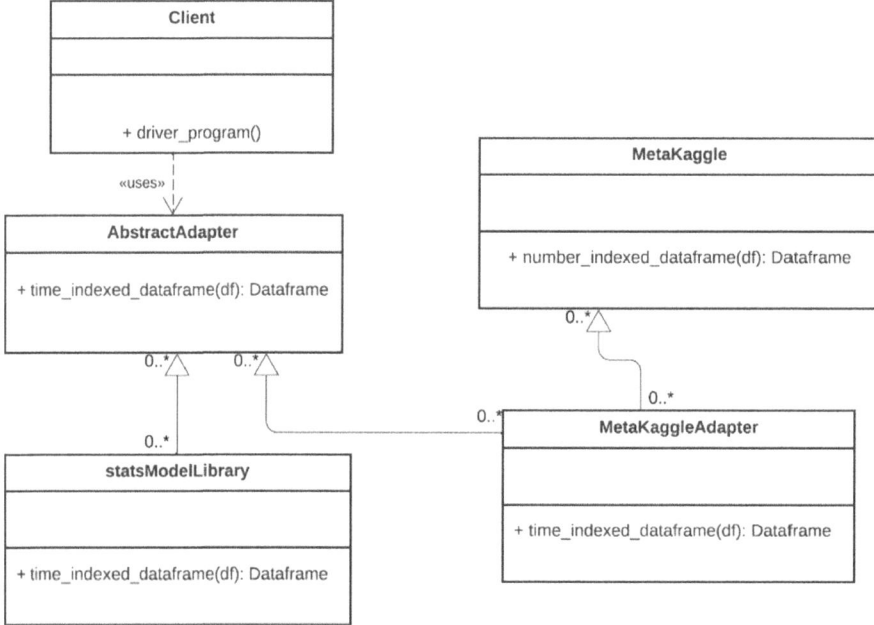

Fig. 4. Factory Method Pattern applied to ARIMA model

An abstract class is defined, which extends into Competition, Dataset, and Kernels subclasses. These suclasses contain concrete implementation of time series. Time indexed dataframe created through the Adapter pattern is passed as input to these subclasses. They are further analyzed using stationary tests and correlograms and an ARIMA model is used for forecasting. The design model of the Factory Method pattern is shown in Fig. 4.

4.5 Adapter Patterns

The adapter pattern helps in resolving compatibility issues between classes and makes classes reusable. The Kaggle dataset contains a dataframe indexed by numbers. The statsmodels library expects a time-indexed dataframe as input. Therefore, an adapter method is used for the conversion of data format. In the adapter method, data is extracted monthly and stored in another dataframe indexed by starting time and date of the month. This dataframe is further passed to the Factory method for analysis and forecasting. The design model of the Adapter pattern is shown in Fig. 5.

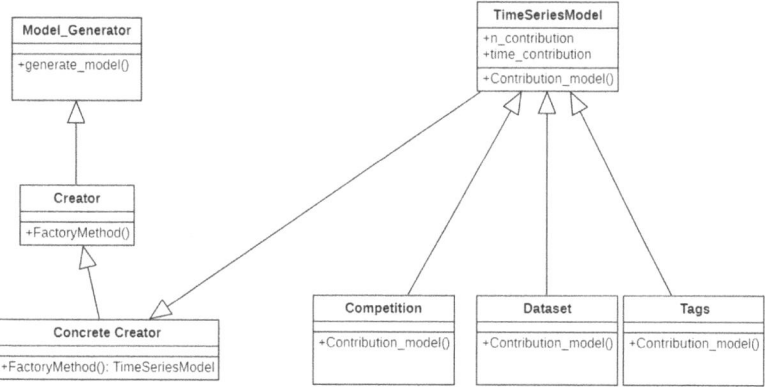

Fig. 5. Adapter Pattern applied to ARIMA model

4.6 Iterator Patterns

The iterator pattern introduces an approach to access object members serially without revealing their hidden design. The iterator pattern is used to avoid multiple loops and gives sequential access to all rows of the dataframe. The design model of the Iterator pattern is shown in Fig. 6. Thus, the forecasting model is designed using the Pipes and Filters architectural pattern as a higher-level design. The system is modeled at a lower

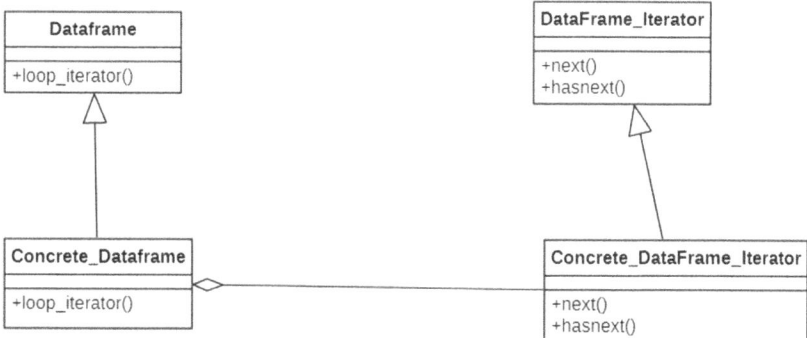

Fig. 6. Iterator Pattern applied to ARIMA model

level with Factory Method, Adapter, and Iterator patterns to provide higher reusability. The experimental results are exhibited in the following section.

5 Results and Discussion

As mentioned in the experimental setup, the results are projected in two scenarios: Performance of the ARIMA model and performance of the proposed system in terms of design pattern based measures.

5.1 Model Performance

Results show that the proposed model has an error of approximately 19%. The mean absolute percentage error of the proposed ARIMA forecasting model is compared with LSTM based forecasting model as shown in Fig. 7. It is observed from the results that the proposed ARIMA-based forecasting model is superior to LSTM. The conjecture for this difference is that LSTM needs large data sets to perform well. On the other hand, the ARIMA model works well even in small and medium datasets.

5.2 Performance of Design Pattern Based Model

The impact of different design patterns on the Cyclomatic complexity of the proposed system is shown in Fig. 8. Results show that each pattern tries to reduce the Cyclomatic complexity and Iterator pattern contributes prominently more than the other two patterns. The result, as shown in Fig. 8, indicates that after the design pattern usage, there is a significant reduction in the Cyclomatic Complexity, which is a good indication of an increase in maintainability. Source Lines of Code (SLOC) is also used to assess the programming productivity or maintainability of the software once it is ready. The system without patterns exhibits 279 SLOC, 5 comments, no multiline strings, and 197 blank lines, thus summing up to 481 lines.

The radon package [11] counts the Logical Lines Of Code (LLOC) before and after the application of design patterns, which shows a minimal increase in LLOC, which is appropriate since code designed using patterns grows bigger. The Maintainability Index is depicted in Fig. 8. As seen in the figure, the maintainability index software metric shows an enhancement in the metric value after the adoption of design patterns, which implies that design patterns have a positive impact on software maintainability. Weighted Methods per Class (WMC) can be calculated as the sum of the cyclomatic complexity of all methods of a class. It forecasts the time and effort needed to implement and maintain a class. As shown in Table 1, the proposed system after the application of design patterns has shown a decrease in WMC, which indicates lesser testing costs. Classes with more methods may be more application-specific, thus restricting reuse [5]. Thus, patterns reduce the number of class methods, permitting more reuse of our proposed system.

If a class is at a lower level in the inheritance tree, it will inherit more withholds, which in turn will make the class more complex and unpredictable in its behavior [5]. *Depth of Inheritance Tree (DIT)* measures the number of super classes that can influence a class. The proposed system has a DIT metric computed as 0, hence making the system less

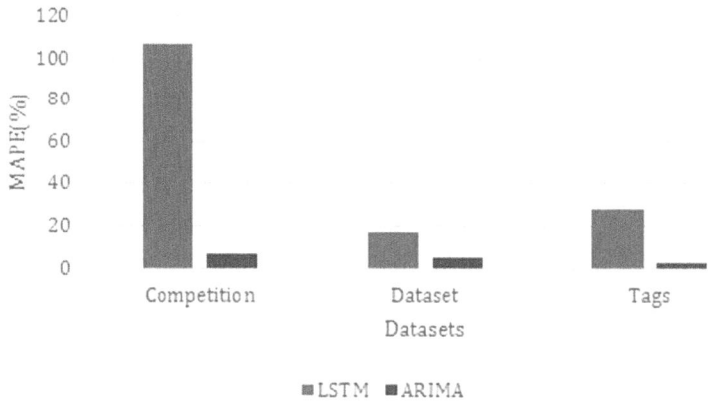

Fig. 7. Comparative analysis of LSTM and ARIMA model

Table 1. Comparative study of the software maintainability of the proposed system with and without design patterns

Metric	Algorithm	Median	Max	Min
WMC	DP	5	7	1
	Normal	7	7	7
DIT	DP	0	0	0
	Normal	0	0	0
NOC	DP	0	0	0
	Normal	0	0	0
RFC	DP	3	6	1
	Normal	3	3	3
CBO	DP	1	3	0
	Normal	0	0	0

complex with foreseeable behavior. Patterns have no impact on the DIT of the proposed system. The design complexity of a class grows with the depth of the inheritance tree since the number of methods and classes affected is high [5]. The system reuse increases if the number of children in the inheritance hierarchy is more [5]. In our proposed system, NOC evaluates to 0, whether implemented with design patterns or not. The possibility of imprecise abstraction of the super class is more if NOC is higher [5], hence, there is no misuse of subclassing in our system. Also, more testing of the methods of the class is required if NOC is large [5]. The testing effort of the proposed system will be comparatively less since the number of children is 0. The testing and debugging of a class get more complex if RFC is high [5]. For our proposed system, RFC remains the same before and after the pattern application. RFC is also proportional to the complexity of a class [5]. Thus, the RFC metric evaluates to 3 for the proposed system, which is considerably a low value, thus signifying lesser complexity. A highly cohesive class improves encapsulation [5]. Patterns reduce LCOM for our proposed system, as shown in Table 2, which in turn increases cohesion, thus enhancing encapsulation. Lack of cohesion indicates a redesign of the class by splitting into subclasses [5]. Complexity rises with low cohesion, thus inflating the probability of errors [5]. The proposed system exhibits LCOM of 0 and 0.33 without and with patterns respectively, thus reducing cohesion to a very small extent. A higher value of afferent coupling. Would lead to stable designs since change in a class will itself propagate to other classes, which makes the class more stable. Thus, our proposed system with patterns shows Ca as 2 than its counterpart without patterns which is 0, indicating that our system is stable. The testing effort of the proposed system will be comparatively less since the number of children is 0. The testing and debugging of a class get more complex if RFC is high [5]. For our proposed system, RFC remains the same before and after the pattern application. RFC is also proportional to the complexity of a class [5]. Thus, the RFC metric evaluates to 3 for the proposed system, which is considerably a low value, thus signifying lesser complexity. A highly cohesive class improves encapsulation [5]. Patterns reduce LCOM for our proposed As a higher value of efferent coupling would lead to unstable designs since changes to heavily mutually dependent software commence an overspread of changes in dependent modules, which will lead to more testing and maintenance efforts [10]. Ce exhibits 2 for the Factory Method pattern, while Iterator and Adapter patterns show 0 values, thus indicating instability in classes implementing the Factory Method pattern. The proposed system computes I = 0 without patterns and I = 1 with patterns, which justifies that a system with patterns is more stable than without patterns.

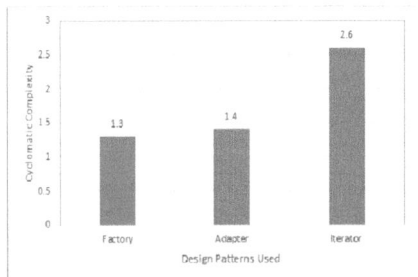
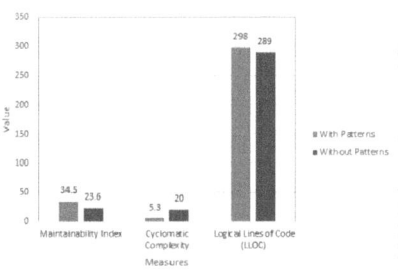

Fig. 8. Comparative study of maintainability index of the proposed system with and without design patterns

Abstractness indicates good design since it tends to increase reusability. The proposed system computes A = 0 without patterns and A = 0.25 with patterns, which justifies that a system with patterns is more reusable than one without patterns. The proposed system illustrates 32% as the reuse percent without patterns and 40% as the reuse percent with patterns, thus justifying better reusability after redesigning with patterns.

Table 2. Comparative study of the software maintainability of the proposed system with and without design patterns

Metric	Algorithm	Value
LCOM	DP	0
	Normal	0.33
Afferent Coupling	DP	2
	Normal	0
Efferent Coupling	DP	2
	Normal	0
Instability	DP	1
	Normal	0
Abstractness	DP	0.25
	Normal	0
Reuse Metric	DP	0.4
	Normal	0.32

6 Conclusion

The objective of this work is to forecast monthly Kaggle competitions, datasets and notebooks in different spectrums. It paves the way for Kaggle users to understand competitions, datasets and notebooks in Kaggle and participate effectively. The paper develops and analyses a time series model to predict different parameters in the Meta Kaggle dataset using ARIMA by checking different statistical properties such as stationarity, seasonality, autocorrelation, and partial autocorrelation of time series data. Furthermore, it aims to develop a reusable system for the ARIMA model using design patterns and evaluate the proposed design pattern-based forecasting ARIMA model using MAPE and software reusability and maintainability metrics. Experiments are conducted on three parameter data sets, tags and competitions, and the results show that the ARIMA model has less error than the other time series model LSTM and the design pattern based ARIMA model improves the maintainability and reusability. In the future, other parameters in Meta Kaggle namely, episodes, forums, kernels, etc., may be considered for analysis. Also, ranking methods may be proposed for competitions that earn more money.

References

1. Avgeriou, P., Zdun, U.: Architectural patterns revisited-a pattern language (2005)
2. Benvenuto, D., Giovanetti, M., Vassallo, L., Angeletti, S., Ciccozzi, M.: Application of the ARIMA model on the COVID-2019 epidemic dataset. Data Brief **29**, 105340 (2020)
3. Buschmann, F., Meunier, R., Rohnert, H., Sommerlad, P., Stal, M.: Pattern-Oriented Software Architecture: a System of Patterns, **1** Wiley (2008)

4. Capiluppi, A., Lago, P. and Morisio, M.: March. Characteristics of open source projects. In: Seventh European Conference on Software Maintenance and Reengineering, 2003. Proceedings, pp. 317–327. IEEE (2003)
5. Chidamber, S.R., Kemerer, C.F.: A metrics suite for object oriented design. IEEE Trans. Softw. Eng. **20**(6), 476–493 (1994)
6. Gamma, E., Helm, R., Johnson, R. and Vlissides, J.: Design patterns: elements of reusable software architecture, Addison-Wesley (1995)
7. Gencer, K., Başçiftçi, F.: Time series forecast modeling of vulnerabilities in the android operating system using ARIMA and deep learning methods. Sustain. Comput. Inform. Syst. **30**, 1005 (2021)
8. Kaggle Homepage, https://www.kaggle.com. Accessed 20 Oct 2023
9. Liao, Z., et al.: Healthy or not: a way to predict ecosystem health in GitHub. Symmetry **11**(2), 144 (2019)
10. Martin Robert, C.: The Dependency Inversion Principle. C++ Report (1996)
11. Radon Documentation, https://radon.readthedocs.io/en/latest/. Accessed 20 Oct 2023

Cyber Security

An Anonymous and Unlinkable Security Protocol for the Communication in Cloud-Enabled Smart Agriculture Environment

Sundararaju Mugunthan[(✉)] and Venkatasamy Sureshkumar

Department of Applied Mathematics and Computational Sciences,
PSG College of Technology, Coimbatore, India
mugunth05@gmail.com, sand.amcs@psgtech.ac.in

Abstract. Emerging technologies including smart perception devices, environment-control actuators, information and communication technologies and large computing resources are the main tools enabling smart agriculture. However, the use of wireless communication makes smart agriculture networks susceptible to various attacks. In this paper, we propose a novel architecture to enable periodic data collection from sensors to cloud using machine-to-machine communication. A robust, anonymous and unlinkable authentication scheme is developed for the proposed architecture. Three-party authentication between the cloud server, gateway and sensor nodes is facilitated by the scheme. The protocol uses session-specific pseudo-names and temporary passwords to achieve anonymity and unlinkability for both sensor nodes and gateways. The protocol also provides easy revocation for removing compromised sensor nodes and gateways. Further, formal and informal proofs are provided, and through performance analysis, it is demonstrated that the proposed protocol outperforms other schemes in terms of security features and performance metrics.

Keywords: Smart Agriculture · Authentication protocol · Machine-to-machine communication · Cloud Server · BAN Logic

1 Introduction

Smart agriculture is deployed in every stage of farming, from the stage of seed sowing to food processing and packaging [12]. Some applications in smart agriculture are nutrition management, precision farming, weather management and livestock monitoring [13]. As smart agriculture is data-driven, it increases the productivity of the farmer by enabling them to make fast decisions based on the data and it also enhances the sustainability of farming activities by reducing the overuse of natural resources [16].

Smart agriculture deploys sensor nodes are used to measure physical aspects such as temperature, humidity, pH, light intensity etc. Due to the limitations in the computational and power capacities of the sensor devices, the collected data is sent to a server through the network layer for further storage or processing. Communication technologies like Bluetooth, WiFi, WifiMax, ZigBee, etc. are used to establish communication between entities [17].

Usually, the user controls the overall operations by monitoring the sensor data and sending necessary control commands to the devices, such as an irrigation controller or weed remover. The user accesses the sensor information by placing a data access request at gateways that are connected to the internet. The gateways relay the request to the respective sensor nodes. The sensor processes the request and returns the sensor data to the gateway, which in turn forwards the data to the user [17].

However, recent advancements in Machine-to-Machine (M2M) communication technology provide exciting opportunities for automation. A distinctive feature of M2M communication is the absence of human intervention. M2M communication is driven by many factors including availability of the high-speed internet, the declining cost of sensor and actuator devices. By enabling a machine to communicate with another machine without human intervention, M2M communication plays an important role in automation [8].

Also, cloud computing technologies are employed in automating smart agriculture systems. Data from various sensors is heterogeneous in nature, and there may be redundant data. Cloud computing can be a solution to automation by monitoring data from sensors and processing and analyzing the collected data to generate models that can be used to predict and make decisions about performing agricultural activities to increase efficiency and productivity.

In smart agriculture, a passive attacker watching all the messages in the network can associate a sensor-actuator pair performing critical tasks by looking at the devices' unique identifiers. In spite of the attacker's inability to access encrypted data, he or she can identify devices that are critical for agricultural activities. This capability will enable him or her to cause more damage by targeting the devices using other attacks, such as jamming attacks or physical attacks. So it is necessary to design security mechanisms in such a way that it is impossible for an attacker to associate any message with a device.

1.1 Security Attacks

Smart agricultural systems are vulnerable to many attacks due to constrains such as limited bandwidth, storage, communication and computation capacity of devices and actuators. Many entities including curious kids to malicious attackers can try to breach the security of the system. As smart agriculture employs various devices, there are many vulnerable points and some of the attacks are given below.

Hijacking and Disruption of Autonomous Systems: Smart agriculture employs various autonomous systems that perform actions such as weeding, spraying fertilizers, watering, etc. By hijacking such autonomous system, an attacker can control it remotely and cause damages like destruction of crops, buildings, financial loss, physical harm to people or cattle, and making the whole system unavailable. Disruption can also be carried out by modifying essential components such as Global Positioning System, camera, sensing devices or remote-control systems. Such disruptions result in incorrect management of crops, soil, or nutrients and damages to equipment and machinery.

Node Capture: Adversary such as an a disgruntled worker or a business rival could capture the physical device and perform hardware or software changes to obtain unauthorized access to the system. The attacker can breach the integrity of the system and can cause damages such as interfering in decision making, damages to crops and financial loss. For example, an adverse actuator that is being controlled by the attacker can never start irrigating the crops or can flood the entire field causing loss of crops.

Fake Node: In order to disrupt the operation of the system an attacker adds a malicious node which is either a new node or a node previously captured by the attacker. Using the fake nodes, attacks are launched to interfere with decision making process by manipulating the data or to cause denial of service by injecting multiple packets. Similarly, malicious gateways may send incorrect control signals to legal actuators or drop legitimate packets and cut off communication between devices.

Sleep Deprivation: In this attack, an adversary exploits the limited power capacity of the nodes which are required to enter sleep mode during the times of inactivity. Attacker sends legitimate requests to the node with the intention of keeping it awake for prolonged period which ultimately resulting in node shutdown. By attacking many number of nodes, an attacker can compromise decision making and significantly reduce the system efficiency.

Denial of Service: An attacker aims to disrupt the availability of a system either by preventing access to services/resources or causing collapse of the resource. Attack is carried out by flooding the routers or servers with too many requests causing network delays, disabled devices and unavailable resources. Such an attack in farms can result in delay of control commands to the actuators, prevention of sensor data from reaching the server and unavailability of services.

Data Transit Attack: An attacker intercepts traffic using malicious access points to gain access to sensitive information such as secret credentials such as secret keys or unique identifiers. As the devices are made by different vendors they may not be fully compatible with each other and unencrypted data transmitted through wireless networks make the system susceptible to attacks. The transit attacks can enable malicious control of devices, corrupt network traffic and sometimes compromise the entire system.

Routing Attacks: In this attack, attacker takes advantage of the traffic path to realise illegal access. In sinkhole attack, the attacker fakes a shorter path using a malicious node prompting legitimate nodes to send their message to it. Once received, the malicious node destroy the messages causing disruption in traffic flow. In wormhole attack, an attacker creates a tunnel between two nodes and draws the traffic through the nodes. These attacks causes delayed or partial delivery of messages, modified messages or receive no message at all.

1.2 Security Goals

Security goals for a agriculture network are as follows.

Mutual authentication: Each communicating entity should be satisfied of others identity i.e., sensors should be able to verify the identities of gateway nodes and cloud server. Similarly, gateway nodes should be able to verify sensors and cloud server. Finally, cloud server should be able to verify the identities of gateway nodes and sensor nodes.

Confidentiality: This security property ensures any information against unauthorized revealing. Confidentiality makes sure only authorized entitites are able to read messages. This is usally achieved by using crytographic operations.

Integrity: Any entity should be able to verify the message received is not modified during transit. Integrity of the data is ensured by use of hash function to produce short summary of the message known as digest. Any mismatch between the message and its digest implies compromise of integrity.

Non-repudiation: It should be impossible for any entity to later deny sending or receiving any messages. This is usually achieved through binding identity or long term secret of an entity with its message digest.

Recentness: Attacker can replay a legitimate message from the past session in the current session. A secure protocol should be able to distinguish a legitimate messages from a different time periods. Failure to distinguish will result in escalation of privilages to unauthorized entity resulting in loss of confidentiality, integrity or privacy. Freshness of messages is usually ensured by use of time stamps and nonces.

Anonymity and Unlinkability: An attacker watching all the messages in a communication channel should not be able to link a particular message with a particular entity. Failure to protect the security properties result in exposing of identities of the entities and overall operations of the system.

1.3 Motivation and Contribution

Our work mainly focuses on the twin objectives of automation and unlinkability. Machine-to-machine communication is vital to automating a system. Automation using cloud services and M2M communication adds value to smart agriculture by removing human supervision and increasing efficiency. In terms of security, an authentication protocol should prevent an attacker from linking any two devices or messages to protect the operation of smart agricultural system.

Existing schemes in the literature try to provide a solution for the user to access data stored in a sensor node. One of the disadvantages of the existing schemes is that, as the number of sensor nodes increases, the task of manually accessing the data from every node becomes laborious, and the repeated human intervention does not help with automation. Automating agricultural operations requires data collection from many sensor nodes, processing, analyzing, predicting and making decisions. Cloud storage is suitable for such tasks. However, to the best of our knowledge, there is no research that aims to secure machine-to-machine communication between sensor nodes and the cloud. Also, important security properties like anonymity and unlinkability of devices have not been fully studied. In fact, providing unlinkability is one research problem.

The novelty of the proposed scheme is that it enables the sensor node to periodically store the sensed data in the cloud without user intervention. By removing user intervention from the system, our scheme enables the cloud to collect data from sensors periodically, which helps to derive insights. To realize autonomous communications, several challenges must be met. These challenges arise due to the unique characteristics of M2M communication and the respective application domain.

The main contributions of the paper are as follows.

- Propose a cloud-enabled architecture for collecting sensor data periodically and storing the data on a cloud server in a smart agriculture environment. The architecture enables automation by removing user supervision through the use of machine-to-machine communication.
- Present an anonymous, unlinkable and secure authentication scheme to enable secure machine-to-machine communication between sensor nodes, gateways and cloud server. The scheme leverages pseudo-names to realize anonymity and unlinkability of sensor nodes and gateways. Use of session-specific temporary passwords enhances security.
- Discuss the security properties of the proposed protocol through informal proofs.
- Prove the correctness of the scheme using the formal method BAN logic.
- Demonstrate the efficiency of the proposed protocol through comparison of the scheme with that of others in the smart agriculture environment.

The paper is organized as follows: Sect. 2 presents the communication architecture of the proposed protocol and related works in the area of smart agriculture. The proposed scheme is presented in Sect. 3. Formal and informal analyses of the scheme are given in Sect. 4. The comparison of various properties of the protocol with other recent schemes in terms of different performance metrics is discussed in 5. Finally, the conclusion of the paper is given in Sect. 6.

2 Communication Architecture and Related Works

This section describes proposed architecture for the establishment of communication among the entities and details about the pertinent works presented in the literature.

2.1 Communication Architecture

The entities considered in this proposed scheme are farming devices such as sensors and actuators, gateway nodes, the user and the cloud. Sensor nodes which measure various parameters such as humidity, temperature etc., and actuators which are mechanical devices such as irrigation controller, pesticide sprayers are installed in the farm. Sensors and actuators communicate with the gateway nodes using wireless communication and gateway nodes are connected to the Internet. The gateway acts as a point of connection for the user, sensor/actuator devices, and the cloud. Sensor nodes sends data to the cloud through the gateway node. The cloud processes the raw data received from the sensor and processes, analyzes, predicts and decides about various agricultural operations. The decisions taken by the cloud are sent to corresponding actuators to change the state of the environment. These commands are relayed to actuators through the gateway node. The communication architecture is presented in the Fig. 1.

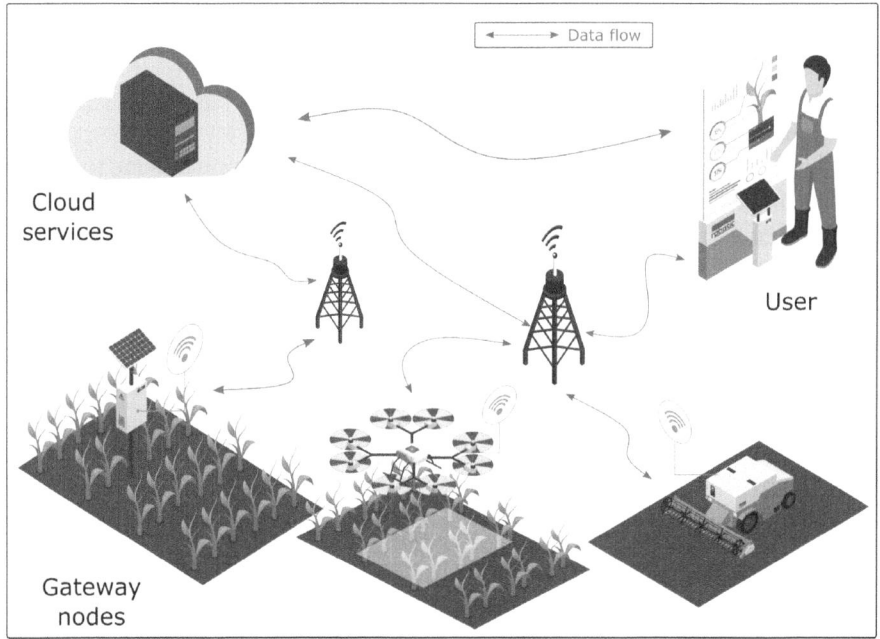

Fig. 1. Communication architecture

2.2 Related Works

Many authentication and key establishment schemes are published for communication in smart agriculture networks.

In 2016, Gope et al. [5] proposed a protocol to provide user authentication in global mobility networks. In this scheme, a mobile user assumed to be connected to a foreign network. The scheme provides authentication between the mobile user and the foreign agent with the help of user's home agent. The protocol uses lightweight operations and the authors claimed their protocol is secure against attacks.

In 2016, Ibrahim et al. [6] presented a scheme to provide anonymous authentication for devices in wireless body area networks using lightweight operations. Also, demonstration of the protocol using NS-2 simulator is also presented in this work.

In 2015, Memon et al. [7] proposed a protocol to authenticate a mobile client with base transceiver station with the help of location based services. In this scheme, a certificateless public key cryptography system is implemented using Elliptic Curve Cryptography(ECC). The authors claimed their protocol is safe from attacks.

However, in 2016 Reddy et al. [9] showed the scheme by Memon et al. [7] is vulnerable to key compromised impersonation attack, privileged insider attack and also suffers from limitations including imperfect mutual authentication and insecure password changing phase. Also, they proposed a scheme based on ECC to provide anonymous authentication for mobile services. The authors claimed their protocol is secure and efficient than Memon et al.

In 2019, Xu et al. [18] proposed a authentication and key agreement scheme for wireless body area network using lightweight operation. The scheme uses only hash and xor operation to provide authentication. Simulation of the protocol using ProVerif tool is presented along with some informal discussions. The author claimed their scheme is secure against various attacks.

However in 2021, Alzahrani et al. [2] demonstrated that the scheme by Xu et al. [18] is vulnerable to multiple attacks such as replay attacks and key compromise impersonation attacks. The authors also claimed that Xu et al. protocol lacks proper privacy. Then the authors presented an authentication protocol for WBANs using lightweight operations.

In 2021, Sureshkumar et al. [15] proposed a authentication protocol for cloud enabled smart agriculture environment using ECC. The scheme intended to enable the communication between IoT devices and user by establishing mutual authentication and key establishment. The authors claimed their protocol is secure and efficient. However, the protocol do not provide provisions for data storage using cloud servers.

The recent survey shows, to the best of our knowledge, that there has been no attempt to secure machine-to-machine communication for a cloud-enabled smart agriculture network. Also, protecting the anonymity and unlinkability of the devices has not been studied as well. This work aims to bridge the gap by proposing an anonymous and unlinkable security protocol for a cloud-enabled smart agriculture network.

3 Proposed Scheme

Our scheme consists of two phases, namely, registration phase and the authentication and key establishment phases. The phases are given below.

3.1 Registration Phase

All the entities have to register before engaging in communication. During the registration phase, secret credentials are stored in the device's memory and on the cloud server, which will be used for communication. The system admin performs the registration and is a trusted entity. Registration is performed through a secure channel.

Gateway Registration: During the registration phase, System Admin (SA) stores a long-term secret x_j and a temporary pseudo-name PID_j for the gateway node GW_j. The pseudo-name is updated after every successful session. The SA also stores the values x_j and PID_j in Cloud Server (CS). The CS identifies gateway nodes by their long-term secret and updates the corresponding pseudo-names after every successful session.

Sensor Registration: Similar to gateway registration, SA stores a long-term secret s_m and a pseudo-name SID_m for the sensor node SN_m. SA also stores the values s_m and SID_m in CS. The pseudo-names of sensor nodes are also updated after every successful session.

3.2 Authentication and Key Establishment Phase

Firstly, the CS and a gateway node GN_j, with the pseudo-name PID_j, perform mutual authentication and establish a session key. Now the CS can access any sensor node that is connected to GW_j by performing mutual authentication.

Step 1: The CS generates a random number R_{cs-gw} and also generates a new temporary password PID_{pw} for the gateway PID_j. The temporary password is session specific and updated for every session. This is used as an additional security measure during authentication. The CS also computes $V_1 = h(x_j \| PID_j \| T_{cs})$, $A_0 = h(x_j \| T_{cs})$, $A_1 = R_{cs-gw} \oplus A_0$, $A_2 = h(R_{cs-gw} \| x \| T_{cs})$, $A_3 = PID_{pw} \oplus A_2$, and $A_4 = h(PID_j \| PID_{pw} \| R_{cs-gw} \| T_{cs})$. The CS sends $M_1 = \{PID_j, V_1, A_1, A_3, A_4, T_{cs}\}$ to gateway node GW.

Step 2: After receiving M_1, GW computes $V_1^* = h(x \| PID_j \| T_{cs})$, and verifies $V_1^* \stackrel{?}{=} V_1$. If this holds true, GW authenticates CS. Then computes the following to retrieve the temporary password and random number. $A_0 = h(x \| T_{cs})$, $R_{cs-gw}^* = A_1 \oplus A_0$, $A_2^* = h(R_{cs-gw^*} \| x \| T_{cs})$, $PID_{pw}^* = A_2^* \oplus A_3$, $A_4^* = h(PID_j \| PID_{pw}^* \| R_{cs-gw}^* \| T_{cs})$, and checks $A_4 \stackrel{?}{=} A_4^*$.

Step 3: Then GW generates a random number R_{gw} and computes $V_2 = h(R_{cs-gw} \| PID_j \| PID_{pw} \| T_{cs} \| T_{gw})$, $B_0 = h(R_{cs-gw} \| T_{cs} \| T_{gw})$, $B_1 = R_{gw} \oplus B_0$, $B_2 = h(R_{cs} \| R_{gw} \| T_{cs} \| T_{gw})$. GW sends the message $M_2 = \{CS, V_2, B_1, B_2, T_{gw}\}$ to CS.

Step 4: After receiving the message M_2, CS computes, $V_2^* = h(R_{cs} \| PID_j \| PID_{pw} \| T_{cs} \| T_{gw})$, and verifies $V_2^* \stackrel{?}{=} V_2$. If this holds true, CS successfully authenticates GW and computes $B_0^* = h(R_{cs-gw} \| T_{cs} \| T_{gw})$, $R_{gw}^* = B_0^* \oplus B_1$, $B_2^* = h(R_{cs-gw} \| R_{gw}^* \| T_{cs} \| T_{gw})$, and checks $B_2^* \stackrel{?}{=} B_2$. If this holds true, the CS successfully authenticates GW.

Both CS and GW compute the session key $SK_{cs-gw} = h(R_{cs-gw} \| R_{gw} \| T_{cs})$.

Step 5: To communicate with the sensor node SN, whose dynamic identity is SID_m, the CS generates a random number R_{cs-sn} and a new temporary password SID_{pw} for the sensor node. Then CS computes, $V_3 = h(s\|SID_m\|T_{cs})$, $C_0 = h(s\|T_{cs})$, $C_1 = R_{cs-sn} \oplus C_0$, $C_2 = h(R_{cs-sn}\|s\|T_{cs})$, $C_3 = SID_{pw} \oplus C_2$, $C_4 = h(SID_m\|SID_{pw}\|R_{cs-sn}\|T_{cs})$, $I_1 = h(x\|R_{cs-gw}\|PID_{pw})$, $I_2 = h(s\|R_{cs-sn}\|PID_n)$, and $I_{gw-sn} = I_1 \oplus I_2$. Then CS sends the message $M_3 = \{V_3, I_{gw-sn}, C_1, C_3, C_4, T_{cs}\}_{SK_{sn-gw}}$ to GW.

In this message, the value I_{gw-sn} facilitates mutual authentication between the gateway node PID_j and the sensor node SID_m. It should be noted that the gateway node can only produce the value $I_1 = h(x_j\|R_{cs-gw}\|PID_{pw})$ which is used to retrieve the value $I_2 = h(s_m\|R_{cs-sn}\|SID_{pw})$. Then the gateway node PID_j uses the value I_2 to authenticate itself with the sensor node SID_m.

Step 6: After receiving the message, GW computes, $I_1 = h(x\|R_{cs-gw}\|PID_{pw})$, $I_2^* = I_{gw-sn} \oplus I_1$, and $V_4 = h(I_2^*\|PID_j\|T_{gw}\|T_{cs})$. GW sends the message $M_4 = \{SID_m, V_3, I_{gw-sn}, C_1, C_2, C_3, V_4, T_{cs}, T_{gw}\}$ to SN.

Step 7: After receiving the message M_4, SN computes $V_3^* = h(s\|SID_m\|T_{cs})$ $V_3^* \stackrel{?}{=} V_3$ If it holds true, the sensor node SN authenticates CS.

Then SN computes, $R_{cs-sn}^* = C_1 \oplus h(s\|T_{cs})$, $SID_{pw}^* = C_2 \oplus h(R_{cs-sn}\|s\|T_{cs})$, $C_3 = h(SID_m\|SID_{pw}^*\|R_{cs-sn}^*\|T_{cs})$, and verifies $C_3^* \stackrel{?}{=} C_3$. If true, SN then computes $I_2 = h(s\|R_{cs-sn}\|SID_{pw})$, $V_4^* = h(I_2\|PID_j\|T_{gw}\|T_{cs})$, and checks $V_4^* \stackrel{?}{=} V_4$. If this holds true, SN authenticates GW. Similar to the gateway node, the sensor node uses the value I_{gw-cs} to retrieve I_1 which is used to authenticate with PID_j.

Step 8: The sensor node SID_m generates a random number R_{sn} and computes, $I_1^* = I_{gw-sn} \oplus I_2$, $V_5 = h(I_1^*\|SID_m\|T_{sn})$, $V_6 = h(SID_m\|SID_{pw}\|R_{cs-sn}\|T_{cs}\|T_{gw}\|T_{gn})$, $D_0 = h(R_{cs-sn}\|SID_{pw}\|T_{sn})$, $D_1 = R_{sn} \oplus D_0$, and $D_2 = h(SID_m\|SID_{pw}\|R_{cs-sn}\|R_{sn}\|T_{cs}\|T_{sn})$. The SID_m sends the message $M_5 = \{V_5, V_6, D_1, D_2, T_{cs}, T_{gw}, T_{sn}\}$ to GW.

Step 9: After receiving the message M_5, GW computes $I_1 = h(x\|R_{cs}\|PID_{pw}\|T_{cs})$, $V_5^* = h(I_1\|SID_m\|T_{sn})$, and checks $V_5^* \stackrel{?}{=} V_5$. If it holds true, GW authenticates SN and sends the message $M_6 = \{V_6, D_1, D_2, Tcs, T_{gw}, T_{sn}\}_{SK_{sn-gw}}$ to CS.

Step 10: After receiving the message, the CS computes $V_6^* = h(SID_m\|SID_{pw}\|R_{cs-sn}\|T_{cs}\|T_{gw}\|T_{gn})$, and checks $V_6^* \stackrel{?}{=} V_6$. If this is true, CS successfully authenticates SID_m and computes, $D_0 = h(R_{cs-sn}\|SID_{pw}\|T_{sn})$, $R_{sn}^* = D_1 \oplus D_0$, $D_2^* = h(SID_m\|SID_{pw}\|R_{cs-sn}\|R_{sn}\|T_{cs}\|T_{sn})$ and verifies $D_2^* \stackrel{?}{=} D_2$.

Then session key between CS and SN is computed as $SK_{cs-sn} = h(s\|R_{cs-sn}\|R_{sn})$.

Finally, the next dynamic identity of GW computed as $PID_k = R_{cs-gw} \oplus R_{gw}$ and next dynamic identity of SN computed as $SID_n = R_{cs-sn} \oplus R_{sn}$.

4 Formal and Informal Analysis

This section aims to establish various properties of the proposed protocol through formal methods and informal discussion.

4.1 Formal Analysis Using BAN Logic

The BAN logic is a formal method that is widely used to verify the correctness of security protocols [14]. In BAN logic, messages exchanged in a protocol are converted to an idealized form. Then a list of assumptions about the protocol and a list of stated goals of the protocol are presented. Then, using a set of inference rules and a set of assumptions, whether the security protocol achieves the stated goals is verified.

Message Idealization. During idealization, parts of the messages or whole messages that are not needed for establishing the stated goals are usually omitted. The messages exchanged during the authentication and key establishment phases of our protocol are idealized as follows.

$M_1 = \{\langle R_{cs-sn}\rangle_{A_0}, T_{cs}\}$
$M_2 = \{\langle R_{gw}\rangle_{B_0}\}$
$M_4 = \{\langle I_1\rangle_{I_2}, \langle R_{cs-sn}\rangle_{C_0}, T_{cs}, T_{gw}\}$
$M_6 = \{\langle R_{sn}\rangle_{D_0}, T_{sn}\}$

Goals. Gateway believes that it shares a session key with cloud server.

$G_1 : GW \mid\equiv GW \xleftarrow{SK_{cs-gw}} CS$.
Cloud server believes that it shares a session key with gateway.
$G_2 : CS \mid\equiv CS \xleftarrow{SK_{cs-gw}} GW$
Sensor Node believes that it shares a session key with cloud server.
$G_3 : SN \mid\equiv SN \xleftarrow{SK_{cs-sn}} CS$
Cloud server believes that it shares a session key with sensor node.
$G_4 : CS \mid\equiv CS \xleftarrow{SK_{cs-sn}} SN$

Assumptions. The following assumptions are used to establish the goals.

Proof of Authentication and Key Establishment. Table 1 presents the step-by-step derivation of goals of authentication and key establishment that is derived using the list of assumptions and rules of inference.

4.2 Informal Analysis of the Proposed Scheme

Informal analysis are discussions to show the robustness of a protocol and informally establish its security features.

An Anonymous and Unlinkable Security Protocol   79

$A_1 : GW \mid\equiv GW \overset{x}{\rightleftharpoons} CS$ $\quad\quad A_2 : GW \mid\equiv \# T_{cs}$

$A_3 : GW \mid\equiv CS \mid\Rightarrow R_{cs-gw}$ $\quad A_4 : CS \mid\equiv \# T_{gw}$

$A_5 : CS \mid\equiv CS \overset{R_{cs-gw}}{\rightleftharpoons} GW$ $\quad A_6 : CS \mid\equiv GW \mid\Rightarrow R_{gw}$

$A_7 : SN \mid\equiv SN \overset{s}{\rightleftharpoons} CS$ $\quad\quad A_8 : SN \mid\equiv \# T_{cs}$

$A_9 : SN \mid\equiv CS \mid\Rightarrow R_{cs-sn}$ $\quad A_{10} : CS \mid\equiv CS \overset{SID_{pw}}{\rightleftharpoons} SN$

$A_{11} : CS \mid\equiv \# T_{sn}$ $\quad\quad A_{12} : CS \mid\equiv SN \mid\Rightarrow R_{sn}$

Mutual Authentication. Mutual authentication between CS and GW is achieved using the values V_1 and V_2 in the messages M_1 and M_2 respectively. The token $V_1 = h(x\|PID_j\|T_{cs})$ is constructed using x which is a shared secret between CS and GW. Thus V_1 assures GW of authenticity of CS. Similarly, $V_2 = h(R_{cs}\|PID_j\|PID_{pw}\|T_{cs}\|T_{gw})$ contains hash values of R_{cs-gw} and PID_{pw} which can only be retrieved by the holder of x. Thus, V_2 assures CS of authenticity of GW. The case is similar for mutual authentication between CS and SN which achieved using secret values s, SID_{pw} and the random number R_{cs-sn}.

Mutual authentication between GW and SN is facilitated by CS provided value I_{gw-sn}. Since CS is a trusted entity, GW and SN use this value to construct the tokens $V_4 = h(I_2\|PID_j\|T_{gw}\|T_{cs})$ and $V_5 = h(I_1\|SID_m\|T_{sn})$.

Replay Attack. Generally, replay attacks are prevented through the use of time stamps or nonces. The proposed scheme uses time stamp as well as temporary passwords which are unique to each session.

The message $M_1 = \{PID_j, V_1, A_1, A_2, A_3, T_{cs}\}$ contains T_{cs} which is the timestamp at cloud server side. If an attacker tries to replay this message with a new time stamp T''_{cs} and new fabricated message $M'_1 = \{PID_j, V_1, A_1, A_2, A_3, T''_{cs}\}$. However this attempt will fail as the integrity check $A_3^* = h(PID_j\|PID^*_{pw}\|R^*_{cs-gw}\|T_{cs})$ will fail as $h(PID_j\|PID^*_{pw}\|R^*_{cs-gw}\|T_{cs}) \neq h(PID_j\|PID^*_{pw}\|R^*_{cs-gw}\|T''_{cs})$ resulting in GW discarding the message M'_1. Same is the case for all the messages in our proposed scheme. Thus our scheme is resilient to replay attacks.

Perfect Forward Security. Given a current session key, an attacker should not be able to construct previous session keys. In other words, each session key should be independent of past session keys. In our scheme, session keys are computed as $SK_{cs-gw} = h(x\|R_{cs-gw}\|R_{gw})$ and $SK_{cs-sn} = h(s\|R_{cs-sn}\|R_{sn})$. Due to the one-way nature of hash function, given a session key, an attacker cannot possibly find the random numbers that is used to generate the key. Apart from the long term secrets, no other random values from previous session are used for current session. This makes each session keys independent of previous session keys.

Modification Attack. Intended recipients of a message should be able to detect any illegitimate changes to that message during transit. This is achieved by

Table 1. Derivation of goals using BAN logic

No. Statement	Reason
$S_1: GW \triangleleft \langle R_{cs-gw} \rangle_{A_0}$	From M_1
$S_2: GW \models CS \mid\sim R_{cs-gw}$	Using S_1 and A_1
$S_3: GW \models \# R_{cs-gw}$	Using A_2 and S_2
$S_4: GW \models CS \models R_{cs-gw}$	In accordance with S_2 and S_3
$S_5: GW \models R_{cs-gw}$	Using A_3 and S_4
$S_6: GW \models GW \xleftrightarrow{SK_{cs-gw}} CS$ [Goal 1]	Using Session Key Rule on S_5
$S_7: CS \triangleleft \langle R_{gw} \rangle_{B_0}$	From message M_2
$S_8: CS \models GW \mid\sim R_{gw}$	Using Message Meaning Rule on A_5 and S_7
$S_9: CS \models \# R_{gw}$	Applying freshness rule on A_4 and S_7
$S_{10}: CS \models GW \models R_{gw}$	Using Nonce Verification Rule on S_8 and S_9
$S_{11}: CS \models R_{cs-gw}$	Using Jurisdiction rule on A_6 and S_{10}
$S_{12}: CS \models CS \xleftrightarrow{SK_{cs-gw}} GW$ [Goal 2]	Using Session Key Rule on S_{11},
$S_{13}: SN \triangleleft \langle R_{cs-sn} \rangle$	From M_4
$S_{14}: SN \models CS \mid\sim R_{cs-sn}$	Applying Message Meaning Rule and A_7 on S_{13}
$S_{15}: SN \models \# R_{cs-sn}$	Using Freshness Rule and A_8 on S_{13}
$S_{16}: SN \models CS \models R_{cs-sn}$	Using Nonce Verification Rule on S_8 and S_9
$S_{17}: SN \models R_{cs-sn}$	Using Jurisdiction Rule and A_9 on S_{16}
$S_{18}: SN \models SN \xleftrightarrow{SK_{cs-sn}} CS$ [Goal 3]	Using Session Key Rule on S_{17}
$S_{19}: CS \triangleleft \langle R_{sn} \rangle_{R_{cs-sn} \| SID_{pw} \| T_{sn}}$	From M_6
$S_{20}: CS \models SN \mid\sim R_{sn}$	Applying Message Meaning Rule and A_{10} on S_{19}
$S_{21}: CS \models \# R_{sn}$	Using Freshness Rule and A_{11} on S_{19}
$S_{22}: CS \models SN \models R_{sn}$	Using Nonce Verification Rule on S_{20} and S_{21}
$S_{23}: CS \models R_{sn}$	Applying Jurisdiction Rule and A_{12} on S_{22}
$S_{24}: CS \models CS \xleftrightarrow{SK_{cs-sn}} SN$ [Goal 4]	Using Session Key Rule on S_{23}

the producing message digest using one-way hash functions. For example, the message M_1 contains the digest $A_3 = h(PID_j \| PID_{pw} \| R_{cs-gw} \| T_{cs})$. The value A_3 ensures any changes done to the values PID_j, PID_{pw} and R_{cs-gw} during transit by any entity other than CS are caught by GW. By including message digest of the contents in all messages, our scheme ensures recipient can verify the integrity of the message and discard modified messages.

Revocation. Some times an attacker can place a counterfeit sensor or gateway node to access sensitive information. It may be also a case that sometimes cloud server wants a sensor to removed from the system whose service is no longer needed. In any case, cloud server should able to revoke sensors and gateways. Our scheme enables the cloud server to achieve this by simply removing the intended device from table of devices which is stored in its memory. By removing the long term secret s and its pseudo identity SID_k, cloud server can revoke the privileges of the sensor node. Similarly, the values x and PID_n should be removed from the table to revoke the respective gateway.

Ephemeral Secret Leakage Attack. A revealing of session nonce values should not result in revealing of long term secret keys of the legal entities. In our scheme, the session key is constructed as $SK_{cs-gw} = h(x \| R_{cs-gw} \| R_{gw})$ and $SK_{cs-sn} = h(s \| R_{cs-sn} \| R_{sn})$. Even if the session random numbers R_{cs-gw} and R_{gw} are exposed, an attacker cannot find the long-term secret x of the gateway due to one-way nature of hash function. And since temporary password PID_{pw} is used for authentication and not x, an attacker cannot possibly learn x_j through the messages and session nonce alone. Similar is the case for the session key SK_{cs-sn} and the sensor secret s_m as well. Thus our protocol is resistent to ephemeral secret leakage attack.

Insider Attack. Sometimes a legitimate entity can also be an attacker. In that case, a secure protocol should prevent the attacker from accessing the long term secrets of other devices and their session keys. In the case of a gateway being an insider, it cannot access the session keys or long term secrets of the sensor nodes. For example, the random value R_{cs-sn} is encrypted as $A_1 = R_{cs-sn} \oplus A_0$. The gateway node would require the long term secret s_j of the sensor node to build A_0 which is not possible. Similarly, the random value R_{sn} is encrypted as $D_1 = R_{sn} \oplus D_0$. The gateway node would require the value R_{cs-sn} and the temporary password of the sensor SID_{pw} to access the value R_{sn} which is not possible. Thus, any attempt by an insider gateway node to build the session key SK_{cs-sn} is not possible. Similar is the case for any insider sensor node to access the long term secret or session keys between the gateway and the cloud server. Thus, our protocol is resilient against insider attacks by a legitimate gateway or a sensor node.

Eavesdropping Attack. This is a passive attack in which the attacker just listens to all the communication and learns sensitive information that is not intended for him/her. After successful authentication of gateway node, its communication with the cloud server is encrypted using $SK_{cs-gw} = h(x\|R_{cs-gw}\|R_{gw})$. Similarly, communication between the cloud server and sensor node is encrypted using $SK_{cs-sn} = h(s\|R_{cs-sn}\|R_{sn})$, which is again encrypted using the key SK_{cs-gw} by the gateway. This double encryption, along with the use of pseudo-names ensure attackers cannot learn any sensitive information nor the identities of the sensors and gateways.

Unlinkability and Anonymity. Unlinkability ensures an attacker cannot link a message to a device, and anonymity ensures an attacker cannot identify an entity from a set of given entities. Failure to preserve unlinkability and anonymity results in attackers learning sensitive information such as device identifiers or locations which will help them to perform more coordinated attacks. Unlinkability is usually ensured by not using the same piece of data across different sessions, and anonymity is ensured by using different identifiers in different sessions or encrypting the identifier. In the proposed scheme, the pseudo-name for gateway is computed as as $PID_k = R_{cs-gw} \oplus R_{gw}$ and sensor nodes as $SID_n = R_{cs-sn} \oplus R_{sn}$. The pseudo names are updated only at the end of a successful session at both the sensor (or gateway) and the cloud server. Pseudo-names for gateways ensure attackers cannot learn the gateway to which a given sensor is associated.

5 Performance Evaluation of the Proposed Scheme

This section deals with the evaluation of the proposed protocol by comparing it with other schemes in terms of security features, computation and communication costs.

5.1 Comparison of Security Features

A comparison of security features is given in the Table 2.

The protocol by Roselin et al. [10] is the most affected protocol and is vulnerable to man-in-the-middle, impersonation, modification and tracing attacks. The only protocol that is vulnerable to replay attack among the compared protocols is Panda et al. [8]. In terms of security features, the protocols Roselin et al. [10], Ryu et al. [11] and Panda et al. [8] provide only two party authentication. Also, the schemes Ryu et al. [11] and Fan et al. [4] require user initiation by providing a password, which makes the schemes unsuitable for automation.

The tracing attack is the most common attack among considered attacks, and it affects all the schemes other than Panda et al. [8] and ours. Successful tracing attacks enable an attacker to identify devices and derive their behavior across sessions, which compromises anonymity and unlinkability. Through the use of dynamic identities, the proposed protocol ensures the anonymity and unlinkability of sensor nodes as well as gateways.

Table 2. Security features and resistance against attacks

	P_1	P_2	P_3	P_4	P_5	P_6	P_7
Esfahani et al. [3]		×	×		×		
Roselin et al. [10]		×	×	×	×	×	
Ryu et al. [11]				×	×	×	
Fan et al. [4]				×	×		×
Adeel et al. [1]		×			×		×
Panda et al. [8]	×		×			×	
Ours							

P_1: Replay attack, P_2: Man-in-the-middle attack, P_3: Impersonation attack, P_4: Modification attack, P_5: Tracing attack, P_6: Three party authentication, P_7: No user intervention

5.2 Computation Cost

The computation resource required to complete an authentication and key establishment phase is known as computation cost. The computation cost of our scheme is compared against other schemes and is presented in the Table 3 and in the Fig. 2a. The computation cost depends on the operation used and the type of hardware. For our scheme, the computational cost values are taken from [14]. Parties communicating for authentication in comparison schemes are given in the Table 4.

Among the compared protocols, the protocol by Esfahani et al. [3] has the lowest computation cost and Roselin et al. [10] has the highest computation cost. The protocols with low computation cost Esfahani et al. [3], Panda et al. [8] and Ryu et al. [11] provide authentication between only two parties and use only the hash function. Among three-party authentication protocols, our protocol uses both hash function and symmetric encryption. Our protocol uses symmetric encryption as it initially performs mutual authentication between the cloud server and gateway. The other two three-party authentication protocols Fan et al. [4] and Adeel et al. [1] use only hash functions. However, all the three-party authentication protocols are comparable in terms of computation, but the other two suffer from vulnerability.

5.3 Communication Cost

Communication cost refers to the number of bits used in one round of authentication. The communication cost of the protocols is given in Table 5 and its visualization is presented in Fig. 2b.

Similar to computation cost, the protocol by Roselin et al. [10] has the highest communication cost. The scheme by Ryu et al. [11] uses the lowest number of bits, and only two messages are exchanged. Similarly Panda et al. [8] also uses

Table 3. Computational cost comparison

Protocol	First party	Second party	Third party	Total (in ms)
Esfahani et al. [3]	$7T_h$	$7T_h$	-	$14T_h \approx 0.072436$
Roselin et al. [10]	$8T_{sym}$	$8T_{sym}$	-	$16T_{sym} \approx 0.343736$
Ryu et al. [11]	$2T_{fc} + 3T_{pm} + 13T_h$	$3T_{pm} + 6T_h$	-	$2T_{fc} + 19T_h + 6T_{pm} \approx 0.098306$
Fan et al. [4]	$5T_h$	$6T_h$	$12T_h$	$23T_h \approx 0.119002$
Adeel et al. [1]	$7T_h$	$6T_h$	$12T_h$	$20T_h \approx 0.10348$
Panda et al. [8]	$6T_h$	$11T_h$	-	$17T_h \approx 0.087958$
Ours	$17T_h + 1T_{sym}$	$11T_h + 1T_{sym}$	$10T_h$	$38T_h + 2T_{sym} \approx 0.187839$

T_{fc} : biometric fuzzy extractor computation time, T_h : hash function execution time, T_{sm} : ECC scalar multiplication, T_{sym} : symmetric encryption/decryption

Table 4. Parties communicating in authentication phase

Scheme	First party	Second party	Third party
Esfahani et al. [3]	Sensor	Router	Authentication Server
Roselin et al. [10]	Sensor	Router	-
Ryu et al. [11]	Patient	Registration Center	-
Fan et al. [4]	User	IoT end device	Trust Authority
Adeel et al. [1]	Device A	Device B	Authentication Server
Panda et al. [8]	Sensor	Controller	-
Ours	Cloud Server	Gateway Node	Sensor Node

only two messages for authentication. It is notable that three-party authentication protocols Esfahani et al. [3], Fan et al. [4], Adeel et al. [1] and ours consume more bits than those of two-party authentication protocols. Our scheme uses the most number of messages among the compared protocols. This is due to the initial mutual authentication between the gateway and the cloud server. However, any number of sensors can be accessed using the same session with the gateway. This reduces the number of messages for further accessing other sensors belonging to the gateway. Our protocol also provides anonymity and unlinkability through the use of pseudo-names which are transmitted at the start of a session. One trade-off of this approach is a slightly elevated communication cost, which is justified.

6 Conclusion

In this work, a robust security protocol for communication in smart agriculture is presented. The proposed protocol enables automation by facilitating cloud servers to periodically collect data from various sensor nodes without user intervention. Firstly, the cloud server mutually authenticates with a desired gateway node, and then it accesses any sensor node that is connected to the gateway. The scheme provides three-party authentication, whereas most of the recent schemes provide only two-party authentication. The proposed protocol enables the cloud

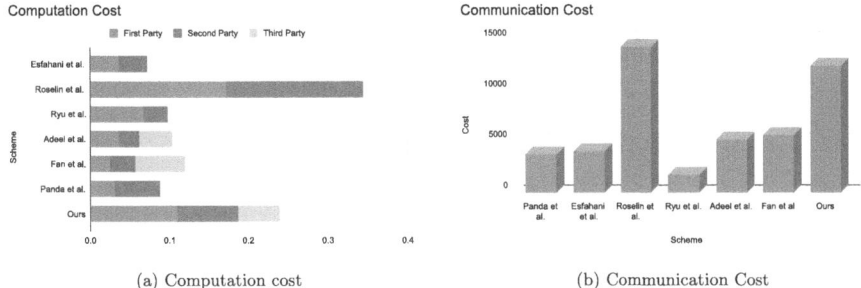

Fig. 2. Cost Comparisons

Table 5. Comparison of communication costs

Protocol	No. of messages	No. of bits
Esfahani et al. [3]	3	4096
Roselin et al. [10]	4	14336
Ryu et al. [11]	2	1728
Fan et al. [4]	4	5635
Adeel et al. [1]	5	5184
Panda et al. [8]	2	3808
Ours	6	12288

The communication cost for every type of message is taken as follows. Random number: 160 bits, identity: 32 bits, timestamp: 32 bits, elliptic curve point: 320 bits, and hash output: 512 bits.

server to initiate the communication and thus requires no human supervision. The use of dynamic identities and temporary passwords marginally increases computation and communication costs. However, a comparison of security features shows the scheme performs better in terms of security features, justifying the elevated cost. Correctness of the protocol is proved using the formal method BAN logic. Informal proofs show the proposed scheme also fulfills the anonymity and unlinkability requirements for both sensor nodes and gateways.

Acknowledgment. This work is supported by PSG College of Technology, Coimbatore, India; and in part, this work is partially supported by Fund for Improvement of S&T Infrastructure in Universities and Higher Educational Institutions (FIST) through Department of Science & Technology (DST), Government of India under the Project SR/FST/COLLEGE-/2021/1139.

Disclosure of Interests. The authors declare that they do not have any commercial or associative interest that represents a conflict of interest in connection with the work submitted.

References

1. Adeel, A., et al.: A multi-attack resilient lightweight Iot authentication scheme. Trans. Emerg. Telecomm. Technol. **33**(3), e3676 (2022)
2. Alzahrani, B.A., Irshad, A., Albeshri, A., Alsubhi, K.: A provably secure and lightweight patient-healthcare authentication protocol in wireless body area networks. Wireless Pers. Commun. **117**, 47–69 (2021)
3. Esfahani, A., et al.: A lightweight authentication mechanism for m2m communications in industrial IoT environment. IEEE Internet Things J. **6**(1), 288–296 (2017)
4. Fan, Q., Chen, J., Shojafar, M., Kumari, S., He, D.: Sake*: a symmetric authenticated key exchange protocol with perfect forward secrecy for industrial internet of things. IEEE Trans. Industr. Inf. **18**(9), 6424–6434 (2022)
5. Gope, P., Hwang, T.: An efficient mutual authentication and key agreement scheme preserving strong anonymity of the mobile user in global mobility networks. J. Netw. Comput. Appl. **62**, 1–8 (2016)
6. Ibrahim, M.H., Kumari, S., Das, A.K., Wazid, M., Odelu, V.: Secure anonymous mutual authentication for star two-tier wireless body area networks. Comput. Methods Programs Biomed. **135**, 37–50 (2016)
7. Memon, I., Hussain, I., Akhtar, R., Chen, G.: Enhanced privacy and authentication: an efficient and secure anonymous communication for location based service using asymmetric cryptography scheme. Wireless Pers. Commun. **84**, 1487–1508 (2015)
8. Panda, S., Mondal, S., Kumar, N.: Slap: A secure and lightweight authentication protocol for machine-to-machine communication in industry 4.0. Comput. Electr. Eng. **98**, 107669 (2022)
9. Reddy, A.G., Das, A.K., Yoon, E.J., Yoo, K.Y.: A secure anonymous authentication protocol for mobile services on elliptic curve cryptography. IEEE access **4**, 4394–4407 (2016)
10. Roselin, A.G., Nanda, P., Nepal, S.: Lightweight authentication protocol (laup) for 6lowpan wireless sensor networks. In: 2017 IEEE Trustcom/BigDataSE/ICESS, pp. 371–378. IEEE (2017)
11. Ryu, J., et al.: Secure ECC-based three-factor mutual authentication protocol for telecare medical information system. IEEE Access **10**, 11511–11526 (2022)
12. da Silveira, F., Lermen, F.H., Amaral, F.G.: An overview of agriculture 4.0 development: systematic review of descriptions, technologies, barriers, advantages, and disadvantages. Comput. Electron. Agricult. **189**, 106405 (2021)
13. Sinha, B.B., Dhanalakshmi, R.: Recent advancements and challenges of internet of things in smart agriculture: a survey. Futur. Gener. Comput. Syst. **126**, 169–184 (2022)
14. Sureshkumar, V., Mugunthan, S., Amin, R.: An enhanced mutually authenticated security protocol with key establishment for cloud enabled smart vehicle to grid network. Peer-to-Peer Network. Appl. **15**(5), 2347–2363 (2022)
15. Sureshkumar, V., Mugunthan, S., et al.: Iot based authentication and key establishment protocol for modern agriculture. NVEO-NATURAL VOLATILES & ESSENTIAL OILS Journal— NVEO, pp. 3446–3457 (2021)
16. Triantafyllou, A., Sarigiannidis, P., Bibi, S.: Precision agriculture: a remote sensing monitoring system architecture. Information **10**(11), 348 (2019)

17. Wolfert, S., Ge, L., Verdouw, C., Bogaardt, M.J.: Big data in smart farming-a review. Agric. Syst. **153**, 69–80 (2017)
18. Xu, Z., Xu, C., Chen, H., Yang, F.: A lightweight anonymous mutual authentication and key agreement scheme for wban. Concurr. Comput.: Practi. Exper. **31**(14), e5295 (2019)

Mitigating Malware Threats in Wireless Sensor Networks: A Fractional Approach with Infected Mutant and Traced Nodes

Abilasha Balakumar[1], Sumathi Muthukumar[2], and Veeramani Chinnadurai[3](✉)

[1] Department of Applied Mathematics and Computational Sciences, PSG College of Technology, Coimbatore, India
[2] Department of Mathematics, PSG College of Technology, Coimbatore 641004, India
msm.maths@psgtech.ac.in
[3] Department of Applied Science, PSG College of Technology, Coimbatore 641004, India
veerasworld@yahoo.com

Abstract. Wireless sensor networks (WSNs) play a crucial role in data collection, but they are vulnerable to malware threats. Our research addresses this challenge through an innovative approach. We introduce a specialized model, Susceptible (S)- Infected (I_1)- Infected-Mutant (I_2)- Traced (T)- Recovered (R), designed to comprehensively analyze malware in WSNs and enhance their security. We introduce an Infected-Mutant state and Traced nodes to quickly find and isolate infected parts. We use Caputo fractional differential equations to study how malware spreads and find ways to control it. We find the reproduction number, and its stability is discussed. The comparative study is discussed. Numerical simulations are used to validate the memory effect in the proposed model.

Keywords: WSNs · Epidemic spread · Fractional Model · Stability · Reproduction number

1 Introduction

In recent years, the deployment of Wireless Sensor Networks (WSNs) has witnessed exponential growth due to their versatility and applicability across various domains, including environmental monitoring, healthcare, and industrial automation. However, this rapid expansion has also made WSNs vulnerable to various security threats, with malware propagation emerging as a significant concern. Malware, short for malicious software, can disrupt network operations, compromise data integrity, and even lead to the failure of sensor nodes. To combat this menace effectively, researchers have developed Malware Spread Epidemic Models specifically tailored to the unique characteristics of WSNs. These models, inspired by epidemiology, draw parallels between the spread of malware in a network and the spread of diseases among individuals [1]. By applying epidemiological principles to WSNs, researchers have made significant strides in understanding and mitigating the impact of malware outbreaks [2].

Using epidemic theory, Tang and Mark [3] investigated the possible risk of virus propagation in wireless sensor networks (WSNs). To describe the dynamics of the viral transmission process from an individual node to the complete system, they suggested a new model termed SIR model with maintenance (SIR-M). Singh A et al. [4] explored the proposed model making use of the stability concept of mathematical equations while studying the impact of the worm with different communication radius and distributed density of the nodes. For the purpose of analyzing the activity of malware propagating in WSN, Awasthi et al. [5] suggested an approach with two exposed compartments. They discussed the impact of bandwidth and the coverage on the spread of malware in the network. Muthukrishnan et al. [6] developed an optimal control problem for the malware spread with tracing measures. In order to establish a non-linear behaviour of malicious software spread and examine the communicative radius of the nodes, Zhou Y et al. [7] proposed an SUIQR epidemic model.

Routing protocols, Data Aggregation, Event History and Energy Management Techniques in Wireless Sensor networks exhibit memory-like behavior. So, the epidemic models based on fractional differential equations are now a fascinating research field since fractional models exhibit non-local behaviour and memory effect.

The malware spread epidemic model on Wireless Sensor Networks employs fractional order differential equations to study the propagation dynamics of malware within sensor networks [8]. In order to lengthen network lifetime, suppress hostile activity, and enhance WSN security, Srivastava et al. [9,10] designed the vaccination model (SEIVR) and looked into the consistency of the network structure under various scenarios. To characterize the behaviour of malware propagation in a wireless sensor network, Zhou et al. [11] created an SEIR fractional model. Based on this model, the most effective control approach is also suggested. Dong et al. [12] developed an epidemic model based on fractional calculus and used fuzzy transmission to analyze the behaviour of wireless sensor network.

Through the thorough investigation into the memory effect within the fractional model, the novelty and contributions of proposed model are:

1. Computer viruses can mutate in similar ways to biological viruses. They can change their code or structure to evade detection from anti-virus software, or to spread more efficiently. In fact, some computer viruses are specifically designed to mutate, making them difficult to remove or contain [13]. So, the infected-mutant state is introduced in the model to explore the dynamics of such mutant virus.
2. Traced compartment helps identify compromised or malfunctioning nodes, allowing for timely isolation and mitigation of potential threats, ensuring the network's reliability.
3. This approach utilizes fractional differential equations to carefully scrutinize the complexities of susceptible-infected-infected mutant-traced-recovered cases, offering advanced techniques for identifying, controlling, and minimizing the impact of malware hazards.

4. The proposed model is compared to the existing model. It shows that our findings have the potential to greatly enhance the security and reliability of wireless sensor networks.

The paper is presented in a structured manner, encompassing various sections. Section 1 serves as an introduction to the topic and outlines previous research on the epidemic model in Wireless Sensor Networks. Section 2 emphasizes the model formulation, while Sect. 3 provides a qualitative analysis of the proposed model. Section 4 is dedicated to the results and discussion of the model. Lastly, the paper concludes with a summary of the findings and future work.

2 Model Formulation

A defence system is crucial to protect WSNs from malware attacks. One proposed solution is a fractional epidemic model known as SI_1I_2TR (Susceptible-Infected-Infected Mutant-Traced-Recovered) to analyze the dynamics of malware spread within the network of area $L \times L$ and communication radius r for each node. This model considers two types of infectious states for sensor nodes: Infected and Infected-Mutant with its density σ_1 and σ_2 in the entire network respectively. Malware is transmitted through nearby active mode sensor nodes and can compromise significant data within the WSN. The total number of nodes is denoted by $N = S + I_1 + I_2 + T + R$.

The dynamics of the equation in the proposed based on states are given by the following non-linear differential equations,

$$\frac{dS}{dt} = M - \beta_1 S I_1 - \beta_2 S I_2 + \mu_1 T + \mu_2 R - dS$$
$$\frac{dI_1}{dt} = \beta_1 S I_1 - (\epsilon + \tau_1 + \tau_2 - d) I_1$$
$$\frac{dI_2}{dt} = \beta_2 S I_2 + \epsilon I_1 - (\gamma_1 + \gamma_2 - d) I_2 \quad (1)$$
$$\frac{dT}{dt} = \tau_1 I_1 + \gamma_1 I_2 - (\theta + \mu_1 + d) T$$
$$\frac{dR}{dt} = \tau_2 I_1 + \gamma_2 I_2 + \theta T - (\mu_2 + d) R$$

where $\beta_1 = \beta(\frac{\sigma_1 \pi r^2}{L^2})$ and $\beta_2 = \beta(\frac{\sigma_2 \pi r^2}{L^2})$.

This paper discusses various factors that affect the spread of a virus in a network. M refers to the birth rate of the nodes (the nodes introduced in the network). β_1 represents the rate at which susceptible nodes become infected, and β_2 represents the rate at which sensor nodes become infected with mutated malware. The death rate of sensors due to energy loss is denoted by d. Additionally, the rates of infected nodes going into a traced state and recovering from it are represented by τ_1 and τ_2, respectively. Similarly, γ_1 and γ_2 denote the rates of mutant nodes going into a traced state and recovering from it. Finally,

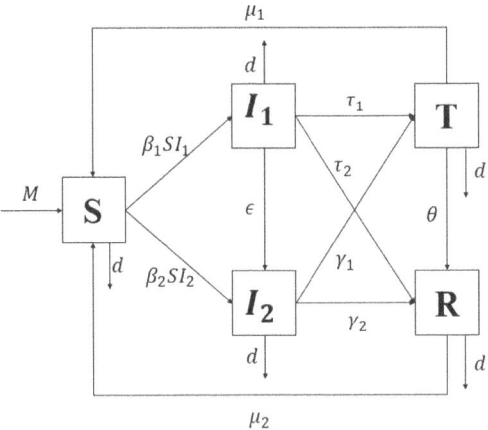

Fig. 1. State Transition Diagram.

ϵ signifies the rate at which the virus mutates. The paper proposes creating a malware remover once infected and mutant nodes have been converted to recovered nodes. The flow between the states with the above mentioned parameters are given in Fig. 1.

The fractional model approach aims to capture the intricate and memory-dependent behavior of malware diffusion, offering insights into the long-term effects and enhancing our understanding of network security dynamics. Hence, the above system is modelled using Caputo fractional differential equations given as follows;

$$\begin{aligned}
{}_0^C D_t^\alpha S(t) &= M - \beta_1 S I_1 - \beta_2 S I_2 + \mu_1 T + \mu_2 R - dS \\
{}_0^C D_t^\alpha I_1(t) &= \beta_1 S I_1 - (\epsilon + \tau_1 + \tau_2 - d) I_1 \\
{}_0^C D_t^\alpha I_2(t) &= \beta_2 S I_2 + \epsilon I_1 - (\gamma_1 + \gamma_2 - d) I_2 \\
{}_0^C D_t^\alpha T(t) &= \tau_1 I_1 + \gamma_1 I_2 - (\theta + \mu_1 + d) T \\
{}_0^C D_t^\alpha R(t) &= \tau_2 I_1 + \gamma_2 I_2 + \theta T - (\mu_2 + d) R
\end{aligned} \qquad (2)$$

Adding all the equations of the 2, we obtain

$${}_0^C D_t^\alpha N(t) = M - dN(t)$$

Hence the possible region is given by,

$$\Theta = \left\{ (S, I_1, I_2, T, R) \in \mathbf{R}^5 \,\middle|\, S(t) + I_1(t) + I_2(t) + T(t) + R(t) \leq \frac{M}{d} \right\}$$

3 Qualitative Analysis

This section covers the qualitative properties of the proposed system (2).

3.1 Basic Reproduction Number

The virus-free equilibrium of the given model is given by, $E_0 = \left(\dfrac{M}{d}, 0, 0, 0, 0\right)$.

The next-generation(NG) matrix approach assesses the basic reproduction number for the particular model. The equations listed below are employed to calculate R_0.

$$ {}_0^C D_t^\alpha I_1(t) = \beta_1 S I_1 - (\epsilon + \tau_1 + \tau_2 + d) I_1 $$

$$ {}_0^C D_t^\alpha I_2(t) = \beta_2 S I_2 + \epsilon I_1 - (\gamma_1 + \gamma_2 + d) I_2 $$

From the above equations, we get

$$ \mathcal{F} = \begin{bmatrix} \beta_1 S I_1 \\ \beta_2 S I_2 + \epsilon I_1 \end{bmatrix} \quad \text{and} \quad \mathcal{V} = \begin{bmatrix} (\epsilon + \tau_1 + \tau_2 + d) I_1 \\ (\gamma_1 + \gamma_2 + d) I_2 \end{bmatrix} $$

By the NGM method, we have

$$ F = J_\mathcal{F} = \begin{bmatrix} \beta_1 S & 0 \\ \epsilon & \beta_2 S \end{bmatrix} $$

$$ V = J_\mathcal{V} = \begin{bmatrix} (\epsilon + \tau_1 + \tau_2 + d) & 0 \\ 0 & (\gamma_1 + \gamma_2 + d) \end{bmatrix} $$

$$ FV^{-1} = \begin{bmatrix} \dfrac{\beta_1 S}{\epsilon + \tau_1 + \tau_2 + d} & 0 \\ \dfrac{\epsilon}{\epsilon + \tau_1 + \tau_2 + d} & \dfrac{\beta_2 S}{\gamma_1 + \gamma_2 + d} \end{bmatrix} $$

At disease-free equilibrium, the largest eigenvalue of the above matrix is the basic reproduction number which is given by

$$ R_0 = \max\left\{ \dfrac{\beta_1 M}{(\epsilon + \tau_1 + \tau_2 + d)d}, \dfrac{\beta_2 M}{(\gamma_1 + \gamma_2 + d)d} \right\} \tag{3} $$

3.2 Stability of the Model

Theorem 1. *(Local stability) Whenever $R_0 \leq 1$, the virus-free equilibrium E_0 is locally asymptotically stable for the system (2).*

Proof. Let us consider the Jacobian matrix at DFE.

$$ J(E_0) = \begin{bmatrix} -d & -\beta_1 S^0 & -\beta_2 S^0 & \mu_1 & \mu_2 \\ 0 & \beta_1 S^0 - (\epsilon + \tau_1 + \tau_2 + d) & 0 & 0 & 0 \\ 0 & \epsilon & \beta_2 S^0 - (\gamma_1 + \gamma_2 + d) & 0 & 0 \\ 0 & \tau_1 & \gamma_1 & -(\theta_1 + \mu_1 + d) & 0 \\ 0 & \tau_2 & \gamma_2 & \theta & -(\mu_2 + d) \end{bmatrix} $$

From the above matrix $J(E_0)$, the eigenvalues $\beta_1 S^0 - (\epsilon + \tau_1 + \tau_2)$, $\beta_2 S^0 - (\gamma_1 + \gamma_2 + d)$, $-(\theta_1 + \mu_1)$, $-(\mu_2 + d)$, $-d$ are obvious with negative real parts.

Based on the Routh-Hurwitz criteria for fractional order differential equations, the system (2) will be locally asymptotically stable at the virus-free equilibrium iff $R_0 \leq 1$. If R_0 exceeds 1, the system becomes unstable. This conclusion validates the theorem.

Theorem 2. *(Global stability) Whenever $R_0 \leq 1$, the disease-free equilibrium E^0 is globally asymptotically stable; however, it becomes unstable when $R_0 > 1$.*

Proof. The Lyapunov function is given as follows,

$$k = c_1 I_1(t) + c_2 I_2(t)$$
$$_0^C D_t^\alpha k = c_1[\beta_1 S I_1 - (\epsilon + \tau_1 + \tau_2) I_1] + c_2[\beta_2 S I_2 + \epsilon I_1 - (\gamma_1 + \gamma_2) I_2]$$
$$\leq (R_1 - 1) I_1 + (R_2 - 1) I_2$$

where $c_1 = \frac{1}{\epsilon + \tau_1 + \tau_2}$ and $c_2 = \frac{1}{\gamma_1 + \gamma_2}$.

It is clear that $_0^C D_t^\alpha k \leq 0$ when $R_0 \leq 1$ and $_0^C D_t^\alpha = 0$ iff $I_1 = 0$ and $I_2 = 0$, the virus-free equilibrium of system (2) is globally asymptotically stable (LaSalle's Invariance principle) (Fig. 2).

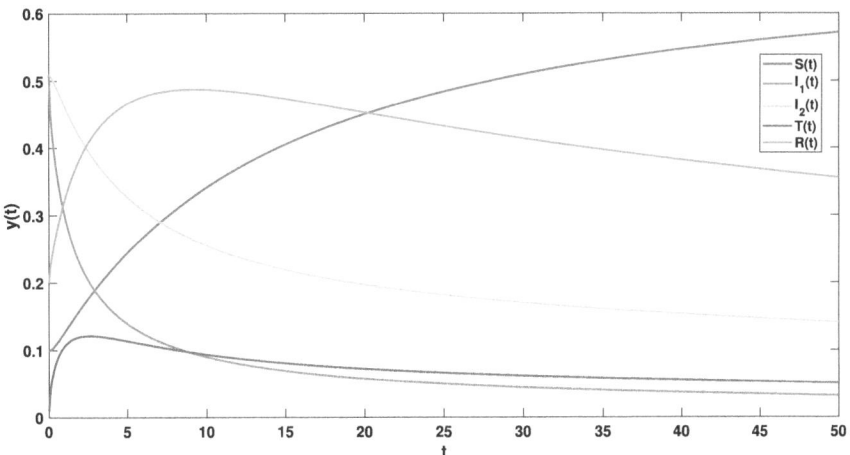

Fig. 2. Plot of all states when $R_0 < 1$

4 Results and Discussions

While mathematical equations can describe the dynamics of disease transmission, many of the fractional epidemic models are complex and may not have analytical solutions. In such cases, numerical simulation becomes a powerful tool

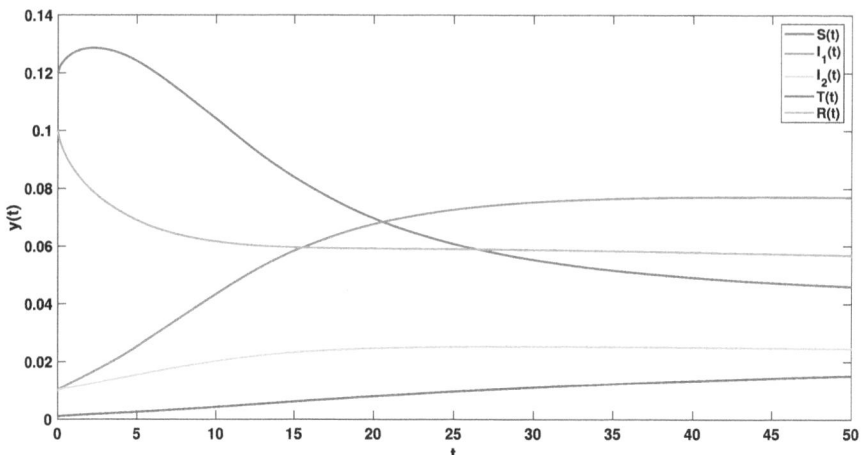

Fig. 3. Plot of all states when $R_0 > 1$

Table 1. Model parameters and its values when $R_0 < 1$ and $R_0 > 1$

Parameter	Value ($R_0 < 1$)	Value ($R_0 > 1$)
M	0.001	0.0015
d	0.01	0.01
β	0.95	0.86
ϵ	0.041	0.41
γ_1	0.025	0.25
γ_2	0.186	0.186
σ_1	0.9	0.5
σ_2	0.75	0.7
τ_1	0.01	0.08541
τ_2	0.04	0.06794
θ	0.015	0.5
μ_1	0.015	0.25
μ_2	0.15	0.15

to approximate and visualize how infectious diseases propagate within a population. We used the FDE12 Matlab function, based on Robert Garappa's Adams-Bashforth-Moulton algorithm, implementing a predictor-corrector method [14]. We begin our results by taking in two cases as (i) When $R_0 < 1$ and (ii) When $R_0 > 1$.

1. Case (i) When $R_0 < 1$
   The initial values of the model: $S(0) = 0.1, I_1(0) = 0.51, I_2(0) = 0.51, T(0) = 0.01, R(0) = 0.2$ and from Table 1, the parameter values are utilized. Using the

above parameter values with $L = 10$ and $r = 10$, we obtained $R_0 = 0.1590 < 1$. The numerical simulation results, employing the versatile framework of fractional calculus and utilizing the generalized Mittag-Leffler function, are depicted in Figure (2). The use of fractional order values allows for an exploration of the network's behavior, similar to the crossover behavior exhibited by the Mittag-Leffler function when extended across different operators. This statistical representation offers practical insights into the WSN's dynamics. As we observe in Fig. 4(a), when the fractional order derivative (α) increases, it influences the population of susceptible nodes and the overall network dynamics. Specifically, as α grows, we witness an increase in the population of susceptible nodes. This alteration is indicative of how fractional order values impact the susceptibility of nodes within the network. Furthermore, the relationship between the fractional order (α) and the infected node population is noteworthy. In Fig. 5(a) and 6(a), we can discern that as the fractional order α increases, the number of infected nodes and infected mutant nodes decreases. This trend underscores the role of fractional calculus in modulating the infectious dynamics of nodes within the WSN. The simulation results in Fig. 7(a) also illuminate the behavior of traced nodes within the WSN. As the fractional order derivative (α) increases, we observe a decline in the population of traced nodes, indicating that the network's stability at equilibrium improves more rapidly with higher α values. Lastly, the proportion of recovered nodes, as depicted in Fig. 8(a), responds to changes in the fractional order derivative. When the non-integer order value (α) increases, the proportion of recovered nodes within the network decreases. This observation highlights the impact of fractional order modeling on the responsiveness and vigilance of nodes.

In summary, the numerical simulations presented in Figs. 4(a)–8(a) demonstrate how fractional order values influence different aspects of a Wireless Sensor Network. These results shed light on the network's susceptibility, exposure dynamics, stability, and alertness, offering valuable insights into the network's behavior under varying conditions of α.

2. Case (ii) When $R_0 > 1$
   The initial values are taken as follows: $S(0) = 0.12, I_1(0) = 0.01, I_2(0) = 0.01, T(0) = 0.001, R(0) = 0.1$. The parameter values from Table 1 and with $L = 10$ and $r = 5$, we obtained $R_0 = 2.6595 > 1$. The plot of all states

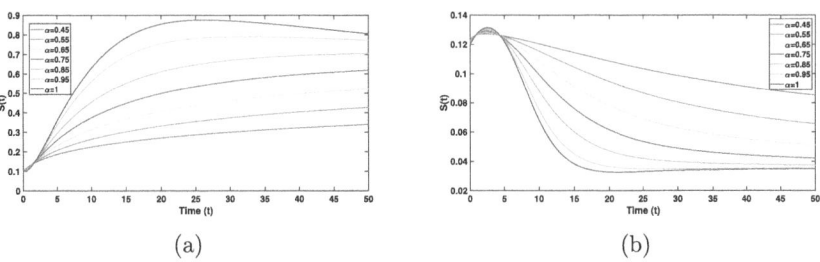

Fig. 4. Simulation of Susceptible state ($S(t)$) for different fractional order values α (a) When $R_0 < 1$ and (b) When $R_0 > 1$

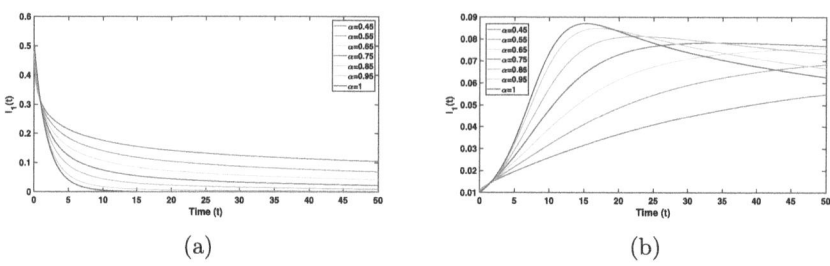

Fig. 5. Simulation of Infected state (I_1) for different fractional order values α (a) When $R_0 < 1$ and (b) When $R_0 > 1$

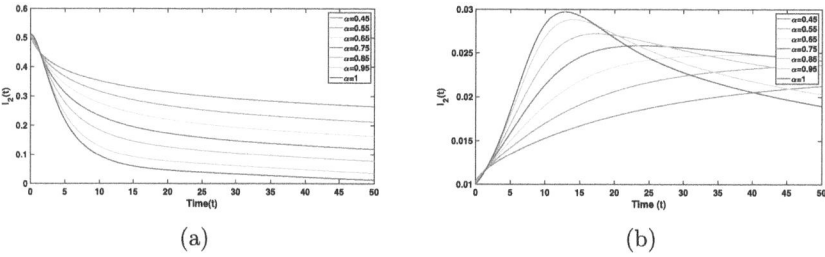

Fig. 6. Simulation of Infected state ($I_2(t)$) for different fractional order values α (a) When $R_0 < 1$ and (b) When $R_0 > 1$

when $R_0 > 1$ is shown in Fig. 3. Figure 4(b) illustrates how the number of vulnerable nodes and the dynamics of the entire network are impacted as the fractional order derivative (α) climbs. In particular, there are less healthy nodes as α increases. The percentage of affected nodes and affected mutant nodes grows as the fractional order (α) increases, as seen in Figs. 5(b) and 6(b). The simulation findings shown in Fig. 7(b) further shed light on the behaviour of traced nodes inside the WSN. We notice an increase in the traced nodes as the fractional order derivative (α) rises. The proportion of recovered nodes also responds to variations in the fractional order derivative, as seen in Fig. 8(b). The percentage of recovered nodes within the network reduces as the non-integer order value (α) rises.

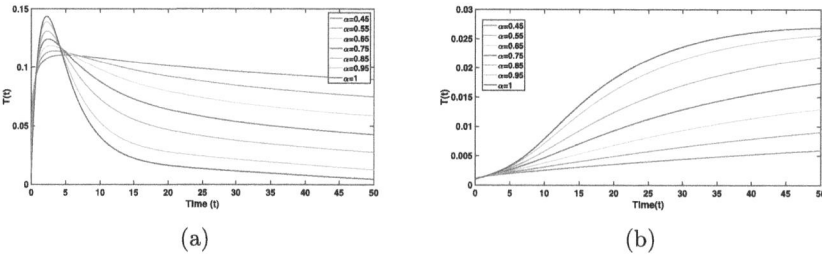

Fig. 7. Simulation of Traced state ($T(t)$) for different fractional order values α (a) When $R_0 < 1$ and (b) When $R_0 > 1$

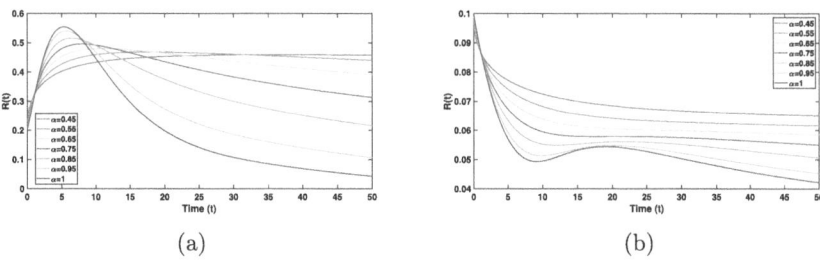

Fig. 8. Simulation of Recovered state ($R(t)$) for different fractional order values α (a) When $R_0 < 1$ and (b) When $R_0 > 1$

When $\alpha = 1$ in both the above cases, the fractional derivative operators (such as the Caputo derivative) reduce to their integer order counterparts (ordinary derivatives). That is, model 2 reduces to 2. Hence, when $\alpha = 1$ in fractional differential equations, we are essentially working with standard, ordinary differential equations. The fractional order dynamics and memory effects, which are characteristic of fractional calculus, disappear, and the equations become more conventional in nature. The proposed model (when $\alpha = 1$) is compared to the existing model [13]. In Fig. 9, the infected state (I_1) of both models is presented. It is evident that the number of infectious nodes decreases compared to the existing model. Figure 10 illustrates the infected-mutant state of both the proposed and existing models, showing a reduction in infected-mutant nodes in the proposed model when compared to the existing one. As tracing serves as a valuable tool for early detection and control, the tracing of infected and infected-mutant nodes significantly reduces interactions (communication) between sensor nodes, and it is clear that identifying cases promptly helps prevent further transmission of the malware, reducing the overall impact of the epidemic.

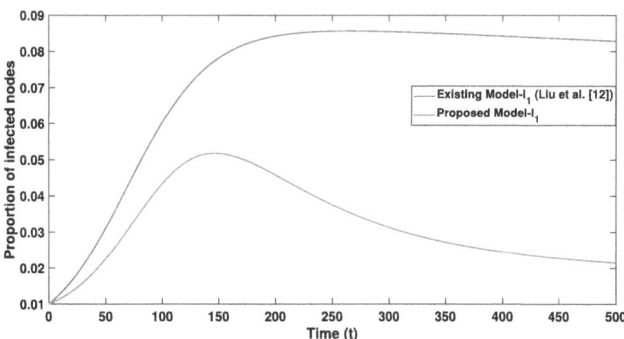

Fig. 9. Plot comparing the existing model [13] and proposed model of I_1

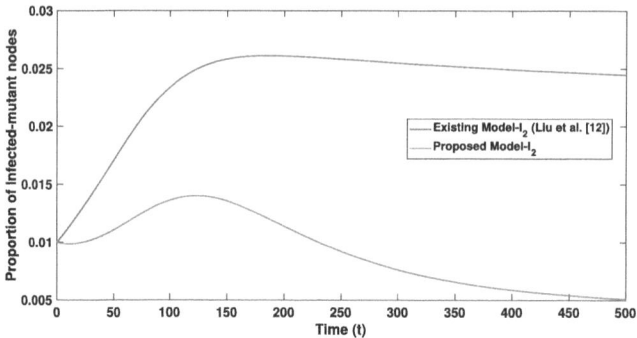

Fig. 10. Plot comparing the existing model [13] and proposed model of I_2

5 Conclusion

Since the selection of the derivative order introduces an extra level of flexibility, fractional-order derivatives tend to be more suitable for modeling compared to their integer-order counterparts. Because they offer a closer alignment with memory, resulting in fewer inaccuracies. Hence, a fractional order SI_1I_2TR epidemic model was proposed as an effective strategy to curtail malware propagation and prolong the longevity of Wireless Sensor Networks (WSN). We have successfully identified the equilibrium state free from malware and determined the reproduction number. We further conducted a comprehensive analysis of both local and global stability for the model. The comparison of the existing model and proposed model was studied. It is clear that the proposed model is more efficient than the existing one. To validate our theoretical findings, we performed numerical simulations, delving into the behavior of all five states under various fractional order values.

Our future research endeavors will center on practical applications, including an examination of the asymptotic behavior of the endemic equilibrium. We will also explore different scenarios involving the basic reproduction numbers of infected (R_1) and mutant-infected (R_2), and the impact of infected-mutant and traced nodes on Wireless sensor networks will be discussed further. To a greater extent, we will investigate the implementation of an optimal control strategy in our forthcoming work.

Funding Information. The authors declare that they have no known competing financial interests or personal relationships that could have appeared to influence the work reported in this paper.

Conflict of Interest. The authors declare that they have no conflicts of interest.

References

1. Muthukumar, S., Myilsamy, K., Balakumar, A., Chinnadurai, V.: Nonlinear analysis and dynamics of COVID-19 mathematical model with optimal control strategies. Optimal Control Appl. Methods (2023)
2. Srinivas, M.N., Madhusudanan, V., Murty, A., Tapas Bapu, B.R.: A review article on wireless sensor networks in view of e-epidemic models. Wireless Pers. Commun. **120**, 95–111 (2021)
3. Tang, S., Mark, B.L.: Analysis of virus spread in wireless sensor networks: an epidemic model. In: 2009 7th International Workshop on Design of Reliable Communication Networks, pp. 86–91. IEEE (2009)
4. Singh, A., Awasthi, A.K., Singh, K., Srivastava, P.K.: Modeling and analysis of worm propagation in wireless sensor networks. Wireless Pers. Commun. **98**, 2535–2551 (2018)
5. Awasthi, S., et al.: An epidemic model for the investigation of multi-malware attack in wireless sensor network. IET Commun. (2023)
6. Muthukrishnan, S., Muthukumar, S., Chinnadurai, V.: Optimal control of malware spreading model with tracing and patching in wireless sensor networks. Wireless Pers. Commun. **117**, 2061–2083 (2021)
7. Zhou, Y., Wang, Y., Zhou, K., Shen, S.F., Ma, W.X.: Dynamical behaviors of an epidemic model for malware propagation in wireless sensor networks. Front. Phys. **11**, 361 (2023)
8. Nisar, K.S., Farman, M., Abdel-Aty, M., Cao, J.: A review on epidemic models in sight of fractional calculus. Alex. Eng. J. **75**, 81–113 (2023)
9. Srivastava, V., et al.: Generalized defensive modeling of malware propagation in WSNs using Atangana-Baleanu-Caputo (ABC) fractional derivative. IEEE Access (2023)
10. Srivastava, V., Tripathi, D., Anwar bég, O.: Numerical study of oxygen diffusion from capillary to tissues during hypoxia with external force effects. J. Mech. Med. Biol. **17**(02), 1750027 (2017)
11. Zhou, Y., Liu, B.T., Zhou, K., Shen, S.F.: Malware propagation model of fractional order, optimal control strategy and simulations. Front. Phys. **11**, 1201053 (2023)
12. Dong, N.P., Long, H.V., Son, N.: The analysis of a fractional network-based epidemic model with saturated treatment function and fuzzy transmission. Iran. J. Fuzzy Syst. **20**(1), 1–18 (2023)
13. Liu, G., Peng, Z., Liang, Z., Li, J., Cheng, L.: Dynamics analysis of a wireless rechargeable sensor network for virus mutation spreading. Entropy **23**(5), 572 (2021)
14. Garrappa, R.: Predictor-corrector PECE method for fractional differential equations, MATLAB Central File Exchange (2022). https://www.mathworks.com/matlabcentral/fileexchange/32918-predictor-corrector-pece-method-for-fractional-differential-equations. Accessed 21 Sept 2022

Exploring Post-quantum Hash-Based Signature Schemes for IoT Motes

P. Thanalakshmi and N. K. J. Ashwinkumaar(✉)

Department of Applied Mathematics and Computational Sciences,
PSG College of Technology, Coimbatore 641004, India
ptl.amcs@psgtech.ac.in, ashwinkumaar789@gmail.com

Abstract. In an increasingly interconnected world, ensuring secure information transmission is paramount. Threats such as data manipulation and impersonation impact applications like e-voting and digital currency. Digital signatures offer crucial non-repudiation and verifiability, especially in IoT contexts. Traditional signature schemes rely on discrete logarithm problems and integer factorization for security, making them widely used. Yet, quantum computers threaten their security, urging a proactive stance to protect IoT communication in the quantum age. Therefore, lightweight IoT applications can benefit from adopting post-quantum signatures. This paper delves into hash-based signature schemes as lightweight alternatives for securing IoT devices, utilizing the EDAS technique for a comprehensive comparative analysis. The goal is to provide efficient cryptographic solutions tailored to lightweight IoT needs.

1 Introduction

The rapid advancement of technology has brought about a transformative shift in our online interactions with information and services. This evolution necessitates robust techniques for authentication and data integrity to counteract malicious activities such as data tampering and identity spoofing, particularly in the background of Internet of Things (IoT) applications. The IoT paradigm, characterized by an extensive network of interconnected smart devices, has emerged as one of the most influential trends of the twenty-first century. A prominent example of IoT's potential is demonstrated in smart cities, where a multitude of compact smart sensors, known as IoT motes, regulate various urban systems, including streetlights, energy distribution, water supply, and waste management. These IoT motes collect and transmit pertinent data to gateways or cloud platforms, where data analytics are conducted, enabling informed actions to be taken through dedicated management systems. This intricate network constitutes the backbone of IoT technology, highlighting the significance of ensuring the integrity and authenticity of the data exchanged.

To address this, digital signatures serve as a fundamental tool to verify the legitimacy of the transferred data. While classical cryptographic signatures like RSA, DSA, and ECDSA have stood the test of time in terms of security, their reliance on the computational complexity of problems such as integer factorization and discrete logarithms makes them vulnerable to quantum computers. The emergence of quantum computers threatens to undermine the security provided by these foundational cryptographic principles. As a result, a proactive strategy is essential to ensure the security of IoT communications in the quantum era. Given the long-term nature of security requirements in IoT motes applications, a shift away from RSA and ECC is imperative, demanding exploration of alternative quantum-resistant techniques.

2 Related Work

Hash-Based Signature (HBS) schemes stand out as robust candidates for quantum-resistant signatures, grounded in secure hash functions. Notably, Grover's quantum attack [1] poses limited threat to the security of hash functions, making HBS a streamlined and dependable security foundation compared to complex number-theoretical schemes. Additionally, lightweight hash function versions empower IoT applications to tailor parameters for resource-constrained devices, thus elevating network performance. The one-way property of hash functions inherent in this scheme ensures robust security encompassing both past and future data secrecy.

The history of hash-based signatures has been extensive. Back in 1979, Merkle presented an innovative signature scheme based on hash functions alone. This method, referred to as the Merkle signature scheme, combines a one-time signature (OTS) used for signing a single message per key pair, along with a path authentication structure that provides a verification pathway. This verification pathway plays a critical role in verifying the connection between the public key and the signature of the particular message.

Over the past four decades, a multitude of security-analyzed schemes have emerged in the field of hash-based signatures. Notable among these are the Lamport OTS [2], the Merkle OTS [3], the Winternitz OTS [4], and the WOTS$^+$ [5]. The Merkle OTS builds upon the Lamport OTS, while the Winternitz OTS generalizes the concept of Merkle OTS. Both the Merkle OTS and Winternitz OTS involve iterative application of an underlying function, with the number of iterations connected to the message intended for signing. Certain few-time signature schemes rely on hash functions, but their growing complexity may not be suitable for lightweight devices.

In the context of IoT applications, research highlights key facets of HBS schemes. Authors in [6] and [7] explore structure and challenges of HBS in IoT. [8] discusses obstacles to HBS adoption, emphasizing standardization's role. Technical aspects are covered in [9] (state management solutions), [10] (optimizing stateless HBS), and [11–13] (implementing and evaluating schemes on IoT platforms). Additionally, broader perspectives encompass post-quantum signature schemes in IoT. [14] addresses challenges in Post-Quantum Cryptography (PQC) for IoT. In [15] author proposes certificateless signature schemes within the context of Industrial Internet of Things.

The paper's structure is as follows: Sect. 3 provides a concise introduction to hash functions and outlines few one-time signature schemes. In Sect. 4, a performance comparison is presented. It also details the schemes' comparison and ranking using EDAS. Concluding remarks are found in Sect. 5.

3 Preliminaries

3.1 Cryptographic Hash Function

The hash function proves to be a potent tool in various applications, serving to decrease the data processing load, guarantee data integrity, and establish robust signature schemes for security. A cryptographic hash function is a mathematical function defined by $h : \{0,1\}^* \to \{0,1\}^n$ with the properties preimage resistance, second-preimage resistance and collision resistance.

3.2 Hash-Based Signatures

Hash-based signature schemes, known for their highly parameterized nature and adaptability, play a crucial role in addressing the specific needs of performance-constrained environments like the Internet of Things (IoT). Their flexibility, particularly in adjusting parameters for balancing between the speed of signing and the size of the key, is vital in achieving low-power and lightweight signatures, essential for IoT applications with limited resources. However, compromises in parameters are constrained in IoT due to devices' extended deployment periods and the imperative to resist potential quantum attacks. Balancing post-quantum security with energy constraints underscores the importance of energy-constrained hash functions in efficient IoT signature implementations. In this context, lightweight hash-based one-time signatures (OTS), such as Lamport OTS, Merkle OTS, Winternitz OTS, and WOTS$^+$, align well with the demands of IoT motes, providing a foundation for enhancing security in future IoT applications.

Lamport OTS. The Lamport One-Time Signature (OTS) scheme involves the utilization of 2k private keys and an equal number of public keys to sign a message of length k bits. Each individual message bit corresponds to a pair of private keys. Specifically, a '0' bit corresponds to the first private key, while a '1' bit corresponds to the second private key. The generation of the public key associated with a given private key requires just one hash computation using a one-way hash function. This scheme follows the approach with the highest storage requirement and the lowest computational cost. The structure of the Lamport OTS scheme is defined through the use of Algorithms 1, 2 and 3 as in [16].

Algorithm 1. Lamport Key Generation

Input: n polynomial in security parameter λ,
Hash function $H : \{0,1\}^n \to \{0,1\}^n$, message $m = (m_0, m_1, \cdots, m_k)$
Output: Lamport key pair (sk, pk)
Choose private key sequence
$sk = (sk_{1,0}, sk_{1,1} \cdots, sk_k, sk_{k,0,1}) \leftarrow (0,1)^{n \times 2k}$
Public key pk is given as
$pk = (pk_{1,0}, pk_{1,1} \cdots, pk_{k,0}, pk_{k,1}) = (H(sk_{1,0}), H(sk_{1,1}), \cdots, H(sk_{k,0}), H(sk_{k,1}))$
return (sk, pk)

Algorithm 2. Lamport Signing Algorithm

Input: message $m = (m_0, m_1, \cdots, m_k)$, private key sk
Output: Lamport signature σ
$\sigma = (\sigma_0, \sigma_1, \cdots, \sigma_k) = (sk_{1,m_1}, sk_{2,m_2}, \cdots, sk_{k,m_k})$
return σ

Algorithm 3. Lamport Verification Algorithm

Input: m, pk, σ
Output: True if σ is valid, else False
return $(H(\sigma_1), H(\sigma_2), \cdots H(\sigma_k)) \stackrel{?}{=} (pk_{1,m_1}, pk_{2,m_2}, \cdots, pk_{k,m_k})$

Merkle OTS. Merkle tree, introduced by Merkle in 1979, is an original method for tree authentication. It uses hash function to create nodes. This binary tree has 2^h leaves at its bottom layer, with height h. Interior nodes derive values through hashing their nearest child nodes. The process goes merging the interior nodes into a binary tree structure using a consistent hash function, culminating in the $h+1$ layer's Root node.

A HBS, combining OTS and Merkle tree, functions like this: Begin with a Merkle tree where the leaf holds a one-time public key. At the top of this "Merkle tree," a single node represents a concise global public key, for authenticating signatures linked to the tree's leaves.

For message signing, utilize the one-time private key to generate a signature. Afterwards, the verifier requires the data associated with the signature along with an authentication path. Before verification, the Root's authentication, like its digital certificate, is sent to verifier. The verifier validates the Root, checks the one-time signature, and then verifies the one-time public key. Merkle OTS is described by the Algorithms 4, 5 and 6 respectively as in [16].

Algorithm 4. Merkle Key Generation

Input: n polynomial in security parameter λ,
Hash function $H : \{0,1\}^{2n} \rightarrow \{0,1\}^n$, message $m = (m_0, m_1, \cdots, m_k)$,
$s = \lfloor \log k \rfloor + 1$
Output: Merkle key (sk, pk)
Choose private key sequence
$sk = (sk_{1,0}, sk_{1,1}, \cdots, sk_k, sk_{k,0,1}) \leftarrow (0,1)^{n \times 2k}$
Compute public key pk
$pk = (pk_1, \cdots, pk_{k+s}) = (H(sk_1), \cdots, H(sk_{k+s}))$
return (sk, pk)

Algorithm 5. Merkle Signing Algorithm

Input: message $m = (m_0, m_1, \cdots, m_k)$,
$m \| checksum = (m_1, \cdots, m_{k+s})$, private key sk
Output: Merkle signature σ
$m_i = 1, i = 1, \cdots, k+s$
$\sigma = (\sigma_{j_1}, \sigma_2, \cdots, \sigma_{j_p}) = (sk_{j_1}, sk_2, \cdots, sk_{j_p})$, where $m_{j_p} = 1, 0 < j_p \leq k+s$
return σ

Algorithm 6. Merkle Verification Algorithm

Input: m, pk, σ
Output: True if σ is valid, else False
return $(H(\sigma_{j_1}), \cdots H(\sigma_{j_p})) \stackrel{?}{=} (pk_{j_1}, \cdots, pk_{j_p})$

Winternitz OTS. The Winternitz scheme and its various adaptations include a parameter referred to as the Winternitz parameter. This parameter dictates the number of bits that are signed concurrently, thereby improving the flexibility of these schemes in comparison to the initial Lamport-Diffie scheme. Opting for larger values of this parameter leads to shorter signatures and keys, but it does come at the cost of reduced signing and verification time. The overall framework of the Winternitz OTS scheme is detailed through a combination of Algorithms 7, 8 and 9 as in [4].

Algorithm 7. Winternitz Key Generation

Input: security parameter n
Hash function $F(n) = f_k : \{0,1\}^n \to \{0,1\}^n | k \in \{0,1\}^n$
Output: Winternitz key pair (sk, pk)
Notation: $f_k^i(x)$ - function is applied iteratively i times to the input x, utilizing k for the initial round and the output is used as key for subsequent iterations. eg. $f_k^2(x) = f_{f_k(x)}(x)$ and $f_k^0(x) = x$
$w \in \mathbb{N}, w > 1$
$x \xleftarrow{\$} \{0,1\}^{(n,l)}$
$sk = (sk_1, \cdots, sk_l) \xleftarrow{\$} \{0,1\}^{(n,l)}$ where l is,
$l_1 = \lceil \frac{m}{log(w)} \rceil, l_2 = \lfloor \frac{log(l_1(w-1))}{log(w)} \rfloor + 1, l = l_1 + l_2$
$pk = (pk_0, pk_1, \cdots, pk_l) = (x, f_{sk_1}^{w-1}(x), \cdots, f_{sk_l}^{w-1}(x))$
return (sk, pk)

Algorithm 8. Winternitz Signing Algorithm

Input: message $M = (M_1, \cdots, M_{l_1})$ in base-w representation, ie. $M_i \in \{0, \cdots, w-1\}$ for $i = 1, \cdots, l_1$,
Output: Signature σ

$C = \sum_{i=1}^{l_1}(w - 1 - M_i)$
$C = (C_1, \cdots, C_{l_2})$ is represented in base w
$B = (b_1, \cdots, b_l) = M||C$
$\sigma = (\sigma_1, \cdots \sigma_l) = (f_{sk_1}^{b_1}(x), \cdots, f_{sk_l}^{b_l}(x))$
return σ

Algorithm 9. Winternitz Verification Algorithm

Input: M, pk, σ
Output: True if σ is valid, else False
Compute $B = (b_1, \cdots, b_l) = M||C$
return $(f_{\sigma_1}^{w-1-b_1}(pk_0), \cdots, f_{\sigma_1}^{w-1-b_l}(pk_0)) \stackrel{?}{=} (pk_1, \cdots, pk_l)$

Winternitz$^+$ OTS: WOTS$^+$ employs a unique iterative approach that facilitates a robust security proof without the necessity for the hash function family used to possess collision resistance. The algorithms denoted as 10, 11 and 12 collectively define the structure of the Winternitz$^+$ OTS scheme as in [5].

Algorithm 10. Winternitz$^+$ Key Generation

Input: security parameter n
Hash function $F(n) = f_k : \{0,1\}^n \to \{0,1\}^n | k \in \kappa_n$ with key space κ_n
Output: Winternitz$^+$ key pair (sk, pk)
Notation: Chaining function $c_k^i(x, r)$:
For i=0, $c_k^0(x, r) = x$
For i>0, $c_k^i(x, r) = f_k(c_k^{i-1}(x, r) \oplus r_i)$
where,
$x \in \{0,1\}^n$, key $k \in \kappa$,
$r = (r_1, \cdots, r_j) \in \{0,1\}^n$ with $j \geq i$
$w \in \mathbb{N}, w > 1$
Compute l: $l_1 = \lceil \frac{m}{log(w)} \rceil$, $l_2 = \lfloor \frac{log(l_1(w-1))}{log(w)} \rfloor + 1$, $l = l_1 + l_2$
Choose $l + w - 1$ random n-bit strings
First l strings are used in $sk = (sk_1, \cdots, sk_l)$ and
Remaining strings, $w - 1$ are used as $r = (r_1, \cdots r_{w-1})$ for chaining function c
$pk = (pk_0, pk_1, \cdots, pk_l) = ((r, k), c_k^{w-1}(sk_1, r), \cdots c_k^{w-1}(sk_l, r))$
return (sk, pk)

Algorithm 11. Winternitz$^+$ Signing Algorithm

Input: message $M = (M_1, \cdots, M_{l_1})$ in base-w representation,
ie. $M_i \in \{0, \cdots, w-1\}$ for $i = 1, \cdots, l_1$,
Output: Signature σ

$C = \sum_{i=1}^{l_1}(w - 1 - M_i)$
$C = (C_1, \cdots, C_{l_2})$ is represented in base w
$B = (b_1, \cdots, b_l) = M \| C$
$\sigma = (\sigma_1, \cdots \sigma_l) = (c_k^{b_1}(sk_1, r), \cdots c_k^{b_l}(sk_l, r))$
return σ

Algorithm 12. Winternitz$^+$ Verification Algorithm

Input: M, pk, σ
Output: True if σ is valid, else False
Compute $B = (b_1, \cdots, b_l) = M \| C$
return $((r, k), c_k^{w-1-b_1}(\sigma_1, r_{b_1+1, w-1}), \cdots c_k^{w-1-b_l}(\sigma_l, r_{b_l+1, w-1})) \stackrel{?}{=} (pk_0, pk_1 \cdots, pk_l)$

3.3 Evaluation Based on Distance from Average Solution (EDAS)

The EDAS method is a notable technique within the Multi-Criteria Decision Making (MCDM) approach, which provides a structured framework for evaluating alternatives based on various criteria. EDAS extends the traditional Decision Analysis for Selection (DAS) method which enables a more comprehensive evaluation and discrimination between alternatives. It enhances evaluation and discrimination between options by normalizing criteria, finding ideal and anti-ideal alternatives, introducing a nuanced weighting approach based on proximity to the ideal and distance from the anti-ideal, calculating relative measures, and aggregating for an overall score. This is useful for comparing digital signature algorithms using criteria like key sizes, processing times, and security levels.

4 Performance Comparison

Table 1 presents the performance assessment of Lamport OTS, Merkle OTS, Winternitz OTS, and WOTS$^+$ with respect to key size (average signature key and verification key sizes), signature properties (average signature size), and time-related metrics (signature time, average key generation time and verification time) as in [16]. In this evaluation, the security level of these schemes is also considered. The variables utilized encompass k representing the length of the message bit, n signifying the length of bits in the input and output of the hash/one-way function, and the parameters w and l as specifically defined within WOTS and WOTS$^+$. The average timings are measured in terms of number of evaluations of hash functions, excluding the time required for generating initial components like private keys and randomized elements. Furthermore, we disregard the computational overhead linked to XOR operations, as their impact is minor compared to the operational cost of the hash function.

Table 1. The performance evaluation of one time hash-based signature schemes

Sign. Scheme	Sign. key	Verify key	Signature	Sign Time	Verify Time	Security Level
Lamport	$2nk$	$2nk$	nk	0	k	n
Merkle	$(k+\log k+1)n$	$(k+\log k+1)n$	$(k/2+\log k+1)n$	0	$(k/2+\log k+1)n$	n
Winterniz	$\ln n$	$\ln n$	$\ln n$	$\frac{l(w-1)}{2}$	$\frac{l(w-1)}{2}$	$n-w-1-2\log lw$
WOTS$^+$	$\ln n$	$(l+w-1)n$	$\ln n$	$\frac{l(w-1)}{2}$	$\frac{l(w-1)}{2}$	$n-\log(w^2l+w)$

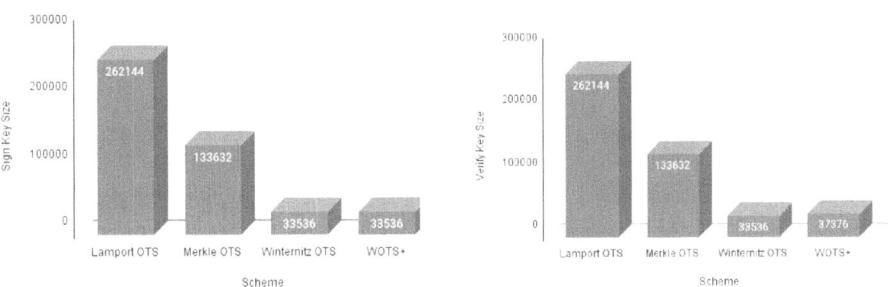

Fig. 1. Signature Scheme vs Avg Sign Key Size.

Fig. 2. Signature Scheme vs Avg Ver Key Size.

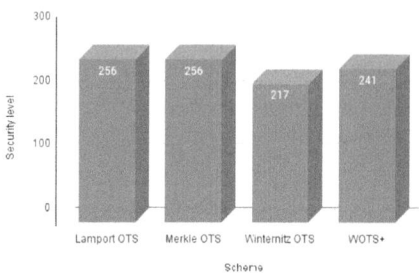

Fig. 3. Signature Scheme vs Security Level.

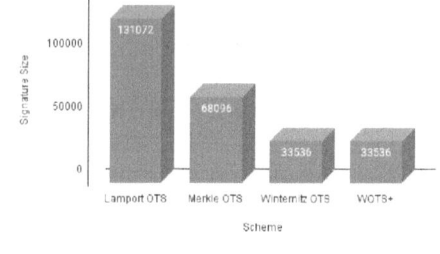

Fig. 4. Signature Scheme vs Avg Sign Size.

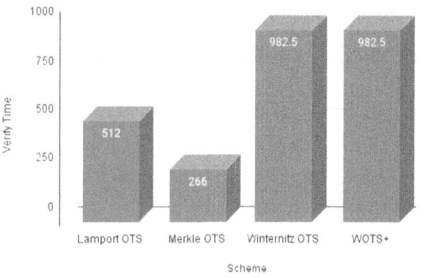

Fig. 5. Signature Scheme vs Avg Ver Time.

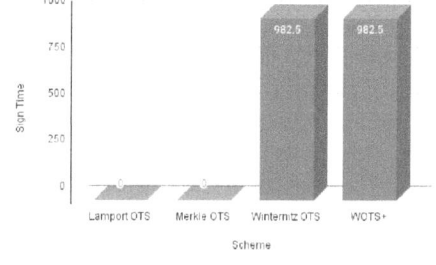

Fig. 6. Signature Scheme vs Avg Sign Time.

Each scheme has its unique advantages based on specific criteria. For example, in Fig. 1, the comparison of schemes based on Average Signature Key size reveals that Winternitz and Winternitz$^+$ have smaller sign key sizes. Figure 2 demonstrates that Winternitz OTS has a smaller verify key size than other schemes. Security levels are similar across all schemes, as indicated in Fig. 3. However, Lamport OTS exhibits larger average signature sizes, shown in Fig. 4. Figures 5 and 6 display the comparison of schemes in terms of average signing and verifying times, revealing that Merkle and Lamport outperform WOTS and its variant in these aspects.

4.1 Ranking Based on the EDAS Method

Using the EDAS technique, we compare signature schemes in this study based on criteria such as key sizes, processing times, and security performance. Weightages are assigned to each criterion: SignKey size (0.15), VerKey size (0.15), Sign size (0.25), Sign time (0.125), Ver time (0.125), and Security Level (0.2). To ensure unbiased comparison, specific values are set $n = 128$, $w = 16$, $k = 512$, ensuring equal security levels across all signature schemes.

Table 2. Comparison of Signature Schemes

Scheme	Sign Key Size	Verify Key Size	Sig Size	Sign Time	Verify Time	Security level
Lamport OTS	262144	262144	131072	0	512	256
Merkle OTS	133632	133632	68096	0	266	256
Winternitz OTS	33536	33536	33536	982.5	982.5	217
WOTS$^+$	33536	37376	33536	982.5	982.5	241

We employ the EDAS method to rank the efficiency of the mentioned signature schemes, considering all criteria. Using the weighted attributes from Table 2, we follow the 7 stages of the EDAS methodology as outlined in [15]. These stages involve determining the average solution, calculating positive and negative distances from the average (PDA and NDA), deriving weighted sum of PDA and NDA values, normalizing weighted sum of PDA and NDA values, and finally obtaining an evaluation score. Upon completion of these stages, the signature schemes will be ranked based on their evaluation scores.

Step 1: Compute average value AV_j of each criterion (Table 3)

$$AV_j = \frac{\sum_{i=1}^{n} X_{ij}}{n}$$

Table 3. Average value of each criterion AV_j

Scheme	Sign Key Size	Verify Key Size	Sig Size	Sign Time	Verify Time	Security level
Weightage	0.15	0.15	0.25	0.125	0.125	0.2
Lamport OTS	262144	262144	131072	0	512	256
Merkle OTS	133632	133632	68096	0	266	256
Winternitz OTS	33536	33536	33536	982.5	982.5	217
WOTS$^+$	33536	37376	33536	982.5	982.5	241
AV_j	115712	116672	66560	491.25	685.75	242.5

Step 2: PDA (Positive distance from average) is calculated as

$PDA_{ij} = \frac{max(0,(X_{ij}-AV_j))}{AV_j}$, when jth criterion is beneficial

$PDA_{ij} = \frac{max(0,(AV_j-X_{ij}))}{AV_j}$, when jth criterion is non-beneficial

where, X_{ij} is value of jth criterion in the performance matrix and AV_{ij} is the average value of jth criterion.

Here, Sign Key size, Ver Key size, Sign size, Sign Time, Ver Time are taken as non-beneficial criteria as the goal is to minimise them. Security Level is taken as beneficial criterion as the goal is to maximise it (Table 4).

Table 4. Positive Distance from Average (PDA)

Scheme	Sign Key Size	Verify Key Size	Sig Size	Sign Time	Verify Time	Security level
Weightage	0.15	0.15	0.25	0.125	0.125	0.2
Lamport OTS	0	0	0	1	0.25337222	0.05567
Merkle OTS	0	0	0	1	0.612103536	0.05567
Winternitz OTS	0.710176991	0.712561711	0.496153846	0	0	0
WOTS$^+$	0.710176991	0.67964893	0.496153846	0	0	0

Step 3: NDA (Negative distance from average) is given by

$NDA_{ij} = \frac{max(0,(AV_j - X_{ij}))}{AV_j}$, when jth criterion is beneficial

$NDA_{ij} = \frac{max(0,(X_{ij} - AV_j))}{AV_j}$, when jth criterion is non-beneficial

where, X_{ij} is value of jth criterion in the performance matrix and AV_{ij} is the average value of jth criterion (Table 5).

Table 5. Negative Distance from Average (NDA)

Scheme	Sign Key Size	Verify Key Size	Sig Size	Sign Time	Verify Time	Security level
Weightage	0.15	0.15	0.25	0.125	0.125	0.2
Lamport OTS	1.265486726	1.246845858	0.969230769	0	0.042239186	0
Merkle OTS	0.154867257	0.145364783	0.023076923	0	0	0
Winternitz OTS	0	0	0	1	1	0.105155
WOTS$^+$	0	0	0	1	1	0.006186

Step 4: Weighted Sum of PDA for each ith scheme is given by

$$SP_i = \sum_{j=1}^{n} w_j PDA_{ij}$$

where w_j is the weights assigned previously (Table 6).

Table 6. Weighted Sum of PDA (SP_i)

Scheme	Sign Key Size	Verify Key Size	Sig Size	Sign Time	Verify Time	Security level	SP_i
Lamport OTS	0	0	0	0.125	0.031672	0.011134	0.167806
Merkle OTS	0	0	0	0.125	0.076513	0.011134	0.212647
Winternitz OTS	0.106527	0.106884	0.124038	0	0	0	0.337449
WOTS$^+$	0.106527	0.101947	0.124038	0	0	0	0.332512

Step 5: Weighted Sum of NDA for each ith scheme is given by

$$SN_i = \sum_{j=1}^{n} w_j NDA_{ij}$$

where w_j is the weights assigned previously (Table 7).

Table 7. Weighted Sum of NDA (SN_i)

Scheme	Sign Key Size	Verify Key Size	Sig Size	Sign Time	Verify Time	Security level	SN_i
Lamport OTS	0.0225	0.0225	0.0625	0.015625	0.015625	0.04	0.17875
Merkle OTS	0.189823	0.187027	0.242308	0	0.00528	0	0.624437
Winternitz OTS	0.02323	0.021805	0.005769	0	0	0	0.050804
WOTS$^+$	0	0	0	0.125	0.125	0.021031	0.271031

Step 6: Calculate normalised values of SP_i and SN_i for each ith scheme (Table 8)

$$NSP_i = \frac{SP_i}{max_i(SP_i)};$$
$$NSN_i = 1 - \frac{SN_i}{max_i(SN_i)}$$

Table 8. Normalised values of SP_i and SN_i (NSP_i, NSN_i)

Scheme	SP_i	SN_i	NSP_i	NSN_i
Lamport OTS	0.167805548	0.17875	0.497276375	0.713742358
Merkle OTS	0.212646963	0.624437478	0.6301598	−2.35949E-10
Winternitz OTS	0.337449267	0.050804037	1	0.918640315
WOTS$^+$	0.33251235	0.271030928	0.985369898	0.565959864

Step 7: Calculate Final Evaluation Score for each ith scheme

$$AS_i = \frac{1}{2}(NSP_i + NSN_i)$$

Table 9. Rank based on AS_i

Scheme	AS_i	Rank
Lamport OTS	0.605509366	3
Merkle OTS	0.3150799	4
Winternitz OTS	0.959320157	1
WOTS$^+$	0.775664881	2

Navigating the complexities of IoT amplifies the challenges in selecting post-quantum signatures. While hash-based signatures, anchored in a secure hash function, offer simplicity within this intricate landscape, the task of choosing an ideal authentication cipher for lightweight security is further complicated by dynamic parameters. In response to these challenges, a proposed solution involves an evaluation framework that employs the EDAS method, assigning weights for a comprehensive assessment. According to the evaluation score using the EDAS method, the top rank is achieved by Winternitz OTS, displaying superior performance compared to others. Winternitz OTS obtains the highest score, as shown in Table 9, surpassing the suggested hash-based signatures. WOTS$^+$ and Lamport rank second and third, respectively, while Merkle OTS secures the fourth position in the ranking.

5 Conclusion

Lightweight signature schemes are pivotal for IoT devices, particularly wearable tech, nodes, and sensors. These schemes ensure data integrity, non-repudiation, and public verifiability in IoT environments. Traditional options like RSA or ECC face vulnerabilities from quantum computing, necessitating the adoption of quantum-resistant techniques for sustained IoT security. However, the complexity of IoT complicates the selection of post-quantum signatures. Hash-based signatures offer simplicity, relying on a single secure hash function. The intricate task of choosing the optimal authentication cipher for lightweight security is further complicated by evolving parameters. To address these challenges, an evaluation framework that assigns weights, employs the EDAS method, and ranks alternatives is employed. Empirical findings strongly favor Winternitz OTS over other hash-based signatures, closely followed by WOTS$^+$ and Lamport in the rankings. Given the results, Winternitz OTS emerges as a recommended choice for lightweight authentication in IoT scenarios.

Acknowledgment. This work is supported by PSG College of Technology, Coimbatore, India; and in part, this work is partially supported by Fund for Improvement of S&T Infrastructure in Universities and Higher Educational Institutions (FIST) through Department of Science & Technology (DST), Government of India under the Project SR/FST/COLLEGE-/2021/1139.

Declaration of Interests. The authors declare that they do not have any commercial or associative interest that represents a conflict of interest in connection with the work submitted.

References

1. Grover, L.K.: A fast quantum mechanical algorithm for database search. In: Proceedings of the Twenty-Eighth Annual ACM Symposium on Theory of Computing, pp. 212–219 (1996)

2. Lamport, L.: Constructing digital signatures from a one way function (1979)
3. Merkle, R.C.: A certified digital signature. In: Brassard, G. (ed.) CRYPTO 1989. LNCS, vol. 435, pp. 218–238. Springer, New York (1990). https://doi.org/10.1007/0-387-34805-0_21
4. Buchmann, J., Dahmen, E., Ereth, S., Hülsing, A., Rückert, M.: On the security of the Winternitz one-time signature scheme. In: Nitaj, A., Pointcheval, D. (eds.) AFRICACRYPT 2011. LNCS, vol. 6737, pp. 363–378. Springer, Heidelberg (2011). https://doi.org/10.1007/978-3-642-21969-6_23
5. Hülsing, A.: W-OTS+ – shorter signatures for hash-based signature schemes. In: Youssef, A., Nitaj, A., Hassanien, A.E. (eds.) AFRICACRYPT 2013. LNCS, vol. 7918, pp. 173–188. Springer, Heidelberg (2013). https://doi.org/10.1007/978-3-642-38553-7_10
6. Butin, D., Gazdag, S.-L., Buchmann, J.: Real-world post-quantum digital signatures. In: Cleary, F., Felici, M. (eds.) Cyber Security and Privacy. CCIS, vol. 530, pp. 41–52. Springer, Cham (2015). https://doi.org/10.1007/978-3-319-25360-2_4
7. Palmieri, P.: Hash-based signatures for the internet of things: position paper. In: Proceedings of the 15th ACM International Conference on Computing Frontiers, pp. 332–335 (2018)
8. Butin, D.: Hash-based signatures: state of play. IEEE Secur. Priv. **15**(4), 37–43 (2017)
9. McGrew, D., Kampanakis, P., Fluhrer, S., Gazdag, S.-L., Butin, D., Buchmann, J.: State management for hash-based signatures. In: Chen, L., McGrew, D., Mitchell, C. (eds.) SSR 2016. LNCS, vol. 10074, pp. 244–260. Springer, Cham (2016). https://doi.org/10.1007/978-3-319-49100-4_11
10. Aumasson, J.-P., Endignoux, G.: Improving stateless hash-based signatures. In: Smart, N.P. (ed.) CT-RSA 2018. LNCS, vol. 10808, pp. 219–242. Springer, Cham (2018). https://doi.org/10.1007/978-3-319-76953-0_12
11. Ghosh, S., Misoczki, R., Sastry, M.R.: Lightweight post-quantum-secure digital signature approach for IoT motes. Cryptology ePrint Archive (2019)
12. Pereira, G., Puodzius, C., Barreto, P.: Shorter hash-based signatures. J. Syst. Softw. **116**, 95–100 (2016)
13. Rohde, S., Eisenbarth, T., Dahmen, E., Buchmann, J., Paar, C.: Fast hash-based signatures on constrained devices. In: Grimaud, G., Standaert, F.-X. (eds.) CARDIS 2008. LNCS, vol. 5189, pp. 104–117. Springer, Heidelberg (2008). https://doi.org/10.1007/978-3-540-85893-5_8
14. Lohachab, A., Lohachab, A., Jangra, A.: A comprehensive survey of prominent cryptographic aspects for securing communication in post-quantum IoT networks. Internet Things **9**, 100174 (2020)
15. Hussain, S., Ullah, S.S., Ali, I., Xie, J., Inukollu, V.N.: Certificateless signature schemes in industrial internet of things: a comparative survey. Comput. Commun. **181**, 116–131 (2022)
16. Li, L., Xianhui, L., Wang, K.: Hash-based signature revisited. Cybersecurity **5**(1), 1–26 (2022)

Computational Models

Describing Regular Closure of Linear Languages by Semi Conditional Insertion Deletion Systems

Indhumathi Raman

Department of Computing Technologies, School of Computing, SRMIST,
Chennai 603203, India
indhumar2@srmist.edu.in

Abstract. The smallest superclass of linear languages LIN which is closed under the regular operations, namely, Kleene star, union, and concatenation, is called the regular or rational closure of LIN and is denoted by $\mathbb{L}_{reg}(\text{LIN})$.

In this paper, the class $\mathbb{L}_{reg}(\text{LIN})$ is described using insertion-deletion system together with semi conditional regulation. A rule in SCID system is applied whenever all strings in its *permitting set* are available as substrings and all strings from the *forbidden set* are absent. We mainly prove that whenever SCID systems simulates the class of linear languages, then with no additional parameters, the SCID system can describe $\mathbb{L}_{reg}(\text{LIN})$. In particular, SCID systems with degree $(2,1)$ and sizes $(2,0,0;1,0,0)$, $(1,1,0;1,0,0)$ and $(1,0,1;1,0,0)$ are shown to describe the class of $\mathbb{L}_{reg}(\text{LIN})$.

Keywords: Ins-del systems · semi-conditional systems · descriptional complexity

1 Introduction

Insertion and deletion operations are considered as building blocks in designing a formal grammar called *insertion-deletion* (in short, ins-del) systems are one of the bio-inspired computing models. It is a grammatical mechanism introduced into formal language theory in [8]. Informally, the insertion operation refers to inserting a string δ within two strings w_1 and w_2 in order to obtain $w_1 \delta w_2$. Nevertheless, deletion operation refers to removal of a substring ζ from $w_1 \zeta w_2$ to get $w_1 w_2$. Both these operations were introduced in a joint manner in [8] as ins-del system. In the field of biology, the insertion operation find application in DNA strands' mismatched annealing; refer [15] and in editing of RNA; refer [2].

The descriptional complexity of an ins-del system is evaluated by *ID size* which is a tuple of six non-negative integers $(r, r', r''; \ell, \ell', \ell'')$ where the six elements in the tuple represent the maximum lengths of (i) insertion string, (ii) left contexts of insertion rules (iii) right contexts of insertion rules (iv) deletion string, (v) left contexts of deletion rules (vi) right contexts of deletion rules, respectively.

An ins-del system can describe the class of recursively enumerable (RE) languages (in this case, we say that the system is computationally complete) with size $(1,1,1;1,1,1)$ (see [17]) but any size which is weaker than this cannot describe the RE languages. This fact has motivated to analyze some regulations in order to achieve the computational completeness with smaller sizes than above. Some common regulations are (i) graph-controlled ins-del systems [6], (ii) matrix ins-del systems [10,16], (iii) random context systems and (iv) semi-conditional ins-del systems (abbreviated as SCID) [7]. The authors of [14] have reported on the use of several variants of context conditions in regulated rewriting.

In this paper, the focus is on SCID systems in which a rule is applied when every string specified in the permitting set is present/available and when every string specified in the forbidden set is absent/unavailable. The permitting and the forbidden set is specified within every ins-del rule and these sets control the application of the rule on the sentential form of a derivation string. The consideration of the permitting and forbidden sets naturally forces to consider additional two parameters in the descriptional complexity of a SCID system as a tuple $d = (p, f)$, called *degree*, where (i) p: the maximum length of a permitting string and (ii) f: the maximum length f of a forbidden string.

Since in a SCID system, the strings/words for a language are derived by checking the presence of permitting words and absence of forbidden words while applying the context-free rules of the grammar, such systems can be used to handle mathematical framework in security systems. Now, consider a security system where the information of what to be permitted and what to be forbidden are available. Now, with that system, if one wants to know how much the system is vulnerable or strong/robust to the threats in the long run, then one can simulate the security system with semi-conditional system and generate the strings to see that any unwanted strings are present in the system to conclude the security system is weak or strong in a long run. The idea is similar to how L-systems (L stands for Lindenmeyar) help to develop fractals and images of flower patterns.

When SCID systems were initiated by Ivanov and Verlan in [7], it was proved that SCID system with size $(1,0,0;1,0,0)$ and degree $(2,2)$, can describe any recursively enumerable language. Further, it was shown that a SCID system of size $(1,1,0;1,1,1)/(1,1,1;1,1,0)$ and degree $(1,1)$ is not able to describe the regular languages and hence will not be able to describe the linear languages. This motivates the present study of SCID systems with degree $(2,1)$ that interpolates between $(2,2)$ and $(1,1)$.

Semi-conditional ins-del systems of degree $(2,1)$ with context-free deletion are not known to be computationally complete if (i) binary length strings are inserted without contexts, or (ii) single length symbols are inserted with either left or right context. In this paper, it is shown that these systems describe regular closure of linear languages.

It is noteworthy that the regular closure class of linear languages lies strictly between the class of regular and context-free languages in the Chomsky hierarchy of formal languages. The classes of *regular* and *context-free* languages hold a special place due to their great practical importance. On one hand, regular languages are very useful in pattern recognition of input of the programming languages in compiler design and on the other hand, many syntactical structures, arithmetic expressions and parsing of the programming languages are represented by context-free grammars. It is interesting to note that the regular and context-free languages are both closed under concatenation and Kleene closure but linear languages are not. This fact makes it interesting to study about linear classes and its smallest superset language class which is also closed under all three regular operations namely union, concatenation and Kleene star operations.

2 Preliminaries

In the theory of formal languages, Σ denotes a finite set of elements called an *alphabet*. Further, the set of all strings is represented as Σ^* and the empty string is represented as λ. The reversals of a string $w \in \Sigma^*$, a language L and a language class $\mathbb{L}$ are denoted as w^R, L^R and $\mathbb{L}^R$ respectively.

A type-2 grammar $G = (N, T, S, P)$ is called *linear* if RHS in every rule are from $T^*NT^* \cup T^*$. Furthermore, we assume that, in the *normal form* for these type of linear grammars, every rule is in one of the three forms, namely $A \to \alpha D$, $A \to D\alpha$ and $A \to \lambda$ where $A, D \to N$, $\alpha \in T$. The class of linear languages is not closed with respect to two operations namely concatenation and Kleene star. This non-closure property of linear languages motivates to construct the classes of formal languages built from linear languages and additionally linking these linear languages by concatenation and Kleene closure. A detailed study of these closure classes and their characterization in terms of finite turn pushdown automaton is given in [12].

The smallest language class (denoted as $\mathbb{L}_{op}(\text{LIN})$) is defined to contain LIN and closed under the *op* operation. Since the class LIN is closed with respect to union, it is true that $\mathbb{L}_\cup(\text{LIN}) = \text{LIN}$. Extending these notations, in this paper, we denote by $\mathbb{L}_{reg}(\text{LIN})$, the superset of LIN that is closed under the three regular operations, namely union, Kleene star and concatenation. $\mathbb{L}_{reg}(\text{LIN})$ is the smallest superclass of languages that contains linear languages and is commonly referred as the rational regular closure of LIN. Clearly, $\mathbb{L}_{reg}(\text{LIN})$ lies between LIN and CF in the Chomsky hierarchy of languages. A characterization of $\mathbb{L}_{reg}(\text{LIN})$ in terms of context-free grammars is shown in [4] which states:

Proposition 1. *[4] A language $L \subseteq T^*$ is in $L \in \mathbb{L}_{reg}(\text{LIN})$ iff there exists a type-2 grammar $\hat{G}(N, T, S, P)$ with $L(\hat{G}) = L$ satisfying:*

- $N := N_0 \cup \hat{N}$.
- $\hat{N}$ *is again a union of* $N_1, N_2, \ldots, N_k$, *such that* P_i *of P are linear rules and only involves symbols.*
- P *is again union of* $P_0, P_1, P_2, \ldots, P_k$.
- *There exists a grammar* $G_R = (N_0, \hat{N}, S, P_0)$ *which is right-linear.* □

This characterization is designed in a dual fashion approach: Initially, G_R produces symbols from $\hat{N}$ serving as terminals for G_R and as nonterminals for G_i.

2.1 Insertion-Deletion Systems

Following [8,15], we define insertion-deletion systems as given below.

Definition 1. *[8, 15] An* ins-del system *is a quadruple* $\gamma = (V, T, A, R)$, *where* V *is an alphabet*, $T \subseteq V$ *is the terminal alphabet, A is a finite language over V, R is a finite set of triplets of the form* $(u, \delta, v)_{ins}$ *or* $(u, \zeta, v)_{del}$, *where* $(u, v) \in V^* \times V^*$, $\zeta, \delta \in V^+$. □

In a rule, $(u, \delta, v)_{ins}$ or $(u, \zeta, v)_{del}$, u and v are called the *left* and *right* contexts of the insertion or the deletion rule. Further, δ and *zeta* are the *insertion* and *deletion*. A string $x \in A$ is called *axiom*. If both contexts are empty for every insertion (deletion) rule, then the insertion (deletion) is termed *context-free*.

2.2 Semi-conditional Insertion-Deletion Systems

Definition 2. *[7] A SCID or a semi-conditional insertion-deletion system of degree* (p, f), $p, f \geq 0$ *is a quadruple* $\Pi = (V, T, A, R)$, *where V is a finite alphabet*, $T \subseteq V$ *is the terminal alphabet*, $A \subseteq V^*$ *is a finite set of axioms, R is a finite set of rules of the form* $[(u, s, v)_t, \mathcal{P}, \mathcal{F}]$ *where* $u, s, v \in V^*$, $t \in \{ins, del\}$, $\mathcal{P}, \mathcal{F}$ *are finite subsets of* V^*. □

The sets $\mathcal{P}$ and $\mathcal{F}$ are called *permitting* and *forbidden* set respectively. For clarity, unique labels are used for rules, even identifying a rule with its label. The ordered pair (p, f) is called the *degree* of the SCID system Π where p is the maximum length of a permitting string in $\mathcal{P}$ and f is the maximum length of a forbidden string in $\mathcal{F}$. The size $(r, r', r''; \ell, \ell', \ell'')$ of an SCID system is same as the size of the underlying ins-del system (which is informally stated in the introduction section) and is formally defined in the following table (Table 1).

Table 1. Meaning of the parameters in SCID size.

$e = \max\{|\delta| : (u, \delta, v)_{ins} \in R\}$	$d = \max\{|\zeta| : (u, \zeta, v)_{del} \in R\}$
$e' = \max\{|u| : (u, \delta, v)_{ins} \in R\}$	$d' = \max\{|u| : (u, \zeta, v)_{del} \in R\}$
$e'' = \max\{|v| : (u, \delta, v)_{ins} \in R\}$	$d'' = max\{|v| : (u, \zeta, v)_{del} \in R\}$

It is denoted by $x \Rightarrow_r y$ when one of the following is true.

1. $x = x_1 u_r v_r x_2$, $y = x_1 u_r s_r v_r x_2$, where $x_1, x_2 \in V^*$ and $t_r = ins$;
2. $x = x_1 u_r s_r v_r x_2$, $y = x_1 u_r v_r x_2$, where $x_1, x_2 \in V^*$ and $t_r = del$.

The language of Π is $L(\Pi) = \{x \in T^* \mid \alpha \Rightarrow^* x \text{ for } \alpha \in A\}$, where $\Rightarrow^* := \bigcup_{r \in R} \Rightarrow_r$.

The families of languages generated by SCID systems of degree at most (i, j) and size at most $s = (r, r', r''; \ell, \ell', \ell'')$ is denoted as $\text{SCID}_{i,j}(s)$.

2.3 Objective

Table 2 shows various RE and nonRE results of SCID from [3,5] and [7]. From Table 2, it is clear that there has been no study on what classes of languages does the SCID systems of degree $(2,1)$ and sizes $(2,0,0;1,0,0)$, $(1,1,0;1,0,0)$ and $(1,0,1;1,0,0)$ generate? This question is answered in this paper by showing that these systems generate $\mathbb{L}_{reg}(\text{LIN})$. It is left open whether these system can generate the class of RE languages or at least the class of context-free languages.

Table 2. Comparing the results of [7], of [3] and of [5].

	Result of [7] (2015)	Result of [3] (2018)	Result of [5] (2019)
1.	$\text{SCID}_{2,2}(1,0,0;1,0,0) = \text{RE}$	$\text{SCID}_{2,1}(1,1,0;1,1,1) = \text{RE}$	$\text{SCID}_{2,1}(2,0,0;2,0,0) = \text{RE}$
2.	$\text{SCID}_{1,1}(1,1,0;2,0,0) \subsetneq \text{RE}$	$\text{SCID}_{3,1}(1,1,0;1,1,0) = \text{RE}$	$\text{SCID}_{2,1}(1,1,0;2,0,0) = \text{RE}$
3.	$\text{SCID}_{1,1}(1,1,0;1,1,1) \subsetneq \text{RE}$	$\text{SCID}_{3,1}(1,0,1;1,1,0) = \text{RE}$	$\text{SCID}_{2,1}(2,0,0;1,1,0) = \text{RE}$
4.			$\text{SCID}_{2,1}(1,1,0;1,1,0) = \text{RE}$
5.			$\text{SCID}_{2,1}(1,0,1;1,1,0) = \text{RE}$

3 Describing Regular Closure Class of Linear Languages

The observations stated below are useful to prove our main results.

Theorem 1. *Let* $s = (r, r', r''; \ell, \ell', \ell'')$ *be the size of some SCID system and* (i, j) *is its degree, then*

1. $\text{SCID}_{i,j}(s) = [\text{SCID}]_{i,j}(s')]^R$, *with* $s' = (r, r'', r'; \ell, \ell'', \ell')$,
2. $\text{LIN} \subseteq \text{SCID}_{i,j}(s)$ *if and only if* $\text{LIN} \subseteq \text{SCID}_{i,j}(s')$.
3. $\text{SCID}_{i,j}(s) = \text{RE}$ *if and only if* $\text{SCID}_{i,j}(s') = \text{RE}$.

Proof. If a conditional rule $p : ((u, s, v)_t, \mathcal{P}, \mathcal{F}) \in \Pi$, where $t \in \{ins, del\}$, then the rule $p^R : ((v^R, s^R, u^R)_t, \mathcal{P}^R, \mathcal{F}^R) \in \Pi^R$. Since LIN is closed with respect to reversal, if $\text{LIN} \subseteq \text{SCID}_{k,l}(s) = \text{RE}$, it is true that $\text{LIN} = \text{LIN}^R \subseteq \text{SCID}_{k,l}(s')$. Further as RE is closed under reversal, whenever $\text{SCID}_{k,l}(s) = \text{RE}$, then $\text{SCID}_{k,l}(s') = \text{RE}^R = \text{RE}$. □

Recalling from [7] that $SCID_{2,2}(1,0,0;1,0,0) = \text{RE}$, the degree of the SCID system is decreased to $(2,1)$ but insertion and/or deletion lengths is raised from one to two. In particular, SCID systems of sizes $(2,0,0;1,0,0)$, $(1,1,0;1,0,0)$ and $(1,0,1;1,0,0)$ are shown to describe the linear class LIN in Theorem 2. A general result is now provided in this paper by showing the following: If there exist a semi-conditional ins-del system of ID size $(r, r', r''; \ell, \ell', \ell'')$ and degree (i, j) describing LIN, then without any additional parameters, the system $\text{SCID}_{i,j}(r, r', r''; \ell, \ell', \ell'')$ will describe $\mathbb{L}_{reg}(\text{LIN})$. Applying this general result (as stated in Theorem 3) on the result of Theorem 2, it is shown that SCID of sizes

$(2, 0, 0; 1, 0, 0)$, $(1, 1, 0; 1, 0, 0)$ and $(1, 0, 1; 1, 0, 0)$ (which are not known to characterize RE and unfortunately, not even CF class) are shown to describe the class $\mathbb{L}_{reg}(\text{LIN})$.

In the following theorems, certain SCID systems are presented to describe the linear languages and later, it is show that these SCID systems with no additional parameters also describe the regular closure of linear languages.

In the paper, the simulations of rules $p: X \to bY, q: X \to Yb, h: X \to \lambda$ in the rule set R are presented which employs the following markers symbols:

$$\begin{aligned} M &= \{m \colon m \in [1 \ldots |R|]\}, & M' &= \{m' \colon m \in [1 \ldots |R|]\}, \\ M'' &= \{m'' \colon m \in [1 \ldots |R|]\}, & M''' &= \{m''' \colon m \in [1 \ldots |R|]\}, \\ \mathcal{M}'' &= M \cup M' \cup M'', & \mathcal{M}''' &= M \cup M' \cup M'' \cup M''', \end{aligned}$$

Similar notations for $\mathcal{M}^{iv}$ and $\mathcal{M}^v$ are also employed.

Theorem 2. *The semi-conditional insertion-deletion systems* $\text{SCID}_{2,1}(2, 0, 0; 1, 0, 0)$; $\text{SCID}_{2,1}(1, 1, 0; 1, 0, 0)$ *and* $\text{SCID}_{2,1}(1, 0, 1; 1, 0, 0)$ *describe all linear languages.*

Proof. Consider $G = (N, T, S, P)$ which is a linear grammar. All rules of P are one of the forms $p: X \to bY; q: X \to Yb; h: X \to \lambda$ labelled uniquely. It is highlighted from [3] the degree $(2, 1)$ SCID systems $\Pi_1 = (N', T, S, R_1)$ of size $(2, 0, 0; 1, 0, 0)$ and $\Pi_2 = (N', T, \{S\}, R_2)$ with size $(1, 1, 0; 1, 0, 0)$ as follows such that $\text{LIN} \subseteq L(\Pi_1)$ and $\text{LIN} \subseteq L(\Pi_2)$.

The simulating rules of R_1 in Π_1 for rules of types $p: X \to bY$ and $q: X \to Yb$ in G are stated in Figs. 1(a) and 1(b) respectively. The simulating rules of R_2 in Π_2 are stated in Fig. 1(c) and 1(d). Rules of type $h: X \to \lambda$ are simulated directly by the SCID rule $h1 = [(\lambda, X, \lambda)_{del}, \emptyset, \mathcal{M}]$. This rule is included in both R_1 and R_2.

The working of $h: X \to \lambda$ in G and the rule $h1 = [(\lambda, X, \lambda)_{del}, \emptyset, \mathcal{M}]$ in R_1 and R_2 are exactly the same and hence the correctness of the simulations are discussed below in order to show that $L(\Pi_1) = L(G)$.

<u>*Simulating* $p: X \to bY$:</u> The simulation rules shown in Fig. 1(a) correctly describes $p: X \to bY$ as follows.

$$X \Rightarrow_1 Xpp' \Rightarrow_2 Xpbp''p' \Rightarrow_3 Xpbp'''p^{iv}p''p' \Rightarrow_4 Xpbp'''p^{iv}p' \Rightarrow_5$$
$$pbp'''p^{iv}p' \Rightarrow_6 pbp'''p' \Rightarrow_7 pbp'''Yp^vp' \Rightarrow_8 pbp'''Yp' \Rightarrow_9 pbYp' \Rightarrow_{10} pbY \Rightarrow_{11} bY$$

<u>*Simulating* $q: X \to Yb$:</u> The rules shown in Fig. 1(b) correctly describes $q: X \to Yb$ as follows:

$$X \Rightarrow_1 Xqq' \Rightarrow_2 Xqq''bq' \Rightarrow_3 Xqq''q'''q^{iv}bq' \Rightarrow_4 Xqq'''q^{iv}bq' \Rightarrow_5$$
$$qq'''q^{iv}bq' \Rightarrow_6 qq'''bq' \Rightarrow_7 qYq^vq'''bq' \Rightarrow_8 qYq'''bq' \Rightarrow_9 qYbq' \Rightarrow_{10} qYb \Rightarrow_{11} Yb$$

We may observe that the q simulation is *mirroring* the p simulation, while the underlying logic is identical. This shows that $L(G) \subseteq L(\Pi_1)$.

Describing Regular Closure of Linear Languages   123

$p1 = [(\lambda, pp', \lambda)_{ins}, \emptyset, (N' \setminus \{X\}) \cup M]$
$p2 = [(\lambda, bp'', \lambda)_{ins}, \emptyset, (N' \setminus \{X\}) \cup M \setminus \{p, p'\}]$
$p3 = [(\lambda, p'''p^{iv}, \lambda)_{ins}, \emptyset, (N' \setminus \{X\}) \cup M \setminus \{p, p', p''\}]$
$p4 = [(\lambda, p'', \lambda)_{del}, \{Xp, pb, bp''', p'''p^{iv}, p^{iv}p'', p''p'\}, \emptyset]$
$p5 = [(\lambda, X, \lambda)_{del}, \{Xp, pb, bp''', p'''p^{iv}, p^{iv}p'\}, \emptyset]$
$p6 = [(\lambda, p^{iv}, \lambda)_{del}, \emptyset, N' \cup M^v \setminus \{p, p', p'''\}]$
$p7 = [(\lambda, Yp^v, \lambda)_{ins}, \emptyset, N' \cup M^v \setminus \{p, p', p'''\}]$
$p8 = [(\lambda, p^v, \lambda)_{del}, \{pb, bp''', p'''Y, Yp^v, p''p'\}, \emptyset]$
$p9 = [(\lambda, p''', \lambda)_{del}, \{pb, bp''', p'''Y, Yp'\}, \emptyset]$
$p10 = [(\lambda, p', \lambda)_{del}, \{pb, bY, Yp'\}, \emptyset]$
$p11 = [(\lambda, p, \lambda)_{del}, \emptyset, (N' \setminus \{Y\}) \cup M \setminus \{p\}]$

(a) Simulating $p : X \to bY$

$p1 = [(X, p, \lambda)_{ins}, \emptyset, M'']$
$p2 = [(\lambda, X, \lambda)_{del}, \{p\}, \emptyset]$
$p3 = [(p, p', \lambda)_{ins}, \emptyset, N' \cup (M'' \setminus \{p\})]$
$p4 = [(p', p'', \lambda)_{ins}, \emptyset, N' \cup (M'' \setminus \{p, p'\})]$
$p5 = [(p', Y, \lambda)_{ins}, \{p'p''\}, \emptyset]$
$p6 = [(p, b, \lambda)_{ins}, \{pp'\}, \emptyset]$
$p7 = [(\lambda, p, \lambda)_{del}, \{bp', Yp''\}, \emptyset]$
$p8 = [(\lambda, p', \lambda)_{del}, \emptyset, M]$
$p9 = [(\lambda, p'', \lambda)_{del}, \emptyset, M \cup M']$

(c) Simulating $p : X \to bY$

$q1 = [(\lambda, qq', \lambda)_{ins}, \emptyset, (N' \setminus \{X\}) \cup M]$
$q2 = [(\lambda, q''b, \lambda)_{ins}, \emptyset, (N' \setminus \{X\}) \cup M \setminus \{q, q'\}]$
$q3 = [(\lambda, q'''q^{iv}, \lambda)_{ins}, \emptyset, (N' \setminus \{X\}) \cup M \setminus \{q, q', q''\}]$
$q4 = [(\lambda, q'', \lambda)_{del}, \{Xq, qq'', q''q''', q''q^{iv}, q^{iv}b, bq'\}, \emptyset]$
$q5 = [(\lambda, X, \lambda)_{del}, \{Xq, qq''', q''q^{iv}, q^{iv}b, bq'\}, \emptyset]$
$q6 = [(\lambda, q^{iv}, \lambda)_{del}, \emptyset, N' \cup M^v \setminus \{q, q', q'', q^{iv}\}]$
$q7 = [(\lambda, Yq^v, \lambda)_{ins}, \emptyset, N' \cup M^v \setminus \{q, q', q''\}]$
$q8 = [(\lambda, q^v, \lambda)_{del}, \{qY, Yq^v, q^vq''', q'''b, bq'\}, \emptyset]$
$q9 = [(\lambda, q''', \lambda)_{del}, \{qY, Yq''', q'''b, bq'\}, \emptyset]$
$q10 = [(\lambda, q', \lambda)_{del}, \{qY, Yb, bq'\}, \emptyset]$
$q11 = [(\lambda, q, \lambda)_{del}, \emptyset, (N' \setminus \{Y\}) \cup M \setminus \{q\}]$

(b) Simulating $q : X \to Yb$

$q1 = [(X, q, \lambda)_{ins}, \emptyset, M'']$
$q2 = [(\lambda, X, \lambda)_{del}, \{q\}, \emptyset]$
$q3 = [(q, q', \lambda)_{ins}, \emptyset, N' \cup (M'' \setminus \{q\})]$
$q4 = [(q', q'', \lambda)_{ins}, \emptyset, N' \cup (M'' \setminus \{q, q'\})]$
$q5 = [(q', b, \lambda)_{ins}, \{q'q''\}, \emptyset]$
$q6 = [(q, Y, \lambda)_{ins}, \{qq'\}, \emptyset]$
$q7 = [(\lambda, q, \lambda)_{del}, \{Yq', bq''\}, \emptyset]$
$q8 = [(\lambda, q', \lambda)_{del}, \emptyset, M]$
$q9 = [(\lambda, q'', \lambda)_{del}, \emptyset, M \cup M']$

(d) Simulating $q : X \to Yb$

Fig. 1. Simulating $p : X \to bY$ and $q : X \to Yb$ by $SCID_{2,1}(2,0,0;1,0,0)$ (in (a), (b)) and by $SCID_{2,1}(1,1,0;1,0,0)$ (in (c), (d)).

The simulation idea is sketched to show the converse. Strings of length two are inserted randomly with at least 1 symbol acting as a marker to stitch the previously introduced string to the correct position. The permitting strings in further steps guarantees that the inserted string was placed only at the particular correct position in the previous step. For instance, pp' was inserted in a random manner by $p1$ rule and Xp in the permitting set of rule $p5$ requires that this insertion was done next to the non-terminal X, particularly on its right.

Similarly, $p^v p'$ in rule $p8$ requires that Yp^v was inserted between b and p'' by rule $p7$ in the previous step, which implicitly implies that bp'' is present due to the application of rule $p2$. The strings in the forbidden set of the insertion rules prevented us from applying of the same rule multiple times. With these details, it is clear that $L(G) = L(\Pi_1)$.

On the other side, while executing $q1$ through $q4$, the rule $X \to qq'q''$ is simulated. Then, we insert the non-terminal Y between q and q'. Similarly, the symbol b is inserted between q' and q''. One may notice that the symbol b could not have been introduced for the second time due to the presence of $q'bq''$ and the absence of $q'q''$ (refer $q5$). On applying rule $q7$, first q is deleted after the presence of the Yq' and bq'' is guaranteed. This ensures that Y and b are introduced correctly. Lastly, the application of rules $q8, q9$ deletes the markers q' and q'' respectively. In summary, the simulation of $q : X \to Yb$ is as: $X \Rightarrow$

$Xq \Rightarrow q \Rightarrow qq' \Rightarrow qq'q'' \Rightarrow qq'bq'' \Rightarrow qYq'bq'' \Rightarrow Yq'bq'' \Rightarrow Ybq'' \Rightarrow Yb$. Clearly, rules in Π_2 similarly.

This shows that LIN $\subseteq$ SCID$_{2,1}(1,1,0;1,0,0)$. The last claim, namely LIN $\subseteq$ SCID$_{2,1}(1,0,1;1,0,0)$ follows from Theorem 1. □

Theorem 3. *Let $r, \ell, i, j \geq 1$ and $r', r'', \ell', \ell'' \geq 0$ with $r' + r'' \geq 1$. If* LIN $\subseteq$ SCID$_{i,j}(r, r', r''; \ell, \ell', \ell'')$*, then* $\mathbb{L}_{reg}$(LIN) $\subseteq$ SCID$_{i,j}(r, r', r''; \ell, \ell', \ell'')$.

Proof. Consider a language $L \in \mathbb{L}_{reg}$(LIN) described by $G = (N, T, S, P)$ as stated in Proposition 1. This G consists of $G_R = (N_0, N'', S, P_0)$ which is right-linear and a set of k linear grammars denoted by $G_m = (N_m, T, S_m, P_m)$ for $m \in [1, 2, \ldots, k]$. Further, we consider a grammar $G'_m = (N'_m, T, S_m, P'_m)$ with $N'_m = N_m \cup \{S_m^A \mid A \in N_0\}$ and P'_m contains rules of the form $S_m^A \rightarrow w$ whenever $S_m \rightarrow w \in P_m$ for $w \in (N_m \cup T)^*$ apart from the rules of P_m.

We assume that LIN $\subseteq$ SCID$_{i,j}(r, r', r''; \ell, \ell', \ell'')$. For each i, the grammar G'_i is simulated by a SCID system $\Pi_i = (V_i, T, \{S_i\}, R_i)$ of size $(r, r', r''; \ell, \ell', \ell'')$. We first consider the case when $e' \geq 1$ and $e'' = 0$.

For G, a semi-conditional ins-del SCID system Π is constructed as follows:

$$\Pi = (V, T, \{S_i A' \mid S \rightarrow S_i A \in P\}, R \cup R'), \text{ where}$$

- $V = \left(\bigcup_{i=1}^{k} (V_i \cup \{S_i^A \mid A \in N_0\})\right) \cup N_0 \cup \{A' \mid A \in N_0\}$;
- $R = \bigcup_{i=1}^{k} R_i$;
- R' contains the below rules: for every $A \rightarrow S_i B \in P_0$:
  - $[(A', S_i^B, \lambda)_{ins}, \emptyset, N'_i \cup \mathcal{M}]$;
  - $[(S_i^B, B', \lambda)_{ins}, \emptyset, B']$;
  - $[(\lambda, A', \lambda)_{del}, B', \emptyset)]$;
  - Further, $[(\lambda, A', \lambda)_{del}, \emptyset, N'_i \cup \mathcal{M}]$ for $A' \rightarrow \lambda \in P_0$.

One may notice that since $L(G_m)$ is described by Π_m, for $m \in \{1, 2, \ldots, k\}$, the Π_m rules are described by R_i rules.

Starting from an axiom $S_i A'$, a string $w_1 \in L(G_i)$ is generated by the simulation of G'_i by Π. In this simulation, when the terminating rule $[(\lambda, X_i, \lambda)_{del}, \emptyset, N_i \cup \mathcal{M}]]$ of L_i is applied, either (i) the rule $A' \rightarrow \lambda$ in G_R is simulated by applying $[(\lambda, A', \lambda)_{del}, \emptyset, N_i \cup \mathcal{M}]]$ which moves the string w_1 to $C1$; or (ii) a rule of the form $A' \rightarrow S_j B'$ is simulated by applying the rules of R'. By the above description, all terminal words of G are derived using Π. For $r' = 0$ and $r'' \geq 1$, the theorem follows using the result from Theorem 1. □

Using the above results of Theorems 2 and 3, it can be concluded that SCID systems of degree $(2, 1)$ and sizes $(2, 0, 0; 1, 0, 0)$; $(1, 1, 0; 1, 0, 0)$; $(1, 0, 1; 1, 0, 0)$ describe the class $\mathbb{L}_{reg}$(LIN). Whether these systems can describe the class of context-free languages or beyond is left open. This is stated formally in the next corollary.

Corollary 1. *Combining the results of Theorems 2 and 3, the following holds.*

- $\mathbb{L}_{reg}(\text{LIN}) \subseteq \text{SCID}_{2,1}(2,0,0;1,0,0)$
- $\mathbb{L}_{reg}(\text{LIN} \subseteq \text{SCID}_{2,1}(1,1,0;1,0,0)$
- $\mathbb{L}_{reg}(\text{LIN} \subseteq \text{SCID}_{2,1}(1,0,1;1,0,0)$. □

4 Conclusion

In this paper, the closure class of linear languages closed under the three operations: union, Kleene star and concatenation, is described using semi-conditional insertion deletion systems of small degree and sizes. The results of this paper prove that the linear languages can be described by SCID systems of the corresponding sizes. It is interested to find

- with what resources, one can describe all context-free languages.
- closure properties and parsing techniques for SCID systems of small sizes.
- how to program biocomputing devices whose underlying system is SCID.

The last study on programming biocomputing devices follow the paradigm of imperative programming which should be performed in presence or absence of certain conditions. This is exactly what semi-conditional grammars can do.

References

1. Alhazov, A., Krassovitskiy, A., Rogozhin, Y., Verlan, S.: P systems with minimal insertion and deletion. Theor. Comput. Sci. **412**(1–2), 136–144 (2011)
2. Benne, R.: RNA Editing: The Alteration of Protein Coding Sequences of RNA. Series in Molecular Biology. Ellis Horwood, Chichester (1993)
3. Fernau, H., Kuppusamy, L., Raman, I.: Computational completeness of simple semi-conditional insertion-deletion systems. In: Stepney, S., Verlan, S. (eds.) UCNC 2018. LNCS, vol. 10867, pp. 86–100. Springer, Cham (2018). https://doi.org/10.1007/978-3-319-92435-9_7
4. Fernau, H., Kuppusamy, L., Raman, I.: Properties of language classes between linear and context-free. J. Autom. Lang. Comb. **23**(4), 329–360 (2018)
5. Fernau, H., Kuppusamy, L., Raman, I.: Computational completeness of simple semi-conditional insertion-deletion systems of degree (2, 1). Nat. Comput. **18**(3), 563–577 (2019)
6. Freund, R., Kogler, M., Rogozhin, Y., Verlan, S.: Graph-controlled insertion-deletion systems. In: McQuillan, I., Pighizzini, G. (eds.) Proceedings Twelfth Annual Workshop on Descriptional Complexity of Formal Systems, DCFS. EPTCS, vol. 31, pp. 88–98 (2010)
7. Ivanov, S., Verlan, S.: Random context and semi-conditional insertion-deletion systems. Fund. Inform. **138**, 127–144 (2015)
8. Kari, L., Thierrin, G.: Contextual insertions/deletions and computability. Inf. Comput. **131**(1), 47–61 (1996)
9. Krishna, S.N., Rama, R.: Insertion-deletion P systems. In: Jonoska, N., Seeman, N.C. (eds.) DNA 2001. LNCS, vol. 2340, pp. 360–370. Springer, Heidelberg (2002). https://doi.org/10.1007/3-540-48017-X_34

10. Kuppusamy, L., Mahendran, A., Krishna, S.N.: Matrix insertion-deletion systems for bio-molecular structures. In: Natarajan, R., Ojo, A. (eds.) ICDCIT 2011. LNCS, vol. 6536, pp. 301–312. Springer, Heidelberg (2011). https://doi.org/10.1007/978-3-642-19056-8_23
11. Kuppusamy, L., Rama, R.: On the power of tissue P systems with insertion and deletion rules. In: Pre-Proceedings of Workshop on Membrane Computing, volume 28 of Report RGML, pp. 304–318. Univ. Tarragona, Spain (2003)
12. Kutrib, M., Malcher, A.: Finite turns and the regular closure of linear context-free languages. Discret. Appl. Math. **155**(16), 2152–2164 (2007)
13. Margenstern, M., Paun, Gh., Rogozhin, Y., Verlan, S.: Context-free insertion-deletion systems. Theoret. Comput. Sci. **330**(2), 339–348 (2005)
14. Meduna, A., Svec, M.: Grammars with Context Conditions and Their Applications. Wiley-Interscience (2005)
15. Paun, Gh., Rozenberg, G., Salomaa, A.: DNA Computing: New Computing Paradigms. Springer (1998)
16. Petre, I., Verlan, S.: Matrix insertion-deletion systems. Theoret. Comput. Sci. **456**, 80–88 (2012)
17. Takahara, A., Yokomori, T.: On the computational power of insertion-deletion systems. Nat. Comput. **2**(4), 321–336 (2003)

Predicting the Toxicity of Biomolecules Using Graph Kernel

R. Manimegalai[✉], A. Susmeta, V. R. Umayal, and M. Venkateshwaran

Department of Computer Science and Engineering, PSG Institute of Technology and Applied Research, Coimbatore 641062, India
drrm@psgitech.ac.in

Abstract. Chemical molecules or bio-molecules can be delineated in the form of a graph. Some of them can be active/inactive, toxic/non-toxic and resistant to a drug/not resistant to a drug. These properties of the molecules can be due to presence of sub structure inside the molecule which causes it to be toxic or non-toxic. So with this help of interpretability of the graph kernel, it will be easy to identify the substructure that has put this graph in a particular class. Moreover when a new bio-molecule or chemical molecule is introduced they can be easily classified as toxic/non-toxic on the basis of presence of that molecule. Thus instead of merely classifying the graph, if the substructures which lead to classification are available and interpretable, then it would be better. The presence of certain substructures that cause toxicity in a chemical molecule, has to be checked. To do this, the sparsity is important because when more and more substructures are taken for classification, it becomes computational expensive. Thus it is necessary to cherry pick the best molecule for the classification of the graph. The main objective is to classify the graph by extracting the most important substructure. In case of multiple important substructures, we use weighted graph classification. The technique is a quick feature extraction method based on the graph isomorphism Weisfeiler-Lehman isomorphism test. The algorithm involves running h iterations of WL-Subtree which in turn means a length feature of color hash for each node. This feature map will basically indicate the similarity of nodes at various depths for two different graphs. We also use the graph edge or node deletion that can be seen as a kind of edit operation.

Keywords: Toxicity predictor · Support Vector Machine · WL Kernel · Graph kernel · Subtree kernel

1 Introduction

The demand for algorithms to analyze and classify graph data is being driven by an increase in applications in chemoinformatics and bioinformatics. The general difficulty of forecasting numerous properties, including the toxicological effects of tiny compounds, while taking into account their molecular graph, which represents the atoms covalent bonds, served as the inspiration for this work's example in chemoinformatics.

Graph classification is typically related to the issue of graph mining, which entails identifying noteworthy patterns in graphs and using them as features to create prediction models.

Pure mathematical analysis as well as chemical applications became crucial with the creation of all the fundamental chemical compound theories, particularly for the study and discovery of previously unknown molecules. Chemical graph theory has advanced more as new substances have been discovered and created. In order to train on data with graph topologies, kernel functions that measure graph similarity are typically integrated into a kernel machine, such as a support vector machine. It has been thoroughly studied in this field how effective classification algorithms based on kernels are in practice. Many distinct graph kernels have been developed, particularly in the last 15 years, either because of their theoretical advantages or because of their adaptability and specialization to a variety of application industries [1]. As the number of approaches grows in use, it becomes increasingly difficult for researchers new to the field and non-expert practitioners to compile a sufficient collection of candidate kernels.

Kernel approaches tied to graph kernels have recently been identified as a promising method for categorizing graph data. Because it is not essential to actually generate the picture of the information that is presented in the feature space, support vector machines (SVM), a type of kernel approach, operate naturally in a Hilbert space of features that may be extremely dimensional. However, they only permit comparisons between polynomially computable substructures of graphs. They respect and employ graph topology. Support vector machines, kernel PCA, and kernel regression are just a few of the many machine learning algorithms known as kernel methods that can be employed with graph-structured data [2]. Based on the algorithms, this model categorizes biomolecules as harmful or non-toxic. It compares the WL subtree feature labeling of the chosen feature graph with the remainder of the graph using a heuristic approach. For classification, a rapid feature extraction technique based on the graph isomorphism test is used. The first generator for chemical graph theory, CONGEN, was created in the 1960s by a Stanford team. As a result, several additional structure generators have been created since then. According to the chemical graph theory, this information produces the structural elements of the desired chemical structures. As a result, the efficacy of the metabolomics data has a significant impact on the accuracy.

2 Literature Survey

Chemical toxicity is a key indicator in the agricultural, environmental, and medical sciences. Toxicology is the primary element that disqualifies the majority of medication candidates and is crucial to the process of discovering new drugs. For instance, a potential cancer treatment drug must be carefully examined since it interacts with a variety of biological targets, including potentially new ones, raising the possibility of various toxicological profiles. To comprehend toxicity forecasting better. Jian Jiang et al. have implemented GGL-Tox in [3], to assess the usefulness and application of MWCGs for the representation and modeling of small molecules. Numerous machine learning algorithms, including random forests, k-nearest neighbors, support vector machines, and others, have been widely employed for toxicity prediction because of the enormous amount of experimental data that is currently available. According to Jiarul Chen et al.'s study on semi-supervised learning-based graph convolutional neural networks for chemical toxicity prediction, one of the five pharmacokinetic properties (ADMET) that must be thoroughly established before a new drug candidate can be approved for clinical trials [3]. Based on the idea that a chemical substance's physical, chemical, and reactivity properties are implicitly specified by its structure and that biological systems influence these properties to determine its biological and toxicological properties. Knowledge graph mining and social network analysis are two frequent uses of Graph Convolutional Neural Networks (GCN). However, we must be aware of this study's limitations. First, a compound's toxicity is influenced by a variety of factors, including chirality and the nature of functional groups. Graph kernels for chemical informatics have been the subject of studies by Liva Raalaivola et al. [4].

For managing structured data with varying sizes, kernel approaches have recently gained popularity as a family of machine learning techniques. The Markovian independence assumptions between the variables are related to the connectivity of the graph, which is how the probabilistic graphical model approach relates random variables to graph nodes. In a survey of graph kernels, is presented by Nils M.Kriege et al. in [5]. A pair (V,E) with finitely many edges (E) and finitely many vertices (V) make up a graph G. A molecule is often represented as a vertex, and a relationship between objects is typically represented by an edge (for example, a molecular bond). In order to do cluster analysis on graphs, graph kernels, more specifically, the Weisfeiler-Lehman kernel convert them into a vector representation. Despite the promising results, the Enriched Weisfeiler-Lehman Kernel for Improved Graph Clustering of Source Code by Frank Hoppner et al. have been criticized for its large dimensionality and high sensitivity [6]. The vector representations are improved and more accurate distance measurements are made possible by the use of an effective subtree distance measure. For molecules, it is suggested to use graph kernels based on tree patterns [2, 7].

3 The Proposed Graph Kernal Method for Predicting Toxicity

The proposed technique uses a graph kernel to extract a biomolecule's key substructures and categorize them as dangerous or nontoxic. The basic objective is to categorize the graph by removing its most significant substructure. When there are several significant substructures, weighted graph classification is used. The method uses the graph isomorphism Weisfeiler-Lehman test and is a rapid feature extraction method as mentioned in Fig. 1 [8]. If a node in a network has relatively little in common with any other node, it can be deleted, an alternative graph in terms of feature maps. The SVM model's complexity is reduced as a result.

Instead of just classifying the graph, the experiment's main goal is to extract the important substructure. This algorithm is based on a heuristic that uses WL-Subtree hashing to determine each node's value [9]. The approach includes performing h WL-Subtree rounds, which results in a color hash feature of length h for each node. This feature map will essentially show how similar the nodes are for two different graphs at different depths. Due to the similarity of their neighborhoods, similar graphs will have a higher similarity score. The concept of the discussed feature can be applied to this. A

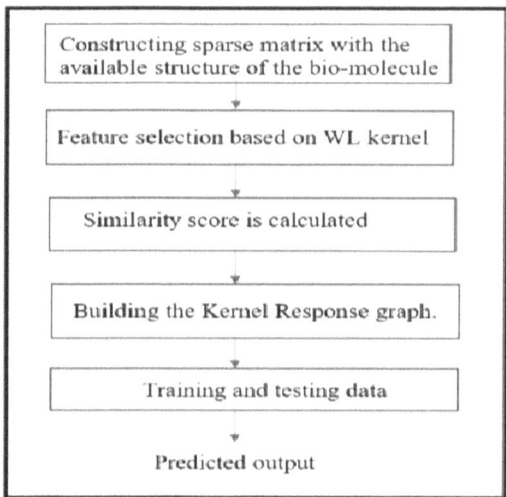

Fig. 1. Steps Involved in the Implementation of Toxicity Prediction

node in a network can be eliminated if it shares very little in common with every other node in the other graph in terms of feature maps. Therefore, by imposing a cutoff on this similarity [10]. The extra nodes are removed from the graph. Consequently, it will be possible to add sparsity to the graphs.

The WL subtree kernel's similarity matrix for the full graph set is first created in order to choose the features. A graph labeled, n-dimensional vector is then used to train an SVM [11]. Class weights are introduced due to the classes' extreme imbalance. The second approach now uses a similarity function with features produced from WL iteration to compare a set of feature graphs to a set of training graphs. The length of the training graph normalizes the similarity score. Now, if a node's similarity score is greater than 25% of the network, it is assumed that it shouldn't be deleted, and the other nodes are eliminated. The first problem is that despite the removal of nodes with low scores, there is no guarantee that the loss will be reduced because there is no direct link between node removal and loss function optimization [12]. Second, it can happen that several significant molecules diffuse among multiple harmful compounds, generating toxicity. However, the system give it low marks, and eventually it will be eliminated [13].

The third is the inclusion of fictitious significant nodes, which serve as a hint that they are present in all molecules but aren't genuinely harmful. The carbon atom which may be found in practically all molecules, is one example [14].

Initially the features are selected by first of all creating the similarity matrix of the WL subtree kernel for the entire graph set. Then an SVM is trained on an n-dimensional vector as mentioned in Fig. 2 with a graph label. Since the classes are highly imbalanced, class weights are introduced. Then after training the SVM, the weight given by the SVM is taken as selection criteria for picking the feature molecule (sorting in decreasing order. But later a more refined method was chosen in which the support vector that was chosen by SVM for classification is taken as the feature. Features are taken from both classes as so that important molecules within each class can be found out as mentioned in Fig. 3.

```
Algorithm SparsityControl( )
{
   Input : vector a(n, x, r), vector b(n, x, r)
   Output : list result(n, x , 1)
           extractSubstructure( )
           for each vector a do
           {
                   initialize the count variable as 0
                   for each vector b do
                   {
                       for each component of selected vector a and b do
                       {
                           if (a==b) count += 1
                           retain the max count
                           if (count/len(b) <= 0.5)
                               append 1 to Result
                           else
                               append 0 to Result
                       }
                   }
           }
           return Result
}
```

Fig. 2. Algorithm for Sparsity Control

The first algorithm is a similarity function which takes two r-dimensional n vectors labeled as a and m vectors labeled as b. Each vector in a is compared against all the vectors in b. If there is a similarity score of more than 0.5 it is taken as an important node marked as 1 and the rest of the nodes as 0. Now the second algorithm takes a set of feature graphs and compares it against a set of training graphs using a similarity function with features obtained through WL iteration. The similarity score is normalized by the length of the training graph. Now if a node has a similarity score of more than 25% of the graph then it is taken as a node that should not be removed and the rest are removed.

4 Experiment Results

We describe our nomenclature before proceeding with results. A graph is made up of three parts: V, E, and l, where V is the collection of vertices, E is the collection of undirected edges, and l: In order to assign labels to graph nodes from an alphabet, a function called V is utilized. The collection of nodes to which a node v has edges linking them is referred to as the node's neighborhood and is indicated by the formula $N(v) = v|(v, v)$ E. We operate under the simple presumption that each network has a maximum degree of d, e edges, and v nodes. The size of G is determined by the cardinality of V. A

```
Algorithm SmilarityControl( )
{
        SparsityControl( )
        for each graph in feature graph(G_f)
        {
          Initialize count zero vector(1, x, n) for each G_f
          for each graph in original graph list(G_l)
          {
            Compute similarity score
            Increment the count vector with similarity score
            Do Normalize
          }
        }
        for each graph in feature graph(G_f)
          Remove the nodes with values in counter vector < 0.25
}
```

Fig. 3. Algorithm for Similarity Function

stroll in a graph is a collection. A subtree design of height 2 rooted at node 1 is shown in Fig. 4. In the unfurled subtree pattern on the right, take note of the node repeats.

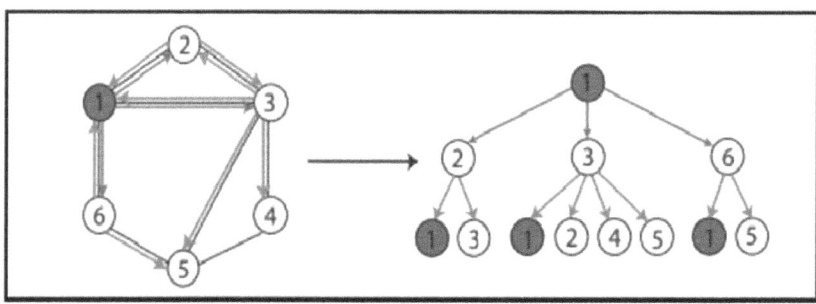

Fig. 4. A Subtree Pattern with a Height of 2 and a Node 1 as its Root.

The Support Vector Machine (SVM) is a well-known supervised learning technique for handling classification and regression problems, despite the fact that it is primarily employed for classification in machine learning. The SVM algorithm looks for the optimum decision boundary or hyperplane that can partition the n-dimensional space into classes in order to quickly categorize new data points in the future. The Support Vector Machine (SVM) algorithm is named after support vectors, which are the extreme cases or points that help create the hyperplane. Figure 5 provides an example of how to divide two different groups using a decision boundary or hyperplane. In this proposed approach, the 1-dimensional variant of the Weisfeiler-Lehman test of isomorphism as in Fig. 6, popularly known as naive-vertex-refinement, is applied. Consider a scenario in which we want to establish whether two graphs, G and G′, are isomorphic. The one-dimensional Weisfeiler-Lehman test is iterated; these iterations are denoted by the letter I and are made up of the stages in Algorithm 1's description. Consider a scenario in which we want to establish whether two graphs, G and G′, are isomorphic.

Algorithm 1 One iteration of the 1-dim. Weisfeiler-Lehman test of graph isomorphism

1: Multiset-label determination
   - For $i = 0$, set $M_i(v) := l_0(v) = \ell(v)$. [2]
   - For $i > 0$, assign a multiset-label $M_i(v)$ to each node v in G and G' which consists of the multiset $\{l_{i-1}(u) | u \in \mathcal{N}(v)\}$.
2: Sorting each multiset
   - Sort elements in $M_i(v)$ in ascending order and concatenate them into a string $s_i(v)$.
   - Add $l_{i-1}(v)$ as a prefix to $s_i(v)$ and call the resulting string $s_i(v)$.
3: Label compression
   - Sort all of the strings $s_i(v)$ for all v from G and G' in ascending order.
   - Map each string $s_i(v)$ to a new compressed label, using a function $f : \Sigma^* \rightarrow \Sigma$ such that $f(s_i(v)) = f(s_i(w))$ if and only if $s_i(v) = s_i(w)$.
4: Relabeling
   - Set $l_i(v) := f(s_i(v))$ for all nodes in G and G'.

Fig. 5. Algorithm for Weisfeiler-Lehman test of graph isomorphism

The one-dimensional Weisfeiler-Lehman test is iterated; these iterations are denoted by the letter I and are made up of the stages in Algorithm 1's description. To do this, the node labels are added to along with the organized set of surrounding node labels. Then, until the node label sets of G and G diverge or n iterations have been completed, these procedures are repeated. Figure 7 and 8 illustrates the steps explianed. However, because the two graphs in the image have different initial label sets, the Weisfeiler-Lehman test would immediately recognize them as being non-isomorphic.

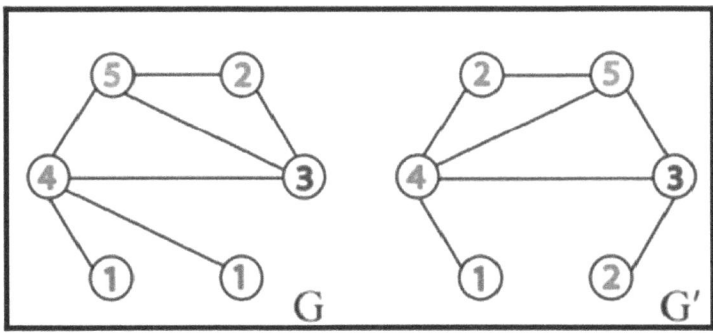

Fig. 6. Working of WL kernel for h Iterations - Given Two Labeled Graphs G and G′

For the compression of labels in step 4 in Fig. 9 and 10, sorting the collection of multisets enables a simple formulation and implementation of f: One maintains a counter variable for f that keeps track of how many different strings f has previously compressed. But, when a new string is encountered, one increases the counter by one and f assigns the new string's value.

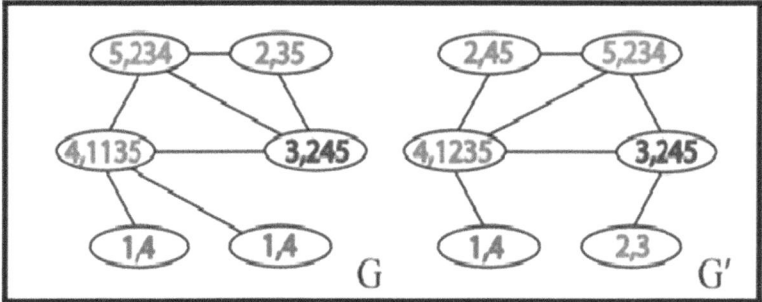

Fig. 7. Multiset-label Determination and Sorting

1,4	→	6	3,245	→	10
2,3	→	7	4,1135	→	11
2,35	→	8	4,1235	→	12
2,45	→	9	5,234	→	13

Fig. 8. Label Compression

The alphabet Σ has to be sufficiently large for f to be injective. Any other injective mapping will produce comparable outcomes. In order for f to be injective, the alphabet Σ must be sufficiently large. For two graphs, $|Σ| = 2n$ suffices. The Weisfeiler-Lehman algorithm terminates after step 4 of iteration i if $\{li(v)|v \in V\}$ 6 = $\{li(v')|v' \in V'\}$ mentioned in Fig. 11, if the sets of freshly produced labels in G and G' are not identical. Hence, the graphs are not isomorphic. After n iterations, if the sets are identical, either G and G' are isomorphic or the algorithm was unable to detect that they are not. As a side note, it points out that for practically all graphs, the 1-dimensional Weisfeiler-Lehman approach has been demonstrated to be a reliable isomorphism test.

Here, conducted is an experimental analysis of the Weisfeiler-Lehman subtree kernel's runtime performance contrasting the actions of two Weisfeiler-Lehman subtree (WL) kernelvariations during runtime [7]. The initial variation computes paired kernel values in O (N 2hm). The second variation simultaneously computes the kernel values on the data set in $O(Nhm + N\,2hn)$. As shown in Fig. 12, it shall refer to the first version as the *pairwise* WL and the second as the *global* WL.

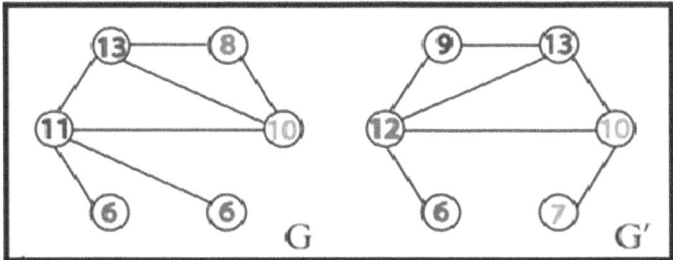

Fig. 9. Relabeling

$$\varphi_{WLsubtree}^{(1)}(G) = (2, 1, 1, 1, 1, 2, 0, 1, 0, 1, 1, 0, 1)$$

$$\varphi_{WLsubtree}^{(1)}(G') = (1, 2, 1, 1, 1, 1, 1, 0, 1, 1, 0, 1, 1)$$

Counts of original node labels | Counts of compressed node labels

$$k_{WLsubtree}^{(1)}(G,G') = <\varphi_{WLsubtree}^{(1)}(G), \varphi_{WLsubtree}^{(1)}(G')> = 11.$$

Fig. 10. Feature Vector Representations of G and G′

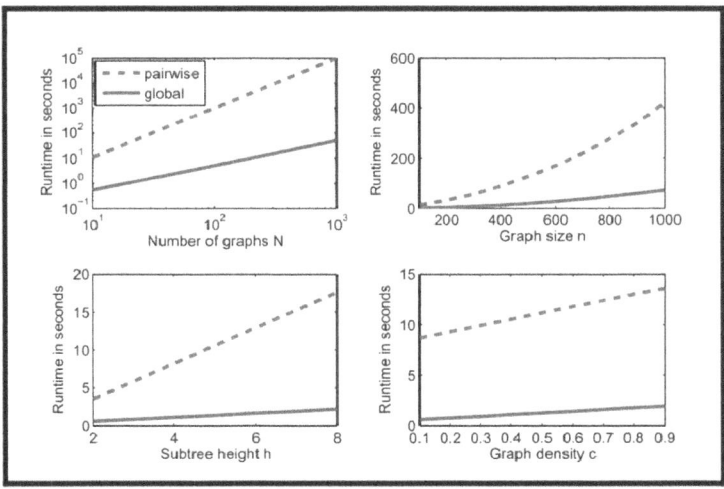

Fig. 11. Runtime in Seconds for Kernel Matrix Computation for the Weisfeiler Lehman Subtree Kernel

The ML model was built on the Tox21 dataset which was taken from [11]. This project uses the AR dataset on which the WL kernel and SVM algorithms have been applied for prediction. The total dataset size is 771 out of which 80% of data is used for training and 20% for testing.

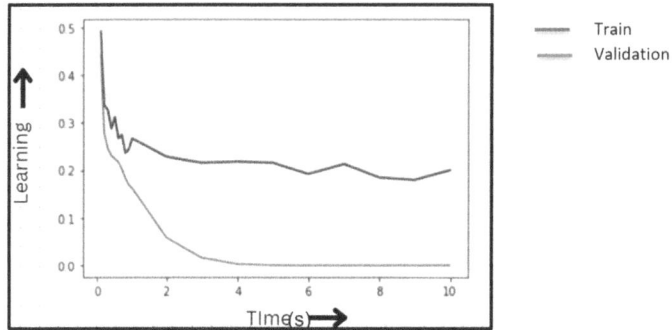

Fig. 12. Fitting the SVM

The algorithm is run for around 10 iterations, the results are plotted below in Fig. 13. The parameter C of SVM is set as 1. There are 397 graphs in total with all the classes. These graphs are split into training and test sets with a ratio of 0.1. The learning curve is a graphical representation that shows how the performance of a model improves as the amount of training data increases. Initially, with a small amount of training data, the model may perform poorly on the test set due to limited information. However, as more training data is used, the model's performance on the test set generally improves, reflecting a decrease in the test error. It helps us understand how the model's accuracy or error changes with respect to the training dataset size.

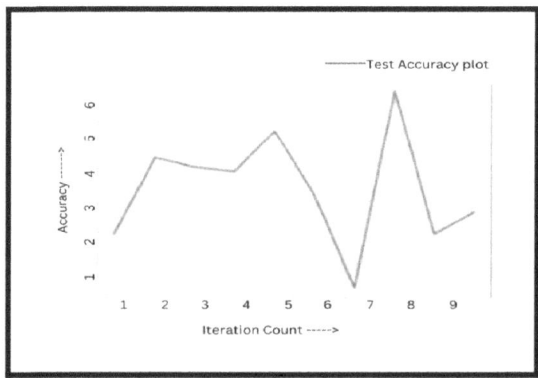

Fig. 13. Test Accuracy Plot on Each Iteration

The graph isomorphism test known as WL (Weisfeiler-Lehman) iterations is used to assess if two graphs are isomorphic or not. The Weisfeiler-Lehman algorithm assigns labels to nodes depending on the labels of their neighbors through iterative refinement. The labels are adjusted at each iteration based on the labels of the surrounding nodes, and the process is continued until convergence. Each node is given a new label at each iteration of the WL algorithm based on the multiset of its current label and the labels of its neighbors. Repeating the procedure until no more improvements are possible. So in Fig. 14, as it can be seen, 6 iterations is the most optimal. The complexity of the graphs under comparison determines how many iterations are necessary for the WL method to converge. In general, more iterations will be needed for more complex graphs. When executing the WL algorithm, the number of iterations can be given as a parameter. The labeled graphs that are produced after the WL algorithm has converged can be compared to determine whether or not they are isomorphic. Two graphs are said to be isomorphic if they have the same set of labels after the same quantity of iterations. They are not isomorphic if not.

```
bal accu--------  0.49480968858131485
100%|██████████| 1063/1063 [00:56<00:00, 18.88it/s]
100%|██████████| 1063/1063 [00:58<00:00, 18.12it/s]
100%|██████████| 1063/1063 [00:56<00:00, 18.83it/s]
100%|██████████| 1063/1063 [00:56<00:00, 18.71it/s]
100%|██████████| 1063/1063 [01:00<00:00, 17.61it/s]
0.997632119505529
-1.1702545266115745
0.0
val accu--------  0.9897260273972602  roc_test-----------  0.5847750865051903
[[289   0]
 [  3   0]]
bal accu--------  0.5
100%|██████████| 1063/1063 [00:57<00:00, 18.54it/s]
100%|██████████| 1063/1063 [00:58<00:00, 18.08it/s]
100%|██████████| 1063/1063 [00:56<00:00, 18.77it/s]
100%|██████████| 1063/1063 [00:56<00:00, 18.70it/s]
100%|██████████| 1063/1063 [00:59<00:00, 17.75it/s]
21.659179726041984
-104.37325788505309
0.0
val accu--------  0.9863013698630136  roc test-----------  0.41753171856978083
```

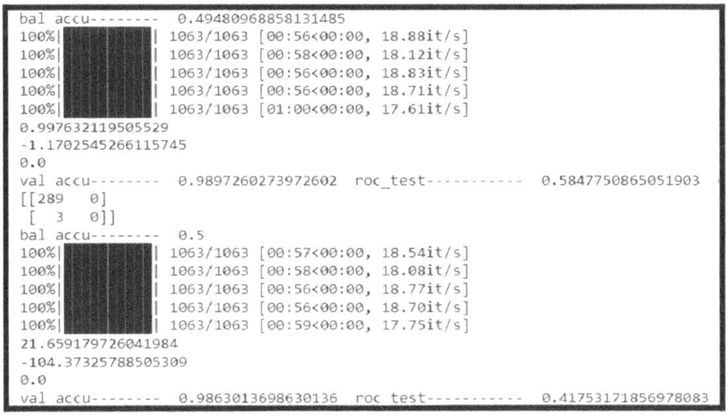

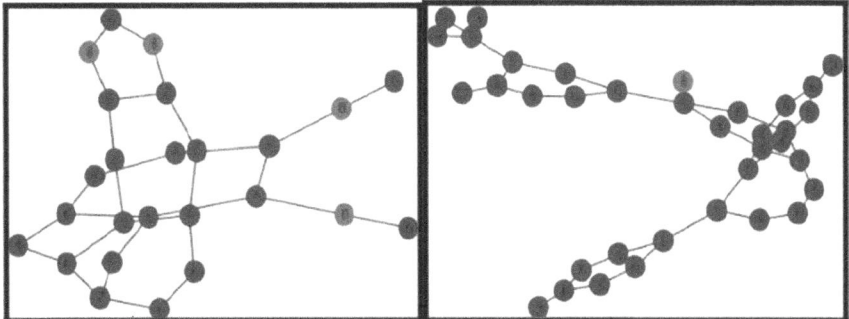

Fig. 14. Value and ROC Accuracy Tests

Fig. 15. Important Nodes in a Molecule (Color figure online)

Precision and AUC-ROC score are two often employed evaluation measures depicted in Fig. 15 for classification models that are associated with *value* and *ROC accuracy*, respectively. The precision of a classification model's accuracy positive predictions is measured. It is calculated as the ratio of the total number of the model's positive predictions to the number of genuine positives i.e., true positives plus false positives. When a model has a high precision score, it is making very few erroneous positive predictions. Area Under the Curve of the Receiver Operating Characteristic, or AUC-ROC score, measures how well a categorization model performs overall. It considers the model's true positive rate (TPR) as well as false positive rate (FPR) for a variety of potential categorization thresholds. Higher AUC-ROC values indicate better performance, which spans from 0 to 1. Figure 15 shows important nodes that are marked by the algorithm in the form of red color and the rest are blue in color. The important nodes are then given further to the classification module where it is grouped as toxic and non toxic substructures. The toxic molecules depicted in this diagram consist of two chemical structures. The nodes highlighted in red within the diagram signify the specific nodes responsible for the toxicity. These nodes exhibit a greater significance and influence towards the conclusion of the weighted WL kernel iterations. When these substructures are present within molecules, they contribute to the manifestation of toxicity.

The identification of substructures that can cause toxicity in a biomolecule is an important aspect of toxicological research. Several substructures or functional groups have been associated with potential toxicity. Here are some examples of substructures that have been linked to potential toxicity in biomolecules. Certain reactive functional groups, such as epoxides, quinones, acyl halides, and nitroso compounds, can form covalent adducts with cellular macromolecules, leading to cellular damage and potential toxicity. Alkylating agents, such as alkyl halides or alkylating drugs, have the ability to transfer alkyl groups to nucleophilic sites in biomolecules, causing DNA damage, protein dysfunction, and potential toxicity. Certain substructures or ligands that possess metal-binding capabilities, such as thiols, dithiocarbamates, or chelating agents, can interact with essential metal ions, disrupting metal homeostasis and resulting in adverse biological effects. Some functional groups, such as aromatic amines or nitro compounds, can be metabolically activated by enzymatic processes, leading to the formation of reactive intermediates that can cause DNA damage or protein dysfunction. It's important to consider that the presence of these substructures does not always indicate toxicity, that is why we use this ML model to increase the accuracy by looking into the effect of the substructures in the neighborhood of the molecules mentioned above.

5 Conclusions

Predicting the toxicity of biomolecules is crucial an an essential step in the drug discovery process is predicting the toxicity of biomolecules. It enables scientists to spot potentially harmful substances early on in the medication development process and save time and money by avoiding molecules with a low likelihood of being safe. Biomolecules, especially hazardous ones, can have a big effect on the environment. Identification and mitigation of novel compounds' environmental effects can be aided by forecasting the toxicity of biomolecules. Regulations for the use and disposal of chemicals, especially harmful ones, are in place in many nations. Biomolecule toxicity forecasting can help ensure legal compliance, prevent fines, and ensure regulatory compliance. For the sake of everyone's health, biomolecule toxicity predictions are crucial. The usage of toxic biomolecules in food, medication, or other consumer goods might have detrimental effects on one's health. Researchers can cut down on the number of animals used in testing by identifying potentially harmful chemicals early in the medication development process. Predicting the toxicity of biomolecules is a crucial step in the development of new drugs, the preservation of the environment, adherence to legal requirements, improvement of human health, and the treatment of animals. It can assist with ensuring that new compounds are secure for usage by people as well as the environment. Overall, the application of the WL kernel to predict the toxicity of biomolecules opens a wide range of exciting research paths, and advancements in this area may have substantial implications for drug discovery, environmental toxicology, and public health.

References

1. Pierre, M., Jean-Philippe, V.: Graph kernels based on tree patterns for molecules. Mach. Learn. **75**, 55–67 (2006)
2. Patle, A., Chouhan, D.: SVM kernel functions for classification. In: International Conference on Advances in Technology and Engineering, pp. 1–9 (2013)
3. Jiang, J., Wang, R., Wei, G.W.: GGL-tox: geometric graph learning for toxicity prediction. J. Chem. Inf. Model. **4**(6), 1691–1700 (2021)
4. Ralaivola, L., Swamidass, S.J., Saigo, H., Baldi, P.: Graph kernels for chemical informatics. Neural Netw. **18**(8), 1093–1110 (2005)
5. Kriege, N.M., Johansson, F.D., Morris, C.: A survey on graph kernels. Appl. Netw. Sci. **5**(6), 10–18 (2020)
6. Höppner, F., Jahnke, M.: Enriched Weisfeiler-lehman kernel for improved graph clustering of source code. In: Advances in Intelligent Data Analysis XVIII, vol. 12080, pp. 248–260. Springer (2020)
7. Shervashidze, N., Schweitzer, P., Jan, E., Leeuwen, V., Mehlhorn, K., Borgwardt, K.: Weisfeiler-Lehman graph kernels. J. Mach. Learn. Res. **1**, 1–48 (2010)
8. Barratt, M.D.: Prediction of toxicity from chemical structure. Cell Biol. Toxicol. **16**, 1–13 (2000)
9. Mayr, A., Klambauer, G., Unterthiner, T., Hochreiter, S.: DeepTox: toxicity prediction using deep learning. Front. Environ. Sci. **3** (2016)
10. Yang, H., Sun, L., Li, W., Liu, G., Tang, Y.: Corrigendum: "in silico prediction of chemical toxicity for drug design using machine learning methods and structural alerts." Front. Chem. **6**, 129 (2018)
11. Wu, Z., Pan, S., Chen, F., Long, G., Zhang, C., Yu, P.S.: A comprehensive survey on graph neural networks. IEEE Trans. Neural Netw. Learn. Syst. **32**(1), 4–24 (2021)
12. Bagherian, M., Sabeti, E., Wang, K., Sartor, M.A., Nikolovska-Coleska, Z., Najarian, K.: Machine learning approaches and databases for prediction of drug-target interaction. Briefings Bioinform. **22**(1), 247–269 (2021)
13. Kang, J., Park, Y.-J., Lee, J., Wang, S.-H., Eom, D.-S.: Novel leakage detection by ensemble CNN-SVM and graph-based localization in water distribution systems. IEEE Trans. Industr. Electron. **65**(5), 4279–4289 (2018)
14. Chavan, S., Friedman, R., Nicholls, I.: Acute toxicity-supported chronic toxicity prediction: a k-nearest neighbor coupled read-across strategy. Int. J. Mol. Sci. **16**, 11659–11677 (2015)

A New Modified Juchez Distribution: Induced Juchez Distribution with Its Properties and Application in Intelligent Irrigation System Data

M. Subhashree(✉) and C. Subramanian

Department of Statistics, Annamalai University, Chidambaram, Tamil Nadu, India
subhashreem17@gmail.com

Abstract. This manuscript presents a unique statistical framework termed the induced Juchez distribution, which represents an innovative alteration of the Juchez distribution. This model is refined through the application of a specific variant of a weighted probability function, referred to as the induced probability function. A comprehensive exposition of various statistical properties is provided, and the parameters pertaining to the probability distribution function are estimated employing the maximum likelihood estimation technique. Ultimately, to substantiate the superior fit of the newly modified Juchez distribution, a practical dataset pertaining to an intelligent irrigation system is illustrated and contrasted with the induced Garima distribution.

Keywords: Induced function · Reliability analysis · Bonferroni and Lorenz curves · Juchez distribution · Order Statistics · Maximum likelihood estimation

1 Introduction

The notion of weighted distribution was originally introduced by Sir Ronald Aylmer Fisher (1934) [1]. The function of weighted distribution encompasses both modeling and the interaction of data. Moreover, the concept of weighted distribution has historical roots in the domain of frequency estimation, which serves as a mechanism for decision-making. In (1954) [2], Epstein, B. and Sobel, M. articulated principal findings pertaining to life tests conducted utilizing exponential distribution. They further established that these outcomes could be employed to estimate the slope while also delineating the boundaries of the stress level. The principles of fiducial distribution and Bayes' distribution within the exponential family were succinctly addressed and exemplified along with the requisite and sufficient conditions for both fiducial and Bayes' distributions by Lindley, D. V. (1958) [3]. Subsequently, this framework was expanded by Rao (1965), as weighted distributions found applications across diverse domains including medicine, reliability, ecology, behavioral sciences, finance, and insurance, etc., thus, facilitating the advancement of statistical models [4].

The gamma distribution, characterized by a scale parameter and a shape parameter, was elucidated by Hogg, R. V. and Craig, A. T. (1978) [5]. The concept of a mixture of two distributions was proposed and expounded upon by Lindsay, B. G. (1995) [6]. The mixing proportion associated with this amalgamation of two distributions was articulated and extensively analyzed by Friedman, J. H. (2009) [7], who also elucidated the derivation of its corresponding new probability density function. A novel family of lifetime distributions was introduced by Abd-Elrahman (2013) through the utilization of order statistics for independent random samples in the survival function, taking into account average renewal failure rates.

Furthermore, he computed the parameters of this new lifetime distribution utilizing maximum likelihood estimation and interval estimation techniques. In conclusion, he presented two real-world datasets to illustrate the enhanced fit of this distribution [8]. In 2020, Brijesh, P. S. and Utpal, D. D. introduced a novel distribution known as the induced Garima distribution, employing a specific variant of a weighted function referred to as the induced function [9].

2 Juchez Distribution

The Juchez probability distribution characterized by a singular parameter, was proposed by Udochukwu. V.E. and Julian. I.M. (2022) [10]. This distribution represents a synthesis of two distributions, namely, the exponential distribution and the gamma distribution, defined by appropriate parameters that include a fixed parameter λ and two shape parameters, specially $\alpha = 2, \alpha = 4$. In the next step, the probability distribution function (p.d.f.) and its cumulative distribution function (c.d.f.) related to this distribution are detailed by

$$f_{JD}(z,\lambda) = \frac{\lambda^4}{\lambda^3 + \lambda^2 + 6}(1 + z + z^3)e^{-\lambda z}; z > 0, \lambda > 0 \qquad (1)$$

$$F_{JD}(z,\lambda) = 1 - \left[1 + \frac{\lambda z(\lambda^2 + \lambda^2 z^2 + 3\lambda z + 6)}{\lambda^3 + \lambda^2 + 6}\right]e^{-\lambda z}; z > 0, \lambda > 0 \qquad (2)$$

3 Induced Juchez Distribution (IJD)

The induced probability function represents a unique instance of a weighted function, akin to length-biased, size-biased, and area-biased functions, as elucidated by Gupta, R. C. and Kirmani, S. N. U. A. (1990) [11]. As established, the probability density function (p.d.f.) of the weighted function is expressed as

$$f_w(z,\lambda) = \frac{w(z)f(z,\lambda)}{E(w(z))}; z > 0, \lambda > 0 \qquad (3)$$

where, $w(z)$ denotes a positive weighted function and

$$E(w(z)) = \int_0^\infty w(z)f(z,\lambda)dz < \infty \qquad (4)$$

In the aforementioned weighted function, by selecting $w(z) = h(z)^{-1}$, where,

$$h(z) = \frac{f(z,\lambda)}{1 - F(z)} \tag{5}$$

is identified as the hazard rate function, the weighted function can be simplified to the induced or equilibrium function. This notion was articulated by Patil, G. P. and Rao, C. R. (1977) [12]. Consequently, the induced function is defined as

$$g^*(z,\lambda) = \frac{1 - F(z,\lambda)}{E(z,\lambda)}; z > 0, \lambda > 0 \tag{6}$$

where,

$$E(z,\lambda) = \int_0^\infty z f(z,\lambda) dz \tag{7}$$

By substituting Eq. 1 into 7, we derive,

$$E(z,\lambda) = \frac{(\lambda^3 + 2\lambda^2 + 24)}{\lambda(\lambda^3 + \lambda^2 + 6)} \tag{8}$$

Now, upon applying the induced function to the Juchez distribution, we ascertain the induced Juchez distribution (IJD) as delineated below:

$$1 - F(z,\lambda) = 1 - \left\{1 - \left[1 + \frac{\lambda z(\lambda^2 + \lambda^2 z^2 + 3\lambda z + 6)}{\lambda^3 + \lambda^2 + 6}\right]e^{-\lambda z}\right\} \tag{9}$$

$$1 - F(z,\lambda) = \frac{(\lambda^3 + \lambda^2 + 6) + \lambda z(\lambda^2 + \lambda^2 z^2 + 3\lambda z + 6)e^{-\lambda z}}{\lambda^3 + \lambda^2 + 6} \tag{10}$$

By substituting 8 and 1 into 6, we acquire, the p.d.f. of IJD as

$$g^*(z,\lambda) = \tfrac{\lambda}{\lambda^3 + 2\lambda^2 + 24}\left[(\lambda^3 + \lambda^2 + 6) + \lambda z(\lambda^2 + \lambda^2 z^2 + 3\lambda z + 6)e^{-\lambda z}\right]; z > 0, \lambda > 0 \tag{11}$$

Further, the c.d.f. of IJD is articulated as

$$G(z,\lambda) = \int_0^\infty g^*(z,\lambda) dz; z > 0, \lambda > 0 \tag{12}$$

$$G(z,\lambda) = \tfrac{1}{\lambda^3 + 2\lambda^2 + 24}\left[(\lambda^3 + \lambda^2 + 6)(1 + e^{-\lambda z}) + \lambda^2 \gamma(2,\lambda z) + \gamma(4,\lambda z) + 3\gamma(3,\lambda z) + 6\gamma(2,\lambda z)\right]; z > 0, \lambda > 0 \tag{13}$$

The graphical depiction of both the p.d.f. and c.d.f. for the IJD across various parameter values λ is illustrated below (Figs. 1, 2, 3 and 4):

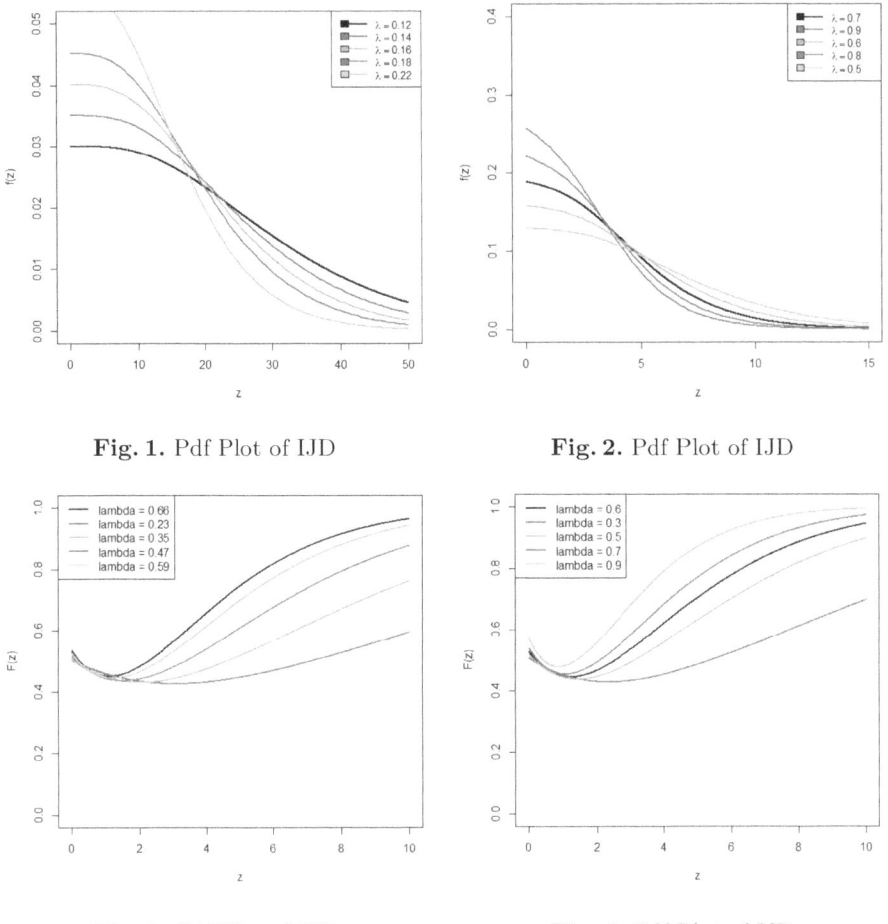

Fig. 1. Pdf Plot of IJD

Fig. 2. Pdf Plot of IJD

Fig. 3. Cdf Plot of IJD

Fig. 4. Cdf Plot of IJD

4 Properties of Induced Juchez Distribution

4.1 Moments

Moments constitute a property of the distribution that characterizes its attributes. They serve an important purpose in evaluating the shape of the dataset and illustrating the spatial dynamics among data points within the distribution. The moments of the IJD have been derived to encapsulate the characteristics of the proposed model. Consequently, the rth order moment $E(Z^r)$ of the IJD is expressed as

$$\mu_r^{'} = E(z^r) = \int_0^\infty z^r g^*(z, \lambda) dz \qquad (14)$$

$$\mu_r^{'} = \frac{1}{\lambda'(\lambda^3 + 2\lambda^2 + 24)} \left[(\lambda^3 + \lambda^2 + 6)\Gamma(r+1) + \lambda^2 \Gamma(r+2) + \Gamma(r+4) + 3\Gamma(r+3) + 6\Gamma(r+1) \right] \qquad (15)$$

In Eq. 15, when r = 1, the 1st moment of IJD is represented by

$$\mu_1' = E(z) = \frac{(\lambda^3 + \lambda^2 + 6) + 2\lambda^2 + 24 + 18 + 6}{\lambda(\lambda^3 + 2\lambda^2 + 24)} = \frac{\lambda^3 + 3\lambda^2 + 54}{\lambda(\lambda^3 + 2\lambda^2 + 24)} \quad (16)$$

where $\mu_1' = E(z)$ is recognized as the mean of the IJD. Similarly, when r = 2, 3, 4 in Eq. 3, the outcomes will be

$$\mu_2' = \frac{2\lambda^3 + 8\lambda^2 + 216}{\lambda^2(\lambda^3 + 2\lambda^2 + 24)} \quad (17)$$

$$\mu_3' = \frac{6\lambda^3 + 30\lambda^2 + 1152}{\lambda^3(\lambda^3 + 2\lambda^2 + 24)} \quad (18)$$

$$\mu_4' = \frac{24\lambda^3 + 144\lambda^2 + 7488}{\lambda^4(\lambda^3 + 2\lambda^2 + 24)} \quad (19)$$

Subsequently, the variance of induced Juchez distribution (IJD) is articulated as

$$Var(z) = E(z^2) - [E(z)]^2 \quad (20)$$

$$Var(z) = \frac{2\lambda^3 + 8\lambda^2 + 216}{\lambda^2(\lambda^3 + 2\lambda^2 + 24)} - \left[\frac{\lambda^3 + 3\lambda^2 + 54}{\lambda(\lambda^3 + 2\lambda^2 + 24)}\right]^2 \quad (21)$$

$$Var(z) = \frac{\lambda^6 + 4\lambda^5 - \lambda^4 + 180\lambda^3 + 120\lambda^2 + 720}{\lambda^2 [\lambda^3 + 2\lambda^2 + 24]^2} \quad (22)$$

4.2 Reliability Analysis

Reliability analysis serves as a metric for assessing the time to failure relative to the existence time. In this segment, we will explicate the reliability tools, including the reliability function, hazard or failure rate, reverse hazard rate, and the Mills ratio of the IJD.

The reliability function of the IJD is derived as

$$R(z) = 1 - G(z, \lambda) = 1 - \frac{[(\lambda^3 + \lambda^2 + 6)(1 + e^{-\lambda z}) + \lambda^2 \gamma(2, \lambda z) + \gamma(4, \lambda z) + 3\gamma(3, \lambda z) + 6\gamma(2, \lambda z)]}{\lambda^3 + 2\lambda^2 + 24} \quad (23)$$

The hazard function, commonly referred to as the hazard rate, instantaneous failure rate, or force of mortality, is defined by

$$h(z) = \frac{g^*(z, \lambda)}{1 - G(z, \lambda)} = \frac{\lambda\left[(\lambda^3 + \lambda^2 + 6) + \lambda z(\lambda^2 + \lambda^2 z^2 + 3\lambda z + 6)e^{-\lambda z}\right]}{[(\lambda^3 + \lambda^2 + 6)(1 + e^{-\lambda z}) + \lambda^2 \gamma(2, \lambda z) + \gamma(4, \lambda z) + 3\gamma(3, \lambda z) + 6\gamma(2, \lambda z)]} \quad (24)$$

Moreover, the Mills ratio of the induced Juchez distribution (IJD) is expressed as

$$Mills\,Ratio = \frac{1}{h(z)} = \frac{[(\lambda^3 + \lambda^2 + 6)(1 + e^{-\lambda z}) + \lambda^2 \gamma(2, \lambda z) + \gamma(4, \lambda z) + 3\gamma(3, \lambda z) + 6\gamma(2, \lambda z)]}{\lambda[(\lambda^3 + \lambda^2 + 6) + \lambda z(\lambda^2 + \lambda^2 z^2 + 3\lambda z + 6)e^{-\lambda z}]} \quad (25)$$

4.3 Moment Generating Function and Characteristic Function

The moment generating function serves to facilitate the computation of moments. It delineates the characteristics of the distribution associated with a random variable and establishes the likelihood of the distribution's occurrence. Assuming Z possesses an IJD, we can ascertain the moment generating function of Z as

$$M_z(t) = E(e^{tz}) = \int_0^\infty e^{tz} g^*(z,\lambda) dz \qquad (26)$$

Utilizing Taylor's expansion,

$$M_z(t) = \int_0^\infty \sum_{j=0}^\infty \frac{t^j}{j!} z^j g^*(z,\lambda) dz \qquad (27)$$

$$M_z(t) = \frac{1}{\lambda^3 + 2\lambda^2 + 24} \sum_{j=0}^\infty \frac{t^j}{j!\lambda^j} (\lambda^3 + \lambda^2 + 6)\Gamma(j+1) + \lambda^2 \Gamma(j+2) + \Gamma(j+4) + 3\Gamma(j+3) + 6\Gamma(j+1) \qquad (28)$$

The characteristic function is employed to delineate the characteristics of the distribution of a random variable, akin to the moment generating function, and is also referred to as an indicator function. It is inherently dependent upon the distribution function, and while it invariably exists, it cannot be infinite, in contrast to the moment generating function which may not always exist. We will derive the characteristic function of the IJD in a similar fashion as

$$\phi_z(t) = \frac{1}{\lambda^3 + 2\lambda^2 + 24} \sum_0^\infty \frac{(it)^j}{j!\lambda^j} (\lambda^3 + \lambda^2 + 6)\Gamma(j+1) + \lambda^2 \Gamma(j+2) + \Gamma(j+4) + 3\Gamma(j+3) + 6\Gamma(j+1) \qquad (29)$$

4.4 Order Statistics

The order statistics serve the purpose of organizing sample values in an ascending sequence. This methodology is employed as a mechanism to reduce the time associated with the analysis of life testing data sets. It encompasses various applications including production workflows, insurance contract evaluations, and the estimation of distribution parameters, among others. Imagine that the symbols $Z_1, Z_2, \ldots, Z_n$ signify variables picked randomly from a continuous set. The function that describes the likelihood density is represented as $f_z(z)$, whereas the total density function is denoted as $F_z(z)$. Within this framework, one might assert that $Z_{(1)}, Z_{(2)}, \ldots, Z_{(n)}$ embody the sequence of order statistics resulting from a random sample.

Consequently, the probability density function pertaining to $Z_{(r)}$ in r^{th} order statistics is elucidated by

$$g^*_{z(r)}(z;\lambda) = \frac{n!}{(n-r)!(r-1)!} g^*(z,\lambda) [G(z,\lambda)]^{r-1} [1 - G(z,\lambda)]^{n-r} \qquad (30)$$

Incorporating Eqs. 11 and 13 into Eq. 30, we obtain,

$$g^*_{z(r)}(z;\lambda) = Term1 * Term2 * Term3 \qquad (31)$$

where,

$Term1 = \frac{n!}{(n-r)!(r-1)!} \frac{\lambda}{(\lambda^3+2\lambda^2+24)}[(\lambda^3 + \lambda^2 + 6) + \lambda z(\lambda^2 + \lambda^2 z^2 + 3\lambda z + 6)e^{-\lambda z}],$

$Term2 = \left[\frac{1}{\lambda^3+2\lambda^2+24}[(\lambda^3 + \lambda^2 + 6)(1 + e^{-\lambda z}) + \lambda^2 \gamma(2,\lambda z) + \gamma(4,\lambda z) + 3\gamma(3,\lambda z) + 6\gamma(2,\lambda z)]\right]^{r-1},$

$Term3 = \left[1 - \frac{1}{\lambda^3+2\lambda^2+24}[(\lambda^3 + \lambda^2 + 6)(1 + e^{-\lambda z}) + \lambda^2 \gamma(2,\lambda z) + \gamma(4,\lambda z) + 3\gamma(3,\lambda z) + 6\gamma(2,\lambda z)]\right]^{n-r}$

Subsequently, the probability density function for the higher order statistic $Z_{(n)}$ can be ascertained as

$$g^*_{z(r)}(z;\lambda) = Term-A * Term-B \qquad (32)$$

where,

$Term-A = \frac{n\lambda}{(\lambda^3+2\lambda^2+24)}[(\lambda^3 + \lambda^2 + 6) + \lambda z(\lambda^2 + \lambda^2 z^2 + 3\lambda z + 6)e^{-\lambda z}],$

$Term-B = \left[\frac{1}{\lambda^3+2\lambda^2+24}[(\lambda^3 + \lambda^2 + 6)(1 + e^{-\lambda z}) + \lambda^2 \gamma(2,\lambda z) + \gamma(4,\lambda z) + 3\gamma(3,\lambda z) + 6\gamma(2,\lambda z)]\right]^{n-1},$

Therefore, the probability density function for the 1st order statistic $Z_{(1)}$ can be determined as

$$g^*_{z(r)}(z;\lambda) = Term-I * Term-II \qquad (33)$$

where,

$Term-I = \frac{n\lambda}{(\lambda^3+2\lambda^2+24)}[(\lambda^3 + \lambda^2 + 6) + \lambda z(\lambda^2 + \lambda^2 z^2 + 3\lambda z + 6)e^{-\lambda z}],$

$Term-II = \left[1 - \frac{1}{\lambda^3+2\lambda^2+24}[(\lambda^3 + \lambda^2 + 6)(1 + e^{-\lambda z}) + \lambda^2 \gamma(2,\lambda z) + \gamma(4,\lambda z) + 3\gamma(3,\lambda z) + 6\gamma(2,\lambda z)]\right]^{n-1}$

4.5 Maximum Likelihood Estimator (MLE) and Fisher Information Matrix

The maximum likelihood estimation represents a methodology for deducing the parameters of a distribution through the maximization of the likelihood function. This statistical approach finds extensive application within the realm of machine learning. A principal advantage of this technique is its convergence to the true parameter value with a probability of one. The maximum likelihood estimator is recognized as the most robust numerical stability estimator for the parameters of the distribution when juxtaposed with alternative estimation techniques. Consequently, the parameters of the Induced Juchez Distribution (IJD) estimated via this methodology are presented below:

Let $Z_{(1)}, Z_{(2)}, ..., Z_{(n)}$ denote the randomly drawn samples of size n from the IJD, thus, the likelihood function for IJD is

$$L(z;\lambda) = \prod_{(i=1)}^{n} g^*(z,\lambda) = \lambda^n / [\lambda^3 + 2\lambda^2 + 24]^n \prod_{(i=1)}^{n} [\lambda^3 + \lambda^2 + 6 + \lambda^3 z_i + \lambda^3 z_i^3 + 3\lambda^2 z_i^2 + 6\lambda z_i] e^{(-\lambda z_i)} \qquad (34)$$

The natural log likelihood function is

$$\log L = n \log \lambda - n \log(\lambda^3 + 2\lambda^2 + 24) + \sum_{i=1}^{n} \log[\lambda^3 + \lambda^2 + 6 + \lambda^3 z_i + \lambda^3 z_i^3 + 3\lambda^2 z_i^2 + 6\lambda z_i] - \lambda \sum_{i=1}^{n} z_i \tag{35}$$

By differentiating Eq. 35 concerning λ, the maximum likelihood estimate for λ can be derived as

$$\frac{\partial \log L}{\partial \lambda} = \frac{n}{\lambda} - \frac{n(3\lambda^2 + 4\lambda)}{(\lambda^3 + 2\lambda^2 + 24)} + \sum_{i=1}^{n} \frac{[3\lambda^2 + 2\lambda + 3\lambda^2 z_i + 3\lambda^2 z_i^3 + 6\lambda z_i^2 + 6z_i]}{[\lambda^3 + \lambda^2 + 6 + \lambda^3 z_i + \lambda^3 z_i^3 + 3\lambda^2 z_i^2 + 6\lambda z_i]} - \sum_{i=1}^{n} z_i = 0 \tag{36}$$

The resolution of the system of non-linear equations is notably complex due to the intricate nature of the likelihood Eq. 36. Consequently, we employ R and Wolfram Mathematica to facilitate the estimation of the requisite parameters.

4.6 Likelihood Ratio Test

The likelihood ratio test constitutes a robust methodology for assessing model assumptions. It delineates the impact of each effect on the model. These effects can be articulated through the derivation of $-2\log$ likelihood of the proposed model. The objective of this test is to appraise the quality of fit between two models by contrasting their likelihood ratios. Envision $Z_{(1)}, Z_{(2)}, \ldots, Z_{(n)}$, as being samples selected at random from the IJD. To evaluate the random samples of size n for IJD, the hypothesis is formulated as

$H_0 : f(z) = f_{JD}(z, \lambda)$ against $H_1 : f(z) = g^*(z, \lambda)$

To ascertain whether the random sample of size n conforms to the Juchez distribution or the induced Juchez distribution, the likelihood ratio is computed as

$$\Delta = \prod_{i=1}^{n} \frac{g^*(z, \lambda)}{f_{JD}(z, \lambda)} = \frac{[\lambda^3 + \lambda^2 + 6]^n}{\lambda^{3n} [\lambda^3 + 2\lambda^2 + 24]^n} \prod_{i=1}^{n} \frac{[(\lambda^3 + \lambda^2 + 6) + \lambda z_i (\lambda^2 + \lambda^2 z_i^2 + 3\lambda z_i + 6)]}{z_i^3 + z_i + 1} \tag{37}$$

Hence, the null hypothesis is rejected if

$$\Delta = \frac{[\lambda^3 + \lambda^2 + 6]^n}{\lambda^{3n} [\lambda^3 + 2\lambda^2 + 24]^n} \prod_{i=1}^{n} \frac{[(\lambda^3 + \lambda^2 + 6) + \lambda z_i (\lambda^2 + \lambda^2 z_i^2 + 3\lambda z_i + 6)]}{z_i^3 + z_i + 1} > k \tag{38}$$

$$\Delta = \prod_{i=1}^{n} \frac{[(\lambda^3 + \lambda^2 + 6) + \lambda z_i (\lambda^2 + \lambda^2 z_i^2 + 3\lambda z_i + 6)]}{z_i^3 + z_i + 1} > k \frac{[\lambda^3 + \lambda^2 + 6]^n}{\lambda^{3n} [\lambda^3 + 2\lambda^2 + 24]^n} \tag{39}$$

$$\Delta = \prod_{i=1}^{n} \frac{[(\lambda^3 + \lambda^2 + 6) + \lambda z_i (\lambda^2 + \lambda^2 z_i^2 + 3\lambda z_i + 6)]}{z_i^3 + z_i + 1} > k^* \tag{40}$$

where,

$$k^* = k\frac{[\lambda^3 + \lambda^2 + 6]^n}{\lambda^{3n}[\lambda^3 + 2\lambda^2 + 24]^n} > 0 \qquad (41)$$

It can be inferred that for an extensive sample size, 2 log follows a chi-square distribution with one degree of freedom. Thus, the chi-square distribution is used to calculate the p-value. If the probability that $p(\Delta^* > k^*)$, where $k^* = \prod_{i=1}^{n} z_i$ falls under the established significance threshold and $\prod_{i=1}^{n} z_i$ is the observed value of the statistic Δ^*, then, the null hypothesis will be dismissed.

4.7 Bonferroni and Lorenz Curves

In the year 1936, Bonferroni, C. E. introduced the Bonferroni and Lorenz curves [13]. The disparities present within a population can be quantitatively assessed through the utilization of these curves. They offer a lucid graphical depiction of disparities in income or wealth distribution. The weight of their influence is markedly clear in the sector of economics. Adjusting p-values effectively is largely dependent on the Bonferroni curve, which helps in minimizing Type I error risks. Conversely, the Lorenz curve illustrates the proportion of the population. The provision of both the Bonferroni and Lorenz curves is attributed to established statistical methodologies.

$$B(p) = \frac{1}{p\mu_1'} \int_0^q z g^*(z, \lambda) dz \qquad (42)$$

and

$$L(p) = \frac{1}{\mu_1'} \int_0^q z g^*(z, \lambda) dz \qquad (43)$$

where,

$$\mu_1' = \frac{\lambda^3 + 3\lambda^2 + 54}{\lambda(\lambda^3 + 2\lambda^2 + 24)}; q = F^{-1}(p) \qquad (44)$$

$$B(p) = \frac{1}{p(\lambda^3+3\lambda^2+54)}\left[(\lambda^3+\lambda^2+6)\gamma(2,\lambda q)+\lambda^2\gamma(3,\lambda q)+\gamma(4,\lambda q)+3\gamma(3,\lambda q)+6\gamma(2,\lambda q)\right] \qquad (45)$$

$$L(p) = p(B(p)) = \frac{1}{(\lambda^3+3\lambda^2+54)}\left[(\lambda^3+\lambda^2+6)\gamma(2,\lambda q)+\lambda^2\gamma(3,\lambda q)+\gamma(4,\lambda q)+3\gamma(3,\lambda q)+6\gamma(2,\lambda q)\right] \qquad (46)$$

5 Data Analysis

This represents a mechanism to regulate the manner in which a statistical model interprets data. In this discourse, we shall analyze the compatibility of the proposed model with the subsequent dataset. Furthermore, a comparative analysis with the induced Garima distribution will be conducted to elucidate the superior fit of the induced Juchez distribution. We shall denote the dataset that encapsulates the mean temperature of the cotton crop, which is integral for the intelligent irrigation system developed by Harshil [14]. The ensuing dataset elucidates the methodology for implementing automatic irrigation in agricultural practices, aimed at conserving time, minimizing water wastage, and alleviating the necessity for manual labor. This dataset guarantees the proficient utilization of resources. The intelligent irrigation system in question represents an ongoing evolution of agricultural methodologies. Its role is paramount in modernizing agricultural practices. The dataset is delineated in the subsequent Table 1:

Table 1. Data of Average Temperature of cotton crop in Intelligent Irrigation System

16	18	22	32	28	23	12	35	45	11	23	34	45	33	45	25	11	41	23	18
36	33	24	15	44	13	29	14	28	31	35	32	10	21	22	21	32	11	13	38
45	39	38	38	44	27	37	29	31	42	40	24	14	31	14	14	17	15	44	12
27	41	29	41	35	30	14	20	15	19	40	29	13	12	32	32	26	30	39	18
25	39	17	16	45	34	22	43	15	29	16	26	15	18	44	41	35	30	18	26
42	35	19	16	18	39	23	12	27	10	39	29	25	27	29	17	20	17	10	17
33	18	40	23	15	25	20	43	32	41	37	43	43	40	43	23	12	13	42	39
16	38	31	37	20	37	43	44	24	20	33	14	36	37	40	27	42	39	17	10
18	10	29	23	28	16	13	36	18	30	44	39	26	42	20	10	41	20	43	28
39	10	29	40	44	21	33	28	19	19	22	36	17	35	35	13	45	42	45	10

In order to facilitate a comparative analysis of the distributions (Table 2), we shall scrutinize specific criteria such as the Akaike Information Criterion (AIC), the Corrected Akaike Information Criterion (AICC), the Bayesian Information Criterion (BIC), and $-2\log L$. The AIC serves to indicate the extent to which the proposed model aligns with the given dataset while accounting for potential overfitting. To mitigate the risks associated with overfitting, we shall compute the AICC. The BIC functions as a metric for evaluating the efficacy of the parameters of the proposed model in relation to the dataset's predictive capabilities. A distribution that exhibits improved fitting characteristics is expected to correlate with diminished values of AIC, BIC, AICC, and $-2\log L$.

Table 2. MLE, -2logL, AIC, BIC and AICC of the induced Juchez distribution of dataset

Distribution	MLE	S.E	-2logL	AIC	BIC	AICC
Induced Juchez	$\hat{\lambda} = 0.1007424$	0.0051172	1649.428	1651.428	1654.726	1651.448
Induced Garima	$\hat{\lambda} = 0.0499704$	0.0032635	1710.535	1712.535	1715.833	1712.555

The aforementioned comparison is also illustrated graphically, (Fig. 5 and Fig. 6) as displayed below:

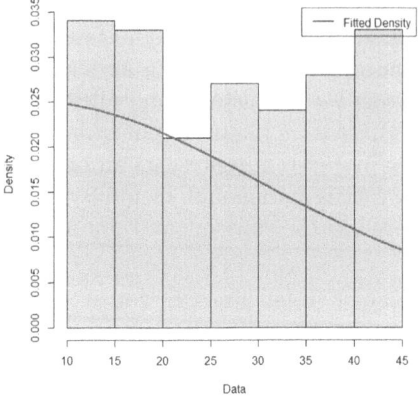 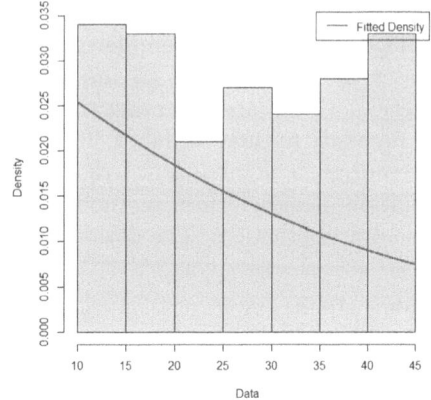

Fig. 5. MLE of Induced Juchez Distribution

Fig. 6. MLE of Induced Garima Distribution

The preceding graph elucidates the enhanced fit of the proposed model in comparison to the induced Garima distribution. Additionally, the curves presented in the two figures elucidate the operational dynamics of the proposed model.

6 Conclusion

In this scholarly article, the derived probability density function (p.d.f.) and cumulative distribution function (c.d.f.) significantly contribute to the theoretical underpinnings of the IJD, thereby establishing a robust foundation for its applicability across diverse domains. The resilience of the parameters associated with this distribution enables it to yield superior results. The maximum likelihood estimator emerges as a potent instrument for the estimation of the distribution's parameters, with its validity corroborated through the likelihood ratio test, thereby reinforcing the integrity of our conclusions. As well, the parameters of this distribution can be estimated through a range of alternative methods, notably the method of moments, least squares estimators, and Bayesian estimation. Several statistical properties are elucidated with clarity. This distribution demonstrates a closer association with real data sets when compared to the induced Garima distribution.

Acknowledgements. We extend our heartfelt gratitude to Dr. Sivabalan Arumugam, Professor, whose assistance in formatting this manuscript in LaTeX has significantly enhanced the quality and presentation of the mathematical expressions contained within this paper.

References

1. Fisher, R.A.: The effects of methods of ascertainment upon the estimate of frequencies. Ann. Eugen. **12**(1), 13–25 (1934). https://doi.org/10.1111/j.1469-1809.1934.tb02105.x
2. Epstein, B., Sobel, M.: Some theorems relevant to life testing from an exponential distribution. Ann. Math. Stat. **25**(2), 373–381 (1954). https://doi.org/10.1214/aoms/1177728793
3. Lindley, D.V.: Fiducial distributions and Bayes' Theorem. J. Roy. Stat. Soc. Ser. B **20**(1), 102–107 (1958). https://doi.org/10.4236/ojs.2016.64058
4. Rao, C.R.: On Discrete Distributions Arising Out of Methods of Ascertainment, In Classical and Contagious Discrete Distributions, Patil. G.P, Eds. Pergamon Press (1965)
5. Hogg, R.V., Craig, A.T.: Introduction to Mathematical Statistics, 4th edn. Macmillan, New York, pp. Remark 3.3.1 (1978). ISBN 0023557109
6. Lindsay, B.G.: Mixture models: theory, geometry and applications, NSF-CBMS Regional Conference Series in Probability and Statistics, Institute of Mathematical Statistics, Hayward, CA, USA, ISBN 0940600-32-3, JSTOR 4153184 (1995)
7. Friedman, J.H.: The Elements of Statistical Learning. Springer Series in Statistics, vol. 2. New York, USA (2009)
8. Abd-Elrahman, A.M.: Utilizing ordered statistics in lifetime distributions production: a new lifetime distribution and applications. J. Probab. Stat. Sci. **11**(2), 153–164 (2013)
9. Brijesh, P.S., Utpal, D.D.: On an induced distribution and its statistical properties. REVSTAT- Stat. J. (2020). https://doi.org/10.48550/arXiv.2010.15078
10. Udochukwu, V.E., Julian, I.M.: Juchez probability distribution: properties and applications. Asian J. Probab. Stat. **20**(2), 56–71 (2022). https://doi.org/10.9734/AJPAS/2022/v20i2419
11. Gupta, R.C., Kirmani, S.: The role of weighted distributions in stochastic modelling. Commun. Stat.-Theory Methods **19**(9), 3147–3162 (1990). https://doi.org/10.1080/03610929008830371
12. Patil, G.P., Rao, C.R.: The weighted distributions: a survey of their applications. Appl. Stat. 383–405 (1977)
13. Bonferroni, C.E.: Statistical theory of classification and calculation of the probability. Publication of the R Institute Superiore of the Science of Economy and Commerce of Florence, vol. 8, pp. 3–62 (1936)
14. Harshil, Intelligent Irrigation System. https://www.kaggle.com/datasets/harshilpatel355/autoirrigationdata

Author Index

A
Ashwinkumaar, N. K. J.   100

B
Balakumar, Abilasha   88
Bhargava, Naman   55

C
Chinnadurai, Veeramani   88

D
Dcouth, Jeswin Roy   15

K
Kumar, Puthin   15
Kumar, V.   3

M
Malar, B.   55
Manimegalai, R.   127
Mohan, Divya   15
Mugunthan, Sundararaju   69
Muthukumar, Sumathi   88

N
Nithishvaran, T. P.   37

P
Priyalakshmi, G.   55

R
Rahman, Manas   3
Raman, Indhumathi   117

S
Sophiya, E.   37
Subhashree, M.   140
Subramanian, C.   140
Sudharsan, S.   37
Sureshkumar, Venkatasamy   69
Susmeta, A.   127

T
Thanalakshmi, P.   100

U
Umayal, V. R.   127

V
Vamsi, M. S. Mohan   37
Varnan, S. K. Mukhil   37
Venkateshwaran, M.   127

© The Editor(s) (if applicable) and The Author(s), under exclusive license
to Springer Nature Switzerland AG 2025
S. Sheen et al. (Eds.): ICC3 2023, CCIS 2423, p. 153, 2025.
https://doi.org/10.1007/978-3-031-88297-5

The manufacturer's authorised representative in the EU is Springer Nature Customer Service Centre GmbH, Europaplatz 3, 69115 Heidelberg, Germany. If you have any concerns regarding our products, please contact ProductSafety@springernature.com

Printed and bound by CPI Group (UK) Ltd, Croydon, CR0 4YY

26/03/2026

02078968-0004